MAMA SAID THERE'D BE DAYS LIKE THESE

365 DAILY REFLECTIONS FROM THE HEARTLAND

LORI LACINA

Lori Lacina

First printed in July 2019
Printed in the United States
ISBN-13: 978-0-692-14513-5 (paperback)

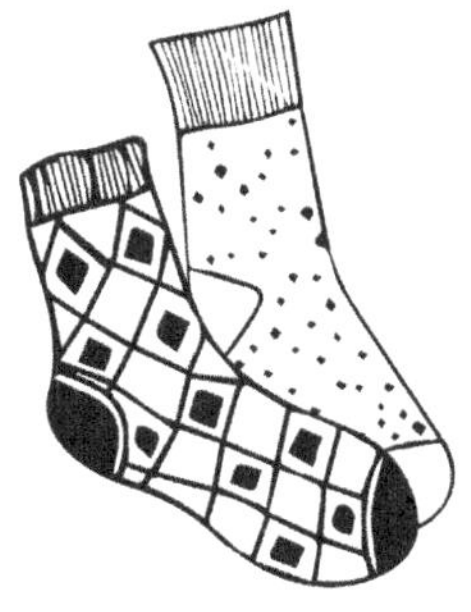

This collection of essays is dedicated to my grandchildren:

Tyler, Emily, Josh, Ben, Allison, and Micaila

Where has the time gone? I can't believe you have all become adults in what seems like the blink of an eye. You have filled my heart with love and my life with laughter and light. This book was a labor of love and I enjoyed every minute I spent writing it, knowing the end result would be part of my legacy to you. It is the fulfillment of a dream that I never quite believed could happen. So hold your dreams close and always remember:

You are never too old to set another goal or to dream a new dream.

— C.S. Lewis

Take the first step towards your dreams and never look back. I am so proud of all of you and the accomplishments of your life thus far. I can hardly wait to see what happens next!! Love you bunches!!

Grandma Lori

JANUARY 1st

Happy New Year!! Here we are, starting a brand new year!

I love a new beginning of any kind: a fresh, crisp clean notebook or journal to write in, a brand new book, the first day of a road trip, new babies, freshly sharpened pencils, newly mown grass, the first green sprouts of the spring flowers, the first heady scent of new lilac blossoms... well, you get the idea.

Starting a new year is all those things and more. True, in one way it is just the next day in the progression of our lives, but it is also something special. It is a chance for a new beginning, trying new things, becoming the best version of yourself. This is the time--take hold of the opportunity to write an amazing story about yourself. Write in ink, scribble, doodle, change your mind, cross things out....but never, never stop writing.

New Year Resolutions do not work for me, and I would venture to guess that is true for many of you. I no longer make a list of things to accomplish or change in the new year. It is such a disappointment when by January 12th, I have reneged or failed on every single one. Kind of ironic in a way, because I am an inveterate list maker who loves lists and crossing off items on lists once completed.

> Watch your thoughts, for they will become actions. Watch your actions for they will become...habits. Watch your habits because they will forge your character. Watch your character for it will make your destiny
>
> — Former British Prime Minister Margaret Thatcher

JANUARY 2nd

THE SECOND DAY of the new year, and I already have big questions for you!! Important questions...life-altering questions....How long does one leave Christmas decorations up?

Pondering, as I make trips too numerous to count, up and down my stairs, how can it be time to put Christmas away? Can you really put Christmas "away?" I hope not, except in the literal sense of the items that are symbols of Christmas. I do it with reluctance, year after year. No matter how bleak and cold the winter is here in the Heartland, Christmas brings light and warmth to a frozen winterscape.

Sigh.....January seems dark and cold without the Christmas accouterments inside, and the nights seem so dark without the cheerful colored lights that decorate the yards and homes.

I try to keep Christmas in my heart always. What else can warm you from the inside out in such a way? The joy, hope, faith, light, and peace makes the world a better place for me and hopefully, for those lives I touch every day. It is a hard job some dreary winter days with Spring's awakening a distant hope.

On your journey today, bring Christmas in your heart to all you meet. Let His light shine through you and warm the hearts of others. On a lighter note, always remember, it is never too cold or dreary for a Dairy Queen!!

JANUARY 3rd

As I MENTIONED EARLIER this year (ahem, two days ago!), there will be no resolutions for this quitter. Instead, I have created something else to live by, to make me step up to the plate, to hold myself accountable. I decided to write a personal credo. Credo is from the Latin, and means "I believe." A personal credo is a little more general than resolutions, but to me, it means what you believe in and how you live your life. So here goes....

I believe in God. I believe no child should go hungry or lack a loving home. I believe that every day on this earth is a gift, another chance to give the world my best self. I believe that we should take joy when it is within our reach. I believe if I can touch just one person's life in a positive way, the ripple effect can be a tsunami. I believe that it is my responsibility to make my little corner of the world better in any way I can. I have faith. I have hope. I have love.

> Carry each other's burdens, and in this way, you will fulfill the law of Christ.
>
> — GALATIANS 6:2

Well, this is a start, needs improvement, just like me. So I will keep working on my credo and on myself. I am definitely a work in progress. On your journey today, think about your personal beliefs and how those beliefs make you the person you are today and help you live the life you want to live.

JANUARY 4th

HAPPY NATIONAL TRIVIA DAY!! One of many holidays I will invite you to celebrate this year!! So in the spirit of this day, here are some little-known facts for you to use to wow your family, co-workers and random strangers.

- There is a 1 in 10,000 chance you will get hit by space junk.
- The 3 Musketeers Bar was originally split into 3 sections: chocolate, strawberry, and vanilla
- Baby porcupines are called porcupettes.
- The original name for butterfly was flutterby.
- There are twice as many kangaroos in Australia as there are people.
- Reno is farther west than Los Angeles.
- Duncan Hines was a real person-a restaurant critic.
- The average cumulus cloud weighs 1.1 million pounds.
- Sea otters hold hands when they sleep to prevent drifting apart.
- 75 New Jerseys would fit into Alaska.
- Alaska is the only state that can be typed on one row of keys. (I know there is at least one of you that will type the other 49 to be sure.)
- A "jiffy" is an actual unit of time-1/100th of a second
- Almonds are a member of the peach family
- Maine is the only state that is a one-syllable word.
- There are no words that rhyme with orange or purple.

Hope you enjoyed the wacky facts. As always, information is deemed reliable but not guaranteed or vetted for accuracy. What would be the fun in that?? Celebrate the day away, my friends!! Throw a trivia party, or a trivial party, your choice. On your journey, embrace the funny, odd, unusual facts about our world, and take a moment to laugh.

JANUARY 5th

I BET many of you are taking a deep breath, trying to get your house back in order after the holidays, and maybe, just maybe, being thankful that the houseful of guests are gone! Don't feel guilty, I am sure you enjoyed having family or friends to stay, but it is a whole bunch of work and does wreak havoc on your personal ecosystem and routine.

I may have a solution for this. How about making the stay for your guests more of a participatory experience? People pay big money to go on "experience" vacations. They go to dude ranches, farms, baseball spring training camp for civilians, and many other places. Why not let them truly experience your life on an up close and personal basis?

Start with an agenda of each day's activities. When they arrive in your guest room, have a nicely folded pile of sheets and pillowcases so they can participate in making their own nest to sleep in. After their initial experience, the possibilities are endless. Cleaning their own bathroom, taking out the trash, and accompanying you to the grocery store.

This takes us to the kitchen, where you can have ingredients for meals grouped together and they can be a chef for the day. I can just see the happy surprise and joy on their faces. It's just like those meal in a kit things you can order to prepare dinner.

Use your imagination and let them experience your life to the fullest. Make it a stay they will never forget! I call this guest adventure, "Some Assembly Required." Your guests will either love the idea or will stay in a hotel the next time they are in town. Either way, it is a win-win for you!!

Remember what Confucius said: " Every house guest brings you happiness. Some when they arrive and some when they are leaving."

JANUARY 6th

If you choose not to find joy in the snow, you will have less joy in your life, but still the same amount of snow.

— Unknown

I came across this quote recently, and knew instantly it belonged in my journal of life quotes!! Also, definitely worth sharing with my readers.

It really rings true for a Heartlander and snow, in the literal sense, but also a metaphor for so many other things in life. Well, technically I don't know if it meets the definition of a metaphor, an English teacher I am not, but it was the only word I could think of.

I think it speaks to not dwelling on things that are out of your control, and keep them from seeping into the joyful parts of your life. To paraphrase something I hear frequently, it is not the rain storm, it's your reaction to it.

So if a rain storm is passing through your life, put your boots on, stomp in the puddles, dance in the rain and laugh about it!! Or you can curl up with a good book, a cup of Irish coffee and a snuggly blanket, either way you have controlled the storm with your reaction.

I try my best to overcome my many gravity storms with jokes and laughter. I maintain these are out of my control, but some would disagree with that. They do not understand my issues with spatial awareness. (Translation: I don't always watch where I'm going.)

On your journey, get up, don't give up and take charge of your day!

JANUARY 7th

ONE OF THE changes in the technology around us is the fact that most late model automobiles have navigation systems, and many folks (including me) also have them on their phone. It can be used for driving, bicycling, and walking. One must be careful which mode it is in. It can be very confusing when the navigation wizard says six hours till your destination, and you know it should only be about 30 miles. Not that I have personally done that.

As we are still in the early stages of this year, and the road trip we call life, I had a thought. (Yep, done for the week.) Wouldn't it be wonderful if we had a navigation system for life? Just enter your destination, and an annoying voice will tell you to go right, or make a U-turn, or come to a stop. Satellite guidance for those directionally impaired, or guidance from above for those of us that need a nudge down the right path, or a reminder to stop and think.

I personally love the navigation for traveling, so easy to get to a specific place!! I think most of us have an internal navigation system to guide us through life. It consists of family, faith, right & wrong, values, community, and love. Look for someone to help you steer if the road is rough. Don't always think you are on the right road just because it is a well-worn path.

> When your values are clear to you, making decisions becomes easier.
>
> — ROY E. DISNEY

On your journey, choose your navigation system, your roads, and your companions carefully...

JANUARY 8th

I AM OFTEN THINKING about words, I mean after all, I use them every day. I like words, and have an affection for words that don't get used often enough in my opinion. So throughout this rambling stream of thoughts I am sharing in this book, be prepared to see some of my favorite words highlighted!!

S is the letter for today.

Here are my favorite "s" words: Sashay, Scoundrel, Smattering, Scamper, Squander, Simper, Skosh, and Serendipity. I mean, when was the last time you heard someone use the word sashay? This word paints a picture for me. I can literally see Miss Susan sashay across the room!! Have some fun, and scatter some of these words in your conversation today.

See how many you can use to make one silly sentence. Let's see: That simpering scoundrel sashayed across the salon to squander a smattering of pennies to the children scampering around the room.

On your journey today, expand your vocabulary, and open your hearts and minds to new ideas!!

JANUARY 9th

MOST OF US that live in the Heartland love the four seasons that we are blessed to experience. That doesn't mean we don't complain once in a while about snow, sleet, cold and dreary days in the winter!!

There is something about a cold winter day, snow softly falling outside that is cozy. It's a day that lends itself to some self-indulgence.

I like to start off a day such as this with an extra cup of morning coffee by the fireplace, watching the snow fall. It is a great time for reflection, evaluation and staring blankly into the great outdoors!!

Another indulgence for me is to spend time in my quilt studio surrounded by piles of colorful fabric, planning, designing and creating a quilt for someone I love. Hours can pass without me realizing it.

It is something I love doing and also acts as therapy to calm any anxiety or worries I may have.

Of course, a snowy day would not be complete without time to snuggle in with a book which can often transparently transform into a nap. I never used to nap as an adult, but now consider it a treat when I am able to have one!!

On your next journey on a snowy day, batten down the hatches and find enjoyment in the small things. May the memories you carry in your heart keep you warm on a cold winter day. One last word of advice, don't make snow angels at the dog park.

JANUARY 10th

WELL, we have made it ten days into the new year! I think that calls for a celebration, of course, I think almost anything calls for a celebration.

I can't think of any reason not to celebrate this crazy trip around the sun we call life!

Life is a journey with many levels of heartache and happiness. As "they" say (I always wonder who "they" are) one can't appreciate the mountain tops until you have walked through the valley. There is some truth to that. I will be ever grateful for my life here in the Heartland. I have traveled many diverse and difficult roads to get to the place I am today. Many of the roads were heartbreaking, but it seems the human heart has a great capacity to heal and eventually be able to welcome joy again. Broken crayons still color.

Wherever you might be on your journey today, be it heartache or happiness, or a little of each, one step at a time, one day at a time. You are not alone on your journey. Many are on the same journey, a step or two behind or a step or two ahead. Travelers on the road of life...

> ...but those who hope in the Lord will renew their strength. They will soar on wings like eagles, they will run and not grow weary, they will walk and not be faint.
>
> — ISAIAH 40:31

JANUARY 11th

It is my wish that you have health, wealth and much to celebrate. I am here to provide you with a list of holidays with which you might not be familiar. How can you celebrate without this knowledge? Some call these bizarre holidays, which seems rude to me. I shall call them Unique Holidays.

January 12- Kiss a Ginger day. (Here ya go Redheads!)

January 24- National Peanut Butter Day (Creamy or crunchy?)

March 12- National Napping Day

March 26-Purple Day

April 20- Lima Bean Respect Day (Now that's a big one!)

July 6- Fried Chicken Day

August 13- Left-Handers Day

September 24- National Punctuation Day (Go wild, use a semi-colon)

December 15- National Cupcake Day

December 30- National Bacon Day

These are just a few possibilities to add to your calendar. There are many more out there. Dare I say, a holiday for all 366 days?

The real question here, is who thinks of these holidays? How do they get on a "Holiday" list? If you are interested in creating your own holiday, I think you should pursue it!! Let me know, I will help you celebrate!!

On your journey, every day should be a celebration of life. Embrace today, fill it with love, laughter, hope, and giving.

JANUARY 12th

I RECENTLY WENT to get the oil changed in my car. When it was completed, they handed me a form that explained my car had been through a 98 point check. All the moving parts and some that don't move were checked, filled, changed and approved. They even washed the car.

I began thinking about this 98 point check. Wouldn't it be great if your doctor gave you a 98 point check up when you went for your annual physical?

Why stop with blood pressure, temperature and pulse? Let's make sure that all the parts that should move are moving and pain-free. Parts that shouldn't move need to be checked that they are in fact in the same place they were last year and where they are supposed to be.

Blood work, vision, mental acuity should top off the list.

For good measure, a massage, manicure, and pedicure would be a nice touch. Am I mixing this up with the spa again?

At my age, I want to leave with that piece of paper that says I am good to go for the next five thousand miles with the checklist of any parts that were replaced, nudged, tweaked or missing. It would also be great to have such a document to add to your travel packing list along with your passport, health insurance card, and drivers license.

On your journey today, embrace your age, experience and wisdom. Walt Disney said, "Laughter is timeless. Imagination has no age, and dreams are forever."

JANUARY 13th

WE MIGHT AS WELL START the year out with one of my favorite television genres. I love crime and mystery shows, but I am not speaking of those today. I do enjoy some of the reality shows. Specifically, Survivor and the Bachelor/Bachelorette series. Go ahead and laugh.

I am not interested in reality shows that follow so-called celebrities lives. I am all about shows where every week someone gets voted off the island or gets sent home without a rose. Since Survivor was the show that piqued my interest in this genre, it is today's topic.

I have seen every season of Survivor since its inception in the year 2000. The series runs twice a year, once in the fall and once in the spring. Do the math. That is a lot of "surviving!" My interest and personal celebrity reached great heights when my grand-niece was a contestant, twice. The second time she was on she was the winner of the million dollar prize.

Contestants live together in a wilderness setting, near the ocean. There are challenges to win rewards and immunity. Every week the group votes one of its own off the island! It takes physical strength, mental strategy, stamina and a little bit of luck to remain until the final episode and win the million dollars. Tribe members range in age from 18 to 70 + years. No worries, I am not going to apply to be on the show. I like my creature comforts, I like to have clean clothes, and most importantly of all, I can't swim. Swimming is key to some of the challenges. Drowning will not get you to the million dollar prize!

I love the strategy and machinations of the tribe members as they plot and scheme about who is going to get voted off at the next tribal council. Feel free to judge me, but if you haven't watched a season of Survivor you might be missing out!!

JANUARY 14th

I THOUGHT since we have our navigation system in place, I would share some helpful (?) hints to make your life easier. I like to call this phenomenon that seems to be sweeping the country, “Life in a Box.”

If you need convenience in any aspect of your daily life, I think it is out there, just waiting for you to express (and pay for) your need.

These boxes are subscriptions to a club that will provide you monthly, quarterly or on demand boxes of stuff. The only one I have personally tried is Stitch Fix which sends you 5 pieces of clothing/accessories. Keep and pay for what you want, send the rest back, postage paid.

There are wine, beer, meal clubs of all types. I even saw a Pickle of the Month Club....there are no words. I was tempted by a monthly club called Scribe. They send you writing accouterments, special pens, journals, paper etc. As a lover of all those things, I found it hard to keep scrolling!

Bookcase Club will send you 2 books a month in the genre of your choice. If you don’t like books they choose, I guess it is just too bad.

Mentorbox contains books, videos, workbooks, workshops geared to the business person.

The concept markets well, we all like to receive a package in the mail, with a nice surprise inside!! I would prefer not to pay for the pleasure, but if that’s what you have to do to get a package, there it is.

Life in a box, who thinks of these things??? On your journey, get outside of your box and live life large. Life is full of surprises and serendipity. Being open to the unexpected turns in the road guarantees you adventures along the way!

JANUARY 15th

WHAT COULD BE BETTER on a cold winter day, than some ice cream? Strawberry ice cream to be more precise! Today is National Strawberry Ice Cream Day. There seems to be no information available about the origins of this very meaningful holiday. It has been reported that First Lady Dolley Madison served strawberry ice cream at the White House in 1813 to celebrate the second inauguration of her husband, President James Madison.

In addition to the deliciousness of strawberry ice cream, it has lots of Vitamin C , potassium, folic acid and fiber. A cup of strawberries contains only 55 calories. I will not venture to guess the number of calories in a cup of strawberry ice cream, but whatever that number is, strawberries are not responsible!!

The strawberry is not really a berry, but a member of the rose family. There is a long scientific explanation why this is so, but it is way above my pay grade to try to tell you. My readers with inquiring minds will do some research!! Others of you will be frantically trying to find some strawberry ice cream!!

As a child, I thought Neapolitan ice cream was quite the treat. Chocolate, vanilla and strawberry together. It was usually served in slices so you would get a portion of each flavor. I recently had some Blue Bunny Neapolitan and it did not disappoint. Blue Bunny is headquartered in Le Mars, Iowa; Ice Cream Capital of the World. It is the largest family owned ice cream manufacturer in the world, founded in 1913 and producing over 150 million gallons of ice cream per year. On my way to procure some now!! Join me in this celebration!! Enjoy some strawberry ice cream, milkshakes or malts. It's the right thing to do!!

JANUARY 16th

Libraries are amazing places, little slices of book heaven that are in every city and town of any size. It really show's a city's commitment to the community when they have a lively and viable library. Today's libraries are not just places to check out books. Movies, CDs, Audiobooks and many other things are ready to be loaned! Computers are available for kids after schools, or anyone else who needs to use one. Libraries host book clubs, craft days, summer reading programs and so much more.

In downtown Kansas City, the facade of the parking ramp for the public library is covered in signboard mylar, constructed to look like a giant row of books on a shelf. The "books" are 25' high and 9' wide. There are 22 books represented on this shelf. It is a sight to behold and worth a stop if you are in the area!

The New York City Public Library was everything I thought it would be when I visited. Of course, the famous lions, Patience and Fortitude (sculpted out of pink Tennessee marble) greet you outside as you arrive. This is the second largest library in the U.S., and the fourth largest in the world. They have 53 million items in 92 locations. Those are the dry facts, but the main library is like walking into a beautiful piece of art. The iconic Rose Main Reading Room has been featured in many movies. The whole building is breathtaking, and a window into a glorious past.

Albert Einstein said, "The only thing that you absolutely have to know is the location of the library." Just more proof that Einstein was indeed a genius of epic proportions!!

Find a cozy nook in your favorite library and steal some reading time out of your busy schedule. Sigh….now if they only served ice cream...

JANUARY 17th

LOOKING FOR A GOOD READ TODAY? Try picking up a cookbook! I have become a fan of cookbooks that have stories along with the recipes. In fact if I am totally frank about this, I have no intention of making some of these recipes but I love the pictures and narratives that accompany them.

There are a couple of cookbooks that I have really enjoyed. The first are the ones written by Ree Drummond, "The Pioneer Woman." Her life story is fascinating and I live vicariously on the ranch with her and her rancher husband and kids. Good recipes and good stories!!

Another one I have really enjoyed is by Beth Howard, Iowa girl who came back from California, rented the American Gothic House and started a pie stand!!! Her first book is about her journey to get here, and the second is a cookbook that is all about pies!! There is nothing not to like about that!!

Thought I would share a recipe for cookies that my Mom used to make. They have become a favorite of my grandkids. I am sure it is not an original recipe, but it is much loved in our family.

Oatmeal Crispies

1 c shortening (I use butter), 1 c brown sugar, 1 c white sugar, 2 eggs, 1 t vanilla, 1 t salt, 1 t baking soda, 1 ½ c flour, 3 c quick oats.

Bake for 10-12 minutes at 350. Baking time really depends on your oven. Take them out before they look too golden brown if you want soft cookies! Enjoy with an ice cold glass of milk or a cup of coffee!!

JANUARY 18th

TYPING CLASS IN HIGH SCHOOL, those were the days, my friends!! I can't remember what grade level, but I think it was a required class. Admittedly, my memory isn't what it used to be, along with a lot of other things. I enjoyed the class very much, and it has served me well all of my life.

Think about it, a whole semester class of just typewriting exercises, or as they would call it now "keyboarding." We were taught to type without looking at the keyboard, and after a semester, one could be very proficient. When I am at school, often the students will comment on how fast I can type. It pays to concentrate on learning a skill, especially one that lasts a lifetime. Typing "The quick brown fox jumps over the lazy dog" never got old…

When I think about the advances I have seen since I began typing, it is truly amazing. Starting out on a manual typewriter, with keys that you needed some hand strength to strike, and when a mistake was made, you need to paint over the error with "white out" and then type over it.

Then came the IBM Selectric typewriters, circa 1980. It had the black ribbon, and a white ribbon for correcting. Thought I was walking in tall cotton when I got one of those.

Then there is today….laptop computers that have applications such as Microsoft Work or Google Docs. These systems not only allow us to create documents, they check our spelling, grammar, punctuation and posture. Well, just kidding about the last one. Or am I? The world has advanced, but the skills I learned on a simple manual typewriter have translated well. Thank you Mr. Walters!

On your journey today, dust off some old skills, try out some new skills, and reflect on the things life has taught you and brought you.

JANUARY 19th

Books, books, books. The only thing I like better than words…because they are full of words. Words that craft unique characters, plots, descriptions, and ideas. My thought when planning this epistle, was to share some of my very favorite books from over the years, hoping to remind you of an old favorite or tantalize you with the prospect of a book you missed.

Here are a few titles for you: "Wild," "The Good Sister," "Defending Jacob," "The Compound," "I Will Always Write Back," "Before We Were Yours," "A Walk in the Woods," and "Light a Penny Candle." Some different genres represented are mystery, historical fiction, autobiographical and young adult. My favorite books are generally mysteries, books set in the Low Country or Scotland, and fictional stories about cooking or quilting. I am so proud of myself, I wrote this whole paragraph without mentioning my all-time favorite classic, "Little Women" by Louisa May Alcott. Oops, didn't quite make it.

An interesting fact is that the average CEO reads about 60, (yes, I said 60) books a year. That tells me that they are astute enough to realize that being a CEO doesn't mean you know everything, and they need to keep up with things in their field of work, technology and the world in general. As President Harry Truman said, "Not all readers are leaders, but all leaders are readers."

So on your journey, let books take you places you could never imagine, introduce you to new ideas and make your life a more interesting place to be.

JANUARY 20th

COLLECTIONS OF THINGS INTRIGUE ME. The definition of collect according to the Merriam-Webster dictionary is to bring or gather things or people to one place. I have had many sorts of collections in my lifetime. When I was a child I collected Barbie dolls and clothes, along with troll dolls. I was enamored with troll dolls. I mean, who wouldn't be excited about a small, squat plastic figure with no clothes and long hair that stood up and could be any color of the rainbow.

I would like to think my collections have grown a tad bit more sophisticated as I have matured, aged, gotten old, however defined. As an older child, I collected glass shoes, I probably had three dozen in all styles and colors. Don't ask me why. I don't know.

My latest collecting interest is pitchers, no not pictures, pitchers. Antique, old, new whatever. They are many shapes, colors, and vintages. I store this collection above my kitchen cupboard where they are displayed for all to see. When there is a need, I pull one out to use as a vase or for drinks. I enjoy them very much. Some are seasonal, some just a pretty color or an unusual shape. It is harmless and amuses me.

My favorite collection over the years is my collection of people. Yes, I have always been a collector of people. If I entice you into my group of friends or acquaintances, you are pretty much there to stay unless you are horribly mean to me or move away and forget about me. The collection waxes and wanes over time. Life circumstances can often separate friends through no fault of either party. I cherish this collection and keep it in my heart at all times. My friends have held me up when I couldn't stand, and helped me sing the song in my heart when I had forgotten the words. May you be blessed with such a collection of friends to travel life's path with you.

JANUARY 21st

Another day, another chance to talk about books. One of the genres I enjoy is the cozy mystery. This is really a subgenre of crime fiction, with less violence and sex. Cozy mysteries can often be identified by the cover. If you see a skein of yarn, a quilt shop, a bookshop or a cottage with a picket fence, there is a very high probability inside a cozy mystery awaits you.

Cozies are true mysteries with suspense, red herrings, and puzzles for the reader to solve along with the protagonist. The protagonist is usually an amateur sleuth in a small village or town. I remember the books and TV show, "Murder She Wrote," and wondering how many people in this small town of Cabot Cove could keep getting murdered. Dangerous place to live if you ask me!!

Cozy mysteries almost always have a happily ever after, crime is solved and justice is meted out to the perpetrators of the crime. Sigh...this may be why I have grown to like them more and more as I have gotten older. Life is not always saturated with happy endings. The news is full of stories that are horrible to hear about and contemplate. Justice for the victims doesn't always occur. In real life, the bad guys do win, more often than they should.

Diane Mott Davidson has a great series that are about food, and contain recipes along with the story. The protagonist is a caterer in Aspen Meadows, Colorado. Good reads and good mysteries. Fun to find a series that is not only a mystery but contains elements of hobbies or other interests you may have. Nancy Pickard is another great cozy mystery author. She has created a great protagonist, a widow who splits her time between Maine and Arizona, and mysteries abound!

Try this genre, hope you like it!! Cozy can be very comfy.

JANUARY 22nd

HERE IS a question that every man I know would like to have answered: What is the deal with women and shoes? I understand their confusion, men usually have 4 pairs of shoes or less…..athletic shoes, black dress shoes, sandals (maybe) and some random pair that even the dog won't chew on.

Women have a deep-seated need for shoes that is part of their genetic makeup when they are born. It is an instinct that we can't ignore, the never-ending quest for the right shoes. Men have shirts and pants, women have outfits….thus the need for the right shoes for a particular outfit. Color, style, season-appropriate are all important. I don't know why that is so hard to understand.

> Of all the wonderful things men and women share, shoes tragically, are not one of them. This is because men lack the shoe chromosome.
>
> — MIMI POND, HUMORIST, AND WRITER

I believe there is another reason why we shop for shoes, that is not generally known in the male population. We can gain weight and lose weight, but we always wear the same size shoes. There is a great deal of comfort in that. Same goes for purses, don't even get me started on that. The never-ending quest for the perfect purse. It is all about the hunt!!

For reasons of national security, I have decided not to divulge the number of pairs of shoes I own. I can assure you however, the number is not in the triple digits….at least not as this book goes to print.

The next time you go shopping for shoes, don't feel a bit guilty.

After all, Cinderella is proof that a new pair of shoes can change your life.

JANUARY 23rd

JANUARY, a new month, a new year, a new appointment for my annual physical. The first question I am asking myself, is why would anyone schedule this appointment for January? Post-holiday, maybe a few too many sweet treats and sumptuous meals combined with cold weather and few opportunities for physical activity, this should go well.

I weighed myself at home on a digital scale. I must have broken it because I didn't get a weight after a number of attempts, but I did keep getting an error message. That seems very rude and uncalled for.

I am getting very tired of inanimate objects telling me what to do and having opinions about me.

Well, nothing more to be done, it is off to the doctor to have my annual exam. (Thought I was done with those when I graduated from college.) The nurse calls my name and leads me down the maze of corridors to the object I fear most: the scale. She gives me a look, as I take off my shoes, jacket, vest, and jewelry. Hey, I am not going to take the blame for accessories increasing what is already going to be too large a number. I wait, while she pushes buttons, writes down a number in kilograms and then converts it to pounds. I can't believe my eyes. I am down a pound since last year. Woo Double Hoo!! I hate to brag, but I am clearly an overachiever.

I can relax now before I see the doctor. Can't wait to receive her congratulations on my over the top efforts this last year, to live a healthy lifestyle and lose some weight. No more anxiety here for this appointment. I am rockin' it today. Maybe, when I am finished, I will celebrate with a Blizzard at Dairy Queen.....

JANUARY 24th

LET'S FACE IT, so many things in life are easier for men. If they need a haircut, they go to the barber, twenty minutes later they emerge with shorter hair but looking basically the same. The cost is minimal.

When a woman needs a haircut, she doesn't just need a haircut, she needs a hairstyle. This will take a minimum of an hour, unless it is a new hairstyle in which case, she needs to pack a lunch. Speaking for myself, I usually am getting a new style, and "gasp" I may be getting highlights and/or lowlights. This is a fancy way of saying I am covering the gray in my hair. Now we are talking two hours minimum. The color is placed, and it must rest for twenty minutes plus, then there is the trip to the shampoo bowl. This usually includes a head massage, which is very relaxing. Finally, we get to the actual cutting of the hairs. Blow drying, styling, and voila, I am a new woman. Let's not talk about the cost, but it is not minimal.

The time we spend together is why many of us have close personal relationships with our stylist. My stylist is family, she is like a devoted niece. We socialize outside the salon, and may have had some adventures together! Other pampering treatments include getting your nails done, and a fancy pedicure on what they call the pedicure throne. I must confess, the last pedicure I had, I got in the chair and looked around for the seatbelt. Some days are like that.

Being taken care of for a few hours is lovely. A glass of wine, refreshed, relaxed and feeling good is hard to beat. One of my favorite things in the salon is a sign that says: "We can't control how old you are, but we can control how young you look." That is why we spend the time and the money. It has been said that you can't turn back the clock, but you can wind it up again!!

JANUARY 25th

HAVING TRAVELED a fair amount in the southern part of the U.S., primarily Florida, I have come to realize that we have so many terms to describe our weather that they never have to use. I mean, how many ways can you say, "Tomorrow's weather will be sunny and 80?"

Here are some of my favorite weather terms that you can only use and appreciate north of the Mason Dixon Line!

Thundersnow: Yes, it can thunder during a snowstorm. It doesn't happen often, but it is very grand and exciting.

Freezing fog: Just what it sounds like, it's foggy (you are driving in solid clouds) the temperature drops and the fog freezes.

Freezing rain: See freezing fog, insert rain instead of fog.

Black ice: Very thin, very clear ice that forms on roadways, matching the color of the road, therefore not seen. I have had personal experience with this phenomenon, it is like unexpectedly riding the Tilt-A-Whirl at the fair, but in your car.

Windchill: This one we know all too well. The temperature might be 5- 15 degrees, but with the winter wind it can feel like it is anywhere from 10 to 40 degrees below zero. Southerners will need to stay inside, Iowans will need a coat.

Ice storm: This is a winter storm that has freezing rain which creates a beautiful but dangerous glaze over everything. Southerners will need to stay inside, and certainly won't be allowed to drive. Iowans will leave ten minutes early to get to their destination.

Sleet: A form of precipitation that is like little ice pellets, often combined with rain and/or snow. Crunchy, noisy and dangerous.

Sprinter: Winter in Spring (April)

Today's winter meteorology lesson has not been brought to you by the Iowa Division of Tourism.

JANUARY 26th

ICED IN, in Iowa. Yep, Freezing drizzle, ice on roads, not leaving the house today. Enforced house arrest by Mother Nature. For those of you not familiar with this ice phenomenon, it is very tricky. Give us 8 inches of snow, and we might slow down, but throw ice all over things and that is a different story. The day is almost done, and I have managed to fill the day quite nicely.

Started the day with a visit from my friendly Mediacom service person. He quickly reprogrammed my new TV and remotes so I could use one remote instead of three to use the TV. I am very happy, it is the little things. I hope they called him in off the road as the day got worse. Skills like that need to be protected.

Had some lunch, took a snooze on the couch, it may have lasted two hours, but there were no witnesses. My favorite soft fleece blanket, a fire in the fireplace and no place to go, perfect napping conditions. After waking up and feeling quite refreshed, I reorganized my quilting studio, for the 597th time, then finished a few quick projects that were on deck, waiting patiently.

Just settled in to watch the evening news before dinner, when what to my wondering eyes should appear but a dark TV screen that proclaimed "searching for signal." Cable has gone out. Did I mention that ice is not good for electricity and cable? Guess it will be a movie night for me.

When unexpected free time comes your way, spend some of it on yourself. No guilt, no explanations. Be productive, be lazy or combine the two! Refresh yourself.

> You can't pour from an empty cup. Take care of yourself first.
>
> — DEVELOPGOODHABITS.COM

JANUARY 27th

FLUENCY IN A LANGUAGE other than your own is an amazing skill. I am not....I used to be fairly immersed in Spanish during high school and college. I even tutored middle school Spanish. But, use it or lose it! It comes back to me if I see or hear something, but our relationship has grown from intimate to amicable divorce.

I enjoy learning about other languages and have been reading about the Chinese language. I recently learned that the Chart of Common Characters of Modern Chinese has only 3,500 characters (letters, so to speak). Are you kidding me? The good news is that about 1,000 aren't commonly used anymore, so you really only need to know about 2,500 to pass a Chinese language test. That's a relief, so much less studying!!

I think of all the words, emotions, and descriptions that we create with only 26 letters in the alphabet, less if you are texting and using emojis...I can only deduce that the Chinese language has many more nuances than English. The pictographs intimidate me. I can barely draw a stick figure, imagine me trying to draw those intricate and beautiful characters! I admire the Chinese and others who can master this.

Although, if those pictographs are on a Chinese keyboard, I am all over it!!

So if you are looking for a learning opportunity or a new hobby, I think I have one for you!! After all, "Thinking, 'here goes nothing,' could be the start of everything." Drew Wagner, Writer

Life is an adventure, don't miss out on a chance to step outside your comfort zone!! If not Chinese, there is something out there to tempt your curiosity!!

JANUARY 28th

PRESIDENTIAL LIBRARIES ARE one of our nation's treasures. These thirteen libraries are administered by the National Archives and every president since Herbert Hoover has one. There are also homes, birthplaces, museums and parks administered by the National Park Service or by private entities. I have visited six of the thirteen, and six or so of the others.

They are situated all across the country, so chances are there is one near you!! We happen to have one in Iowa, about ten miles from where I live: The Herbert Hoover Library and Museum, as well as a park where he was born and is buried. It is one of the smaller ones, but definitely worth a visit to learn about this Quaker man from a small village in Iowa who became President. I had the pleasure of serving as a docent in his museum, telling the story of his life. During my years of service, I met President Ronald Reagan, President Gerald Ford, Helen Thomas, Roger Mudd, Stephen Ambrose and Cabinet Secretary Elizabeth Dole. Great perks for a volunteer gig!! I actually drove Secretary Dole to the Cedar Rapids airport, which is indeed, another story!!

My favorite Presidential places are:

- Home of Pres. George Washington, Mt. Vernon, VA
- Home of Pres. Thomas Jefferson, Monticello, VA
- Franklin D. Roosevelt Presidential Library/Museum in Hyde Park, NY
- Ronald Reagan Presidential Library/Museum in Simi Valley, CA
- John F. Kennedy Presidential Library/Museum in Boston, MA

The stories told here are more than the story of one man. They are a treasure chest of memories, artifacts, pictures, culture and the history of those times which belong to all of us as Americans. Take a plane, take a train, take a road trip, it will be worthwhile.

JANUARY 29th

Books, books, books and more books. As they say, so many books, so little time. Today's reader has so many options, it makes it easier to read and also more complicated.

There is the "real" book that I can physically hold, turn the pages, close the book when I have finished with a satisfying thump, and place on my bookshelf. I grew up reading this way, accumulating books as if they were treasures....which they are....There is really nothing quite like this experience.

I will confess, that I do cheat on my real books. I read books on my Kindle and iPad, especially when traveling. I can literally take thousands of books with me, ensuring I will never run out of reading material. Very comforting to an avid reader. My apologies to real books, you are my first love, but sometimes one is tempted to stray. There is also a financial benefit to this option as Kindle books are less expensive.

I also love to listen to audiobooks in the car, even just driving around town on my way to school, the grocery store or daily errands. I find I am much more patient waiting in traffic if I am listening to a book. This is really important during road construction season, or as we call it, summer.

So many books, so many options, so little time!!

> Books are the plane, and the train, and the road. They are the destination and the journey. They are home.
>
> — Anna Quindlen, Writer

May you find the gift of an exceptional book to read on your journey today. Drink in the words and let them take you to a new destination.

JANUARY 30th

When I travel, there is one important item that I never forget to pack. I always bring a couple of decks of cards. They are extremely portable, easy to pack and take up very little room. You just never know when you might be stuck in an airport, watching a rainstorm from your hotel room or run across the possibility of a rousing card game. I for one, don't want to miss out.

Fifty-two cards and endless possibilities. There are some unique and interesting "coincidences" if we compare a deck of cards to the world around us. I find this sort of thing fascinating, so here we go!!

There are 52 cards in a deck, and 52 weeks in the year. There are four different suits. These suits are from the French, originally used hundreds of years ago. Opinions vary as to what these suits might coincide with. Four seasons and four elements (earth, water, wind, fire) have been mentioned. Thirteen cards in each suit could represent the thirteen phases of the lunar cycle. The cards are two colors, representing night and day.

Maybe it is all just one coincidence after another....or is it? I find coincidences highly suspicious. I like to think the meaning of the design of a deck of cards is deeper than "face value."

There is nothing like the companionship of sitting around the table, talking and playing cards with family or friends. It's social, it's inexpensive and family-oriented entertainment. I grew up playing cards with multiple generations of my family and these memories are some of my fondest. The next time you find yourself at home with the choice of re-runs or screen time, find yourself a deck of cards and gather the troops. Shuffle 'em up and start a new tradition or revive an old one.

JANUARY 31st

Remind me each day of the fable of the hare and the tortoise, that I may know that the race is not always to the swift.

— The Quiet Mind Calendar, 1964

It is so easy to get caught up in the madness that is today's world. But it is only that way because we allow it to be so. Get the most done, be the first to do, to have, to go, and that's in our leisure time!!! Throw in the work day, appointments, child/grandchild activities and the best words I have for that hot mess are pandemonia on steroids.

If I don't think carefully about my schedule, I can fall into that trap as well. I am officially retired from my career as a banker but have been working as a guest teacher. The beauty of that system is I can work when I want to..except as I have become friends with many of my work colleagues at school, I struggle to say no when they ask me to fill in.

This long-winded rambling is meant to recognize the fact that we need to make mindful choices about how we spend our time and with whom. Time is our most valuable currency. The pocketbook that is filled with time, is not a bottomless container. We will all run out of time someday, so we need to make the best of what we are given. Slow down, enjoy the everyday moments instead of rushing through them. Spend this currency on people and activities that are important to you.

The bad news is time flies. The good news is you're the pilot.

— Michael Altshuler

FEBRUARY 1st

HELLO FEBRUARY!! I have to say, for a short month, you have it going on girl!! Let's see, Heart Month, Go Red Friday, Groundhog Day, I Don't Need a Jacket Day, International Jello Week, Super Bowl Sunday, Valentines Day, Lincoln's Birthday, Washington's Birthday, Boy Scout Day, Wave ALL Your Fingers at Your Neighbor Day (hey, I don't make this stuff up) and sometimes even Leap Day. Whew!!

I like February, it is January's nicer sister. When you live in the Heartland, January can be brutal. February always seems to bring a hint of spring and has a softer personality. We begin to see the snow melt, might even have some downright toasty days. Hey! If you have had 40 below 0 windchills, 33 degrees is toasty.

Valentines Day is the most publicized holiday in February. It is overdone in such a way to put pressure on people in a relationship to have something fantastical planned for that day. It also seems designed to make those without a special someone feel left out of the game. My advice is to celebrate it if you want to, ignore it if you want to, but don't let one day on the calendar define who you are and how much fun you "should" have. Not a bad day to treat yourself. Have some wine and chocolate, or Diet Pepsi and Cheetos, whatever floats your boat!!

February gives you a plethora of holidays to celebrate. Pick one, pick them all and celebrate life!

FEBRUARY 2nd

HAPPY GROUNDHOG'S DAY!! I have never really understood this "holiday." It is evidently an old tradition, but a very strange one. Why are we asking a groundhog how many more weeks of winter are in store? Why do we think he knows? For all we know, he is just toying with us!

Punxsutawney Phil lives in the town library in Punxsutawney, Pennsylvania. He has a "friend" Phyllis who lives with him. She, however, is not allowed to give her opinion about the potential continuation of winter or early spring. It's all about Phil.

It wasn't until this year that I learned about Phil and his swanky home. I never gave it much thought, but wondered how they caught a groundhog every year and got him to look at his shadow. I mean, the whole idea becomes crazier the more you think about it.

I also still don't understand if he sees his shadow why that means more winter. Wouldn't that mean the sun is out? I am so confused.

There is more good news about Phil. There is an official Groundhog Club that you can join for a mere $15 a year. I don't know much more about it, but one could assume there are perks galore in this rather elite club of groundhog-ophiles!

Don't ask me about the movie, *Ground Hog Day.* Never saw it, don't understand the premise. I think I have groundhog-a-phobia. It's a chronic condition, with no known medical solutions. I am okay with that.

On your journey today, watch out for groundhogs, they might be full of themselves on this day and looking to do some serious mischief.

FEBRUARY 3rd

Don McLean wrote a song entitled "American Pie," which has a reference in it to an event with an Iowa connection, an event known around the United States. On this day in 1959, a plane leaving after a concert at the Surf Ballroom in Clear Lake, Iowa crashed...on board were Buddy Holly, Richie Valens, and The Big Bopper, stars of the rock and roll scene in the mid-1950s. One of the lines in McLean's song says, "the day the music died" referring to this tragedy.

I started thinking about other days that the "music died." The one that stands out for me is the day Elvis Presley, the King of Rock and Roll died, on a hot August night in 1977. A talented musician who changed the face of music, taken too soon.

The music in the hearts of a hopeful nation died when John F. Kennedy was assassinated in Dallas, Texas in 1963. The youngest president, the face of a new generation represented our hopes and prayers for this great country and ourselves. What would it be like today if he had not been killed, and had been able to execute his plans for the future?

We will never know and we are poorer because chances for a better America were lost.

In your personal life, hold tight to the music of your hopes and dreams. Sing them loudly every day. Write new lyrics when you need to. There is always another verse within you. Have a friend help you sing the song of your heart when your voice wavers and hope seems lost.

One of my personal heroes, who I had the good fortune to meet, said this, "Life is one grand sweet song, so start the music." President Ronald Reagan

Yes indeed, start the music and never let it stop.

FEBRUARY 4th

TODAY SEEMS like another good day for words...well isn't every day?? The letter "C" is on my mind, so many crisp and creative words begin with the letter "C."

Here are some of my favorites: Crunching, Cattywampus, Capricious, Capitulate, Charisma, Cherish, Chipper and Comport, not to be confused with Compote. How much more interesting our conversations would be if we used more of these descriptive words!! Use one, use them all in your conversation today, you will be a winner!!

Silly sentence: My cat was cattywampus on the cart, looking very chipper and crunching capriciously on cat food.

This is also fun to do with your children or grandchildren. Use age appropriate vocabulary words and help them study or grow their vocabulary. Your vocabulary can never be too large or too interesting!!

> Prose, words in their best order. Poetry, the best words in the best order.
>
> — SAMUEL TAYLOR COLERIDGE

FEBRUARY 5th

PRODUCTIVE DAY, or wasted day? (Makes me want to break out in song with Freddie Fender's rendition of "Wasted Days and Wasted Nights.") How can I get so much accomplished some days while other days I pretty much just take up space?

I have decided one of my solutions to procrastination is procaffeination. I wasn't even sure procaffeination was a word, but the thirty-seven spell checks that seem to be hard at work when I write, let it pass. It is a fact that I not only want but need my morning dose of that delectable concoction we call coffee. I can drink it hot, on the rocks, flavored, unflavored, whatever you've got.

Another solution to procrastination that is pure genius was suggested by Marie Bostwick (best selling author) in her blog. She called it the "Seventeen Minute Procrastination Cure." Don't you already love it? Her advice is to set your kitchen timer for seventeen minutes. During that time, no phone, no email, work on your task. Knock it off one chunk at a time. Very clever.

If I am watching television, I trick myself into work during the commercials. I fold laundry, empty the dishwasher, dust, and many other small chores that can be done during that time. Makes the work seem less tedious when you chop away at it, bit by bit, and before you know it, it's all done. I don't really think it is ever "all" done, but you get the idea! At least for a short spot of time, I have the illusion I am done!

My hope for you today is a day that you enjoy and feel good about. Some days are for productivity, some days are for friendship and laughter, some days are about you and your needs for the day. Give the world the best version of yourself today, it will make a difference.

FEBRUARY 6th

I CAME across an interesting idea and thought I would share it. This is the time of year when Christians are preparing to observe Lent, which is the prelude to Easter. Depending on the complicated calculation of the calendar, Lent can begin anywhere from early February to mid-March, hence an early post to plant a seed for you.

Lent is 40 days long, and some people "give something up " for Lent. It might be soft drinks, coffee, something that they really enjoy. I used to give up french fries, which evidently was funny, as people teased me about it. I am not a chocolate lover, and I REALLY love french fries. Let's look at the giving up of something in a different way.

Starting on the first day of Lent, choose one item from your home that you don't use or really need and put it in a box or storage bin. Continue this practice for 40 days. At the end of the 40 days, donate the items to the local charity of your choice.

Two birds with one stone, as they say, can be accomplished. Clearing out your home, and donating the items to people who really need them, seems like a pretty wonderful idea. It may seem silly, why not just clean out your closet and be done? Sometimes that seems overwhelming, and it gets pushed to the bottom of our to-do list. I love the idea of one thing at a time, even on the most hectic of days that can be accomplished. (Just between you and me, you don't have to stop at the 40 days!!)

> Small acts, when multiplied by millions of people, can transform the world.
>
> — HOWARD ZINN, PLAYWRIGHT, AND SOCIAL ACTIVIST

Be one of the millions, help transform your little corner of the world and encourage others to do the same.

FEBRUARY 7th

Start writing no matter what. The water does not flow until the faucet is turned on.

— Louis L'Amour

If you want to write, these words are excellent advice. Mr. L'Amour should know. He has written over 100 books, 400 short stories, poetry and who knows what else??? I have never read any of his books since most of them are Western stories, but I might need to.

I have always enjoyed writing. When I was in elementary school (or as we called it back in the "olden days", grade school) I wanted to write books. Part of that was probably due to my love affair with the school and public libraries. My second choice was to be a librarian….Hmmm…..I worked in the banking industry for 27 years, retiring as a Vice President. While there, I taught classes at Kirkwood Community College and for the Iowa Bankers Association. Guess I strayed from my original path.

My retirement "job" has been acting (and I do mean acting) as a guest teacher for the last decade or so, primarily at a middle school. Still missing the mark on my career goals. What do I want to be when I grow up?

I have kept a file for years with quotes, ideas and nonsense, thinking someday I would do something with it. That day has come. It is never too late to strive for a dream. I was fortunate to have the flame of desire to do this nurtured and kindled by a wonderful man who I am lucky to have in my life. He listened to my dreams, and helped me get started making them come true.

On your journey today, figure out what you want to do when you grow up, turn loose the horses and go for it!! I'm rooting for you!!

FEBRUARY 8th

When I was growing up, Jell-O salads were the trendy dish. An endless variety of Jell-O with fruits, vegetables, whipped cream, cream cheese, and shredded cheese graced many a Sunday dinner table and church potlucks. There were whole cookbooks filled with Jell-O recipes. I am pretty sure my mom had a mold in which to create fancy looking Jell-O salads. Actually, they could be a salad or a dessert depending on the ingredients. Some years ago, a new twist was added, changing the recipe slightly, you could make Jell-O Jigglers, that you could pick up with your fingers and eat.

An interesting celebration that you may have been missing out on is International Jell-O Week, which is the second full week of February. A whole week to reflect, enjoy, devour and wax poetic about Jell-O.

In 1897, the first four original flavors were strawberry, raspberry, orange and lemon. Today there are twenty-two flavors of this slippery, fruity salad/dessert.

Salt Lake City, Utah has the highest per capita consumption of Jell-O in the world. I am not sure what the average lifespan is in Utah, but there must be some reason they are eating all that Jell-O, and I think it bears looking into!! I am especially bemused by this, as I am not a connoisseur of the gelatinous foods. I did however once give someone an Easter basket filled with every variety of Jell-O I could find. It was very colorful, and no eggs were harmed in the making of it.

Just wanted to give you another holiday to put on the calendar, a reason to celebrate and have some fun!! Wow your friends with your new knowledge. Have a Jell-O themed party...there is just no end to the fun you can have!!

FEBRUARY 9th

If I were the President of the United States of America...when you have resumed your composure and the laughter has stopped, here is my brief version of a State of the Union Address.

Good evening fellow Americans. I am directing this speech to you and not to the members of Congress. The state of the union is a bizarre twisted version of what our founding fathers intended. I intend to fix a few things immediately, in the name of all that is fair and good.

1. Effective immediately, members of Congress will not have any better or less expensive access to health care than the average American. They will not vote on their own pay raises, they will get a cost of living raise like most of you. They will not receive a pension for life for serving one or two terms. Their retirement pension will be dictated by years of service at their Social Security mandated full retirement age.
2. All celebrities, politicians, political activists and "friends" of Congress will be prosecuted to the full extent of the law until their income taxes are paid in full. It is a travesty that some are allowed to owe millions of dollars in back taxes, while the average citizen pays their taxes every year.
3. Private national accounting firms will audit each department of the federal government and identify excess and inappropriate spending. The budget of the federal government will be streamlined and non-essential departments will be eliminated. Our top priorities will be Education, National Defense, Homeland Security, Healthcare and Transportation Infrastructure.

Good night and God Bless these United States of America.

FEBRUARY 10th

MAGAZINES, love them or hate them?? It seems to me that each month, there are more ads and less content. I have let most of my subscriptions lapse due to the fact that I just don't care!! I feel like I am not getting much enjoyment from them anymore. However....I have come across some publications that I enjoy and thought you might as well.

"Daphne's Diary" published in the United Kingdom was a pleasant surprise. It is chock full of stories, DIY, gardening, travel and interesting paper cutouts to name a few. It is a very upscale interactive bookazine (I can't bring myself to call it a magazine, so that is my made up word for this) for grown-up people!! It is a little pricey for an issue, but there is so much to read and do, it will last for a while. I think it is worth it. If you journal or scrapbook, you will definitely enjoy this. If you are not a crafty person, I think you will still like it. Did I mention there are no advertisements?

"Project Calm (Mindfulness Through Making)" is another bookazine I enjoy. Similar in theory, but a different approach to content. Inspiration is found on every page, as well as stories, paper cut-outs/projects, bookmarks, postcards and more that are for, again, grown-up people!!!

Slow your pace, and relish something new and unique. Give the gift of time to yourself.

> Teach me the art of taking minute vacations...of stopping to savor the simple beauty of the daily round.
>
> — THE QUIET MIND CALENDAR, 1964

FEBRUARY 11th

As much as I love the Heartland, and can't imagine myself living anywhere else, a break from the winter is wonderful. It helps you get through the rest of the cold weather with a renewed purpose. We escaped just in time this year, in front of a snowy, cold week.

Being in warm weather in February does bring some challenges as I am not as young as I used to be. No bikinis for this Heartland girl for the last many years. I worry about how I will look on the beach as an "older" person.

So, the time has come, we have arrived in the Sunshine State and are ready to make our first trip to the beach. (In my case, that can be like packing for a short vacation!) We gather chairs, sunglasses, towels, books, phones, liquid refreshment of the cold and sometimes adult variety, and last but not least my courage. The beaches in Florida aren't always busy this early in the month, but if the weather is exceptionally warm, there can be a crowd. So with trepidation in my heart, we find a place to set up our chairs and belongings. I take off my swimsuit cover-up and sit down to read. Time passes, and I wait... What a relief, I have been here fifteen minutes and nobody has hollered "Help! Beached Whale!" so I think I am okay. Whew...that was a close one.

It is hard getting older, so many things that don't work the way they used to, or look the way they used to. The hardest part is that in my heart and mind, I am still young, funny and 3 gallons of crazy in a 2-gallon bucket. So no matter what your age, live life in color!!

On your journey today, pedal hard, coast when you can and take your hands off the handlebars every once in a while.

FEBRUARY 12th

I FEEL it's safe to confess here that I am someone who likes to shop. Online, in-store, window shopping, it all appeals to me. One of my favorite stores to browse through, which may surprise you is an office supply store.

I am fascinated and often covet the many things I find at my local Staples store. Notebooks, fun paperclips, pens, post-it notes in every color and shape, planners, folders and all sorts of things to organize your office and yourself.

Granted, I don't work in an office anymore, I have a pseudo home office but work is minimal. I am definitely not running Barnes and Noble from my small, postage stamp sized desk in my very small sitting room. However, if you saw my office supplies, you might wonder.

Starting with pens, I am very picky about the pens I write with. I am not a brand snob, but the pen has to feel a certain way when I write with it. I prefer blue ink over black for my daily lists, schedule, and random notes. I will write with black if the feel is right, but I am not going to be happy about it. Paperclips are another obsession. I prefer the plastic, colored clips in the larger size. They are useful in every situation where papers need to be held together.

I think this fascination (some might say obsession) with office supplies has to do with my OCD tendencies. I love things to be organized. I am most vulnerable to the purchasing of office supplies when I feel out of control about a project, or life itself.

As A.A. Milne put it, "Organizing is what you do before you do something, so that when you do it, it's not all mixed up."

FEBRUARY 13th

February in the Heartland....or Hawkeye cruise leaving from Puerto Rico with friends who asked us to go?? It was a hard question, but we rose to the occasion and said yes, we will endure the hardships of an ocean cruise for our dear friends.

This was a few years ago and quite an adventure for me. I had never been on a cruise. We had lots of Ports of Call, saw many beautiful islands including St. Maarten, St. Kitt, Barbados, and others. We had not signed up for any of the day excursions. We enjoy finding our way into town and exploring on our own, with one exception. We couldn't pass up the opportunity to do a zip line course.

The ziplining adventure took place in St. Kitt. Neither my traveling companion nor I had ever been ziplining, so what better place to try it out??? We arrived in a van from the cruise ship. Along with fifteen strangers, who bonded quickly as we were crammed into a very old Toyota pickup truck. The ride up the mountain was at least 30 minutes. There was no road. It was a rutted cow path with rocks everywhere. At this point, we decided if we survived the ride up the mountain, the zip line course would be a breeze!! With only minimal bruising, cursing and praying, we made it to the top. That pickup was one tough truck!!

There were about 7 ziplines to get back down the mountain. Imagine ziplining over a tropical paradise, with the ocean in view. It was staggeringly spectacular!! I will never forget the beauty of the island and the thrill of the zip line through the jungle!!

Mark Twain said, "Twenty years from now, you will be more disappointed by the things you didn't do, than the ones you did. So throw off the bowlines. Sail away from the safe harbor. Catch the trade winds in your sails. Explore. Dream. Discover."

FEBRUARY 14th

AHHHH....SWEET Valentine's Day....flowers, chocolates, dinner, wine with the one you love....or is it? We were spending Valentine's Day in Florida and decided to have dinner at an Italian restaurant. It was a beautiful night, so after dinner, we decided to stroll around the circle. This is a beautiful area with lots of outdoor dining and shops.

The previous few days we had noticed a number of dogs being pushed in strollers, quite a number actually. If your eyesight were a little compromised, your first thought might be, now ***that's*** an ugly baby! It is very confusing to see!

So off we strolled, enjoying the night, the white lights everywhere, and the warm summer breeze. Then we saw it....A couple at an outdoor table, with three, yes, three strollers at their table. Each stroller contained, yes, you guessed it, a dog. Each stroller was decorated with a string of battery operated heart lights while the occupants were properly bedecked in their Valentine finery. The strollers had a high seat so the dogs are sitting at table height.

I am sure the neighboring tables were thrilled to have their nice dinner punctuated with dog "conversation." I had to walk by a second time to make sure I wasn't hallucinating. I didn't think I had that much wine at dinner!!

I understand that people love their pets.....but seriously??? Dogs are not people and shouldn't be treated as such. Are these people afraid to be alone with each other? Do they know how to make conversation? Having dogs at your dinner table pretty much eliminates the need and possibility of that happening. Leave the dogs at home with their chew toys and invest that time and effort on your dinner companion. No hate mail please, I like dogs, but I am not taking one out to dinner.

FEBRUARY 15th

I LOVE poetry by Robert Frost. I would like to share one of his poems with you today, that I find thought provoking and humorous.

"Fire and Ice" by Robert Frost

Some say the world will end in fire,
Some say in ice.
From what I've tasted of desire
I hold with those who favor fire.
But if it had to perish twice,
I think I know enough of hate
To say that for destruction ice
Is also great
And would suffice.

I like this poem because it can be interpreted different ways. Upon first reading, taking it literally, it seems it is about the end of the world due to human greed and destruction.

I think the poet is using the world as a metaphor for relationships. I have definitely been in relationships that ended in fire, and some in ice!! Sometimes both….Hate and holding a grudge are two of the most destructive emotions in my opinion. These emotions solve nothing, and destroy the person holding on to them.

I wish I could know your thoughts after reading this poem. One of the wonderful things about poetry, is seeing how it is interpreted from different perspectives. Black, white, shades of gray, or flames of red in this case, what do you see?

FEBRUARY 16th

I AM sure that I would be remiss, being from Iowa, in writing this crazy collection of essays, if I did not write about "loose meat" sandwiches. It seems this delectable taste treat was invented around 1920 in Sioux City, Iowa and called a tavern sandwich. I did not grow up calling them a tavern sandwich or a loose meat sandwich. We called them Maid-Rites which is the name of a franchise restaurant chain with headquarters in Urbandale, Iowa.

Eating at the Maid-Rite was a treat growing up. We often ate at one in Washington, Iowa (a town made famous by my being born there…). Not only did we get to have the special sandwich, but they had Lemon Pepsi, Chocolate Pepsi, and Cherry Pepsi. Those were the days my friend!! Give me a Maid-Rite sandwich with cheese and the works, a Lemon Pepsi and I am good to go!!

The loose meat/Maid-Rite/tavern sandwich which is comprised mainly of crumbled ground beef, onions and sometimes a mystery ingredient is not to be confused with the Sloppy Joe. The Sloppy Joe usually has some sort of sauce mixed in that is tomato based. Yummy in its own right, but it is not now, nor will ever be a Maid-Rite.

Maid-Rite restaurants are hard to find these days, they are mostly a memory. Fortunately, there are still many local restaurants in Iowa that serve up a delicious loose meat sandwich!!

You don't have to be from Iowa to enjoy this tasty treat, but you may have to come to Iowa to have one!! Remember, happiness is stringing together all the little things. On your journey, kick up your heels (don't hurt yourself), rock the boat and find yourself a loose meat sandwich.

FEBRUARY 17th

SEEMS LIKE THERE SHOULD BE A "HOLIDAY" today...wait....there is....It is Random Acts of Kindness Day. Although every day should contain random acts of kindness, I guess it is a good idea to be reminded of that.

The unexpected gift, comment, surprise can make a sad day better, and a good day extraordinary. I try to embrace this practice, but it is easy to let everyday life get in the way.

Did some brainstorming for ideas for random acts, and thought I would share with you…

- Leave an anonymous treat for a co-worker.
- Buy a bunch of inexpensive flowers and hand them out as you walk down the street.
- Give a stranger a compliment (be careful here).
- Leave some change by the vending machines.
- Send some texts just to say " hi, thinking of you."
- Take treats to your local fire or police department
- Pay for a meal for someone you spot in a restaurant.
- Walk up to military personnel and thank them for their service.
- Walk up to police on duty and thank them for their service. (I also usually get a picture out of the deal, but that is another story!)
- Leave a treat in the mailbox for the mail carrier.
- Pay for coffee for a stranger.

We are all on this journey together, make someone's load a little lighter, make them smile, it is really a gift to yourself.

FEBRUARY 18th

> Reading forces you to be quiet in a world that no longer makes place for that.
>
> — John Green

I can't imagine a world without books, a world without reading. Books are a path to other worlds, cultures, places, knowledge, pleasure, and understanding. Reading helps build vocabulary, prevent boredom, and keeps the brain active. Books have been important in my life since I was a child. Weekly trips to the public library where I could check out a stack of books almost as tall as I was. My mother shared and indulged my love of reading.

It's a different world now. It can be hard to find the time, that quiet moment to block out the world and become immersed in a story that enthralls, amuses and grants escape from our daily routine. Books are also protection from that chatty person sitting next to you on your flight to Iceland. When the power goes out in the Heartland during an ice storm, voila, open a book!! Also, the neighbors rarely complain that I am reading too loud.

There is a debate today concerning real books vs e-books. I am such a fan of real books. However, electronic books make so much sense when traveling. I can take thousands of books with me wherever I go. But for me, bottom line, there is nothing like browsing through "real" books at the local bookstore or library. Turning that first page with eager anticipation….it never gets old!

On your journey today, choose a genre, choose a book, choose to read.

Your world will began expanding immediately and your brain will thank you.

FEBRUARY 19th

ANOTHER HOLIDAY TO CELEBRATE!! Today is Chocolate Mint Day as proclaimed by the U.S. Confectioner's Association!! This may be a little known holiday, but who cares?? A day to recognize the importance of these two important flavors and the mixing of them!! Chocolate is not one of my favorite things, but I do like this combo!!

Here is a chocolate mint cookie recipe I have been making over the years, pretty simple and very yummy!

Ingredients: ¾ cup of butter, 1 ½ cups of brown sugar, 2 eggs, 2 ½ cups of flour, 1 ¼ tsp baking soda, 2 T water, 2 cups semi-sweet chocolate chips, ½ tsp salt, 3 (4.5-ounce packages Andes Mints)

1. Over medium heat, cook sugar, butter and water stirring til melted. Remove from heat, stir in chocolate chips til melted. Cool for 10 minutes.
2. Pour chocolate mixture into large bowl, beat in eggs, one at a time. Combine flour, baking soda and salt, stir into chocolate mixture. Cover and refrigerate at least 1 hour.
3. Roll cookie dough into walnut sized balls. Bake on greased cookie sheets (or parchment paper) at 350 degrees for 8-10 minutes. Don't overbake.
4. When cookies come out of the oven, press one chocolate mint wafer into top of each cookie and let sit for a minute. When mint is soft, swirl with a toothpick to make a pattern.

There is a chocolate mint plant you can grow indoors. It is described as peppermint with chocolate overtones. You can use it as an herb just like the peppermint plant. Who knew??? Enjoy the cookies, throw an Andes mint or three in your morning coffee and celebrate the day.

FEBRUARY 20th

We have been traveling to Florida for a number of years, staying in different places on the Gulf Coast. We finally found the perfect place to be our home away from home. This small condo group is right on the beach, with a nice heated pool and near many amenities that we enjoy.

Upon arrival, we noticed a sign in the elevator inviting one and all to the "Sunset Social" held at 5:30 p.m. every Wednesday. Bring a snack to share and your own adult beverage. The gathering is held in the large community room that is all windows facing the beach. I had dragged my feet about going last year but finally assented to go and be "social" this time around. But off we go snack in one hand, wine glasses in the other.

I was deeply involved in a conversation when it appeared the sun was going to start its stunning descent into the sea. Voices became hushed and then silent as some thirty of us watched the spectacular sight that is a Florida sunset. The sun slowly descends, appearing to rest on the ocean, and then quickly disappears. It leaves behind beautiful trails of pinks, oranges, and lavenders. It was still quiet, and somebody said, "You know, the sun will still set even if we are talking!" Technically he was right, but I was delighted to share this experience, knowing everyone in the room was appreciating the handiwork of the Master, in absolute silence.

Turned out, like many things that I think I don't want to do, I was glad we went for the fellowship and the ritual setting of the sun. I will be looking forward to it next week, with our fellow travelers who have all gathered here in the Sunshine state. We share stories about home, about our personal journey, break bread together and marvel at the unique beauty of the sun setting over the Gulf of Mexico.

May you find beauty in your world that leaves you awestruck.

FEBRUARY 21st

"MEMORIES PRESSED between the pages of my mind. Memories sweetened through the ages just like wine." The first lines of a popular song, "Memories," written by Billy Strange and Mac Davis, and originally recorded by Elvis in 1968. This song came to mind when I was thinking about memories, and trying to recall what is my first actual memory. There are events I think I remember but know that it is only because I have heard the story so many times.

My first actual memory happened somewhere around the ages of 3-4 years old. I was sitting on the steps of the Clover Farm, a neighborhood grocery store on Summit Street in Iowa City. I was looking at books with a friend Joyce. We ended up attending school grades K-12 together. We weren't close friends as we got older, but for some reason, this memory is a fond one.

It is fascinating what the brain remembers and shares with us. Another distinct memory I have, is my birthday when I was 6 or 7. I was clearly a renaissance woman at a tender age. My birthday wish list included a hula/grass skirt, and a cowgirl holster with guns. I received both of those items, and often wore them together. A memory that seems consistent with the woman I would become, and makes me giggle anytime I think of it. If only my mom had taken a picture....sigh...

Take a moment to lose yourself in your memories. Record favorite memories in a journal. Doesn't have to be fancy or Pulitzer prize- winning literature, get it down on paper. Your future self and your family will appreciate stories from your past and from your present.

Take heed of this quote from Cesare Paves, Italian poet and novelist: "We don't remember days, we remember moments." Make more moments every day. Live life large!!

FEBRUARY 22nd

Today I am thinking about small things that make me smile....

- A quiet morning with nowhere to go
- Finding money in a wallet you haven't used in awhile
- Receiving a card in "real" mail
- A new book
- Fresh flowers for no reason
- A good movie
- A rainstorm, a book and time
- A new friend
- A blossoming tree
- A blank notebook and a new pen
- Falling snow, fireplace, hot toddy
- Laughter of children
- Smell of newly mown grass
- Peonies
- First day of a road trip
- Blank notecards
- A to-do list that is done
- Freshly painted room

Just a few things that are special and make me happy. Make your own list, remembering the things that make you smile.

> Happiness is found in the simplest of things. Happiness is found in gratitude, in a kept promise, in a good conversation, in love, in friendship, in an achieved goal, in a found memory; in all the simple magnificence of life.
>
> — Dr. Steve Maraboli

FEBRUARY 23rd

One flag, one queen, long may she reign!! (Long has she reigned!!) I am a self-proclaimed Anglophile, and for years I have had a fascination with the British monarchy. I find the rigid protocol, ceremonies, pomp and circumstance so compelling. It is unlike anything here in America, so a curiosity indeed.

I don't know why I didn't think of this years ago, but I decided to write a letter to Queen Elizabeth. The writing of the letter is a bit more difficult than it sounds. There is a protocol (imagine that) for writing to the Queen. It is not totally inappropriate if you don't follow the protocol as an American, but it will just reinforce the opinion of the British that we are the uncivilized, rebellious child that left the nest some 300 years ago!!

I wrote my letter to the Queen and her husband, wishing them a healthy and happy New Year, and expressing my interest and admiration for the royal family. I also commented on what wonderful men her grandsons had turned out to be. Then, insert drum roll, I signed it as directed: I have the honour to be, Madam, Your Majesty's humble and obedient servant.

I mailed it. I waited, patiently, knowing it could take some time to reach Her desk, and hopefully respond. I waited. Imagine my delight, upon collecting my mail one day, I spotted an unusual looking envelope that had a big red ink stamp on it that said "Royal Mail."

Color me excited. I held my excitement in check, looked at my other mail, and sat down with the Royal letter to fully savor and appreciate the moment. The letter was on very heavy stationary with Buckingham Palace and the Royal Crest at the top. The Queen thanked me for my kind words and New Year wishes. It wasn't personally signed, but all in all still very exciting to get a letter from the Queen!!

FEBRUARY 24th

As someone who enjoys making quilts, I am always on the lookout for quilt shops as we travel. Each shop is unique, and shops in different parts of the country often yield different fabrics, some unique to their geographical location.

I had a very interesting adventure in one particular shop while on vacation. I will call it "Sarah's Quilt Shop, in honor of my great-aunt Sarah, a lovely Mennonite lady. I always enjoy going to Sarah's as it is located in an Amish area. There are usually 4-6 Amish women sitting at an old-fashioned quilting frame, hand stitching a quilt, just as their mothers, grandmothers and all those who came before them did. It is a step back in time and a calming scene to watch.

Sarah's also sometimes has "Amish" themed fabric. My last visit there, I saw some items for sale with some of this fabric. I wanted to purchase the actual fabric to make a quilt myself. I asked one of the Amish workers if they had this fabric, as I would like to buy some. She looked around to see if anyone else was within earshot, and the motioned for me to come to the back room of the shop, where the fabric resided. She called the owner to the back to ask if I could buy some. I explained I had Mennonite and Amish relatives and would really like to have some of this fabric.

After some discussion, she agreed I could buy two yards of the coveted fabric, with the caveat that I not tell anyone where I got it. Hence, the pseudonym used above for the shop name, and no mention of the locale. I didn't realize there was an underground, secret market for hard to obtain fabric. I felt honored to be welcomed to the sisterhood of forbidden fabric. I have yet to make anything with this special fabric. I am waiting for the perfect quilt idea to percolate in my brain.

FEBRUARY 25th

I HAVE HEARD many times news stories about people arrested for murder, fraud, conspiracy and whatever buffet of crimes they may have committed. One man had eleven, yes I said eleven, aliases and apparently identification to go with them. This is amazing to me.

I have enough trouble keeping track of my one real identity and all the documents, passwords, and records that go with it!!

I do however, have a lot of nicknames used or created by friends, most of them nice. I certainly don't have identification for them, and if I did, that might raise some eyebrows. Maybe it would make me famous since they are all one-word nicknames. I could be the next Cher, Elvis, Beyonce...all those people who are so amazing, they only need one name.

My best-suited nickname for that would be "LoLa", a compilation of the first syllables of my first and last names. That might just be enough to jumpstart my rise to stardom....or therapy....or an admiring glance from the police officer pulling me over....

Nicknames are fun if the creator is someone who adores you, and it is a nice name. As kids, the nicknames for our peers were not always kind. If we called someone Stupid Head, that was about as low as it could go. Ahhhh.....the good old days....You could call someone a name like that, and be best friends again within the hour. I am happy that my adult friends have christened me with nicknames that make me smile.

On your journey, today, wear a bright color, have a bright idea, and let your light shine on those around you.....and think up a nickname or two!

FEBRUARY 26th

I LOVE to listen to casual conversation about the differences between the male brain and the female brain. There are certainly differences, but I am not sure if everyone agrees on what the differences are!!

My girlfriends and I can carry on conversations about multiple topics simultaneously, switching back and forth without missing a beat. We can make random conversational jumps to a topic discussed thirty minutes ago, and everyone gets it. Based on my observation of men, this is not true about them. I have heard it said that a woman's brain (yes, sometimes it is directed at me pointedly), is similar to having 43 web browsers open at the same time, all the time, while men use one web browser at a time, sometimes.

I saw an explanation that made sense to me, in an article from Psychology Today, authored by Dr. Gregory Lantz. "The right and left hemispheres of the male and female brains are not set up exactly the same way. Females tend to have verbal centers on both sides of the brain, while males tend to have verbal centers on only the left hemisphere. This is a significant difference." The article continues on to say females use more words when describing something. Ha! What father, husband, boyfriend, brother couldn't have told you that?? In fact, women speak about 20,000 words a day, in contrast to the 7,000 words men speak. Again, is this a surprise to anyone? It's just nice to have it quantified. Give me the facts!!

On your journey today, meet with someone for coffee and conversation, ice cream and conversation, happy hour and conversation! There is nothing like a good conversation with someone important in your life. Words, laughter, sometimes tears can combine in the most magical way. Make some magic today!!

FEBRUARY 27th

Oscar Wilde, an Irish playwright and poet once said, "If one cannot enjoy reading a book over and over again, there is no use in reading it at all." I agree, that many books are worth reading over and over again, but that isn't necessarily true for all books and all readers.

I have a number of books that I have read a dozen times or more. My all-time favorite, "Little Women," by Louisa May Alcott. I probably read that once every year. Why in the world would anyone continue to read the same books over and over? Personally, the place I am in, on life's game board influences what I get out of a book, the details I notice, and the perspective I take from it. Also, reading a favorite book again is like putting on those old comfy pajamas, slippers, and talking to a good friend.

I also know people who will finish every book they start, even if they dislike it and are not enjoying it. Not this reader!! If it doesn't grab me in the first 50-75 pages, we are breaking up!! There are too many books I will enjoy, that are waiting impatiently to be read!! I admire their tenacity and patience, but not skills I possess in this instance.

A series I have read more than once is the seven-book saga that starts with the book "A Woman of Substance," by Barbara Taylor Bradford. These books are complex and span three generations of families, so I definitely pick up nuances and character traits I missed before.

On your journey, today, read early, read often!! A quote from an unknown source sums it up, "I always read books twice. The first time you appreciate the story. The second time you appreciate the writing."

Go forth and read and read and read!!!

FEBRUARY 28th

Ralph Waldo Emerson said, "Live in the sunshine, swim in the sea, drink in the wild air." I couldn't agree more, and while you are living, swimming and drinking....take a look at the world around you with careful intent to really notice specific objects.

Day after day, we travel the same places as we go to work, run errands or take a walk in the neighborhood. Objects may be invisible to us, since we are in familiar terrain, we often don't really look, and therefore don't actually see the things around us.

Next time you are out and about, try noticing specific items. Here are some suggestions:

- A blue door
- Puddles
- Huge tree
- Cloud formations
- Random wildflowers
- A cluster of parked bicycles
- Empty park benches
- Green space
- Neighbor's garden
- Outside art
- The perfect house/lawn
- A small shop
- Clothes on a clothesline
- Big pile of rocks
- Children laughing
- People waiting at a bus stop

Life is all around, just waiting to be noticed. Take a look.

FEBRUARY 29th

HERE WE ARE, once in a four year time span at this special day. I love the unique and unusual, and February 29th or "Leap Day" as it is called certainly fits the bill. I am including this day in case you are reading this book during a Leap Year. If you are reading this book and it is not a leap year, stop reading this page!!

I am not a scientist, astrologer, or an expert on the waxing and waning of the moons. There are a lot of other things I am not, but that would fill another book. The simplest way it has been explained to my non-scientific brain is that the earth does not orbit the sun in exactly 365 days. It actually takes 365 days and just under 6 hours to make the trip. So to keep our calendar in alignment with the rotation of the earth around the sun, every four years we add a day.

Too bad in our own lives that we can't just add a day when we need one. I know a lot of students of all ages that would love an extra day now and then before a test. But alas, this day adding phenomenon is handled by those left-brain people.

There are also some fun, crazy historical remnants associated with this day. My favorite is that during Leap Year, a woman may ask a man to marry her. This might not be so uncommon in today's world, but, hey ladies, this gives you official permission!!

Enjoy your extra day this year, do something for yourself, your family, your friends or your community. Pay it forward!

MARCH 1st

WELL, I have done it again. I was browsing through the floral department at the Hy-Vee store, which is always dangerous. After admiring the ivies, the philodendrons, the big, beautiful Norfolk Pine, I decided to bring home a shamrock plant. Not the first one I have owned….definitely won't be the last.

I am the Hospice House for plants. This is where plants come to spend their final days. I am the last step on their journey back to Mother Earth. I love plants, but evidently that isn't enough to be a plant owner. Give me a healthy, thriving green plant, and I can and will change that. I have faced the truth, my home is where plants come to die.

I have managed to keep a prayer plant (maybe this one is getting help from a higher power) and an aloe plant alive for months, yes in the plural, months. Not really sure how, but I ignore them until they are screaming for water, and that seems to be working. I am afraid to try Miracle-Gro or other plant food. That seems like a job for someone with a higher security clearance and pay grade than me!

Why do I keep bringing plants to my home to die? Every time, I have hopes that this one will be different. I really enjoy having plants and the benefits they bring to your home. Organic, good for air quality, and someone to talk to when the power goes out. Maybe I should talk to them more, and tell them how beautiful they are. Works for people.

On your journey today, nurture a green plant, buy some flowers and let nature bring some life to your home.

MARCH 2nd

SCOTCHAROOS, the Rice Krispie treat that is impossible to beat!! This dessert treat, allegedly invented in Iowa is legendary. There is no real evidence where this treat originated, but what I have read seems to lean towards Iowa. In fact, the Urban Dictionary says, "A tasty Midwest treat, most commonly found in the great state of Iowa." Note: I rarely quote the Urban Dictionary, but in this particular instance, it supports my claim!

There are several versions of this delectable treat. Chocolate and Rice Krispies are in both, then depending on your favorite, there will be either peanut butter or butterscotch chips added to the mix. Or, you can go hog wild and use peanut butter AND butterscotch chips!! Count me in!!

These bars can be found in the Midwest at many potlucks, Little League games, graduation parties, picnics and for no reason at all!! There are many recipes out there, but I use the original recipe from the Kellogg's Rice Krispie box. As we say here in the Heartland, if it ain't broke, don't fix it. If you have not made or tasted these, check out the recipe and you will be guaranteed chocolatey, butterscotchy, crunchy, peanut buttery heaven.

As I write this, my mouth is watering! If I had the ingredients for these on hand, my kitchen would be a gooey mess right now!! Where's my grocery list??

It is permissible to take them across state lines to share with the uninitiated, So on your journey today, make some treats, share them with friends and family everywhere, it's the Iowa way!!

MARCH 3rd

Happy March 3rd!!! I am told that March 3rd is "Peach Blossom Day." A lovely sounding day on what is normally a dreary, not-spring-like day. I don't know anyone who celebrates this day, but I may start!!

It seems like a perfectly peachy day to talk about words that begin with the letter "P." Here are some of my favorite words:

Preposterous	Propensity
Plop	Pique
Prevaricate	Perky
Pratfalls	Pithy
Plucky	Perspicacious

Have some fun with these words today. Try to work every single one into a conversation or text. If you don't know the meaning, look them up. I love learning new words. We are never too old to learn, unless it's about programming a new TV, then I am too old.

On your journey today, prepare a peach pie, gather a committee to plan Pi Day, and avoid pratfalls as you plop down to eat the pie. (Or as my friends often do, shake your head, nod and smile, and humor me!!!

MARCH 4th

TODAY IS March Forth and Do Something Day!! Don't you just love a good homophone? (I had to do a little dictionary work, because I can get confused about the differences between homophone, homonym and homograph. I will not attempt to explain it here, frankly because it would take the whole page, and still not make sense. You will just have to trust me on this one!) March Forth is mostly an imaginary holiday, but I don't require things to be factual or real to celebrate them. I am flexible that way, plus I get to enjoy a cornucopia of extra holidays that way. As we used to say back in the 'hood, "My mother didn't raise any dummies." Which also elicits the obvious response…. No need to go there.

This is your day! March Forth into your life, and do whatever you are aching to do. Check that bucket list and see if there is something that you can check off today. Start a new hobby or lose yourself in an old one. Indulge your dreams today and make something happen for yourself. The stars are the limit, so set some big goals for yourself today. What have you always wanted to do or try? Sign up for tap dance class, learn to play the ukulele, stop by the art supply store, visit the local hobby shop, try a DIY project, and enjoy yourself. Perfection is not required to have fun or create something. Perfection is not expected from we who are mere mortals.

I have not seen the movie, "Ferris Bueller's Day Off," but I would like to share a quote that seems perfect for this day: "Life moves pretty fast. If you don't stop and look around once in awhile, you could miss it." True words.

On your journey today, March Forth and seize the day for yourself. Do something that will stir your senses, ignite your passion and polish this day to a high shine.

MARCH 5th

I RECENTLY READ A VERY funny article in "The New Yorker" by Kathryn Schulz. The topic was losing things. She estimates that in our lifetime, we will spend six months looking for items we have misplaced/lost!! Phones, remotes, shoes, keys, socks, purses, wallets, jackets, glasses, well you get the idea!!

I like to look for these misplaced items as I am trying to get out the door so that I can be late for whatever appointment, meeting or lunch that is on my schedule. Logic would dictate remaining calm, not my modus operandi. If I don't find said item in the first two places I look, I immediately declare DEFCON 1. Panic sets in and pandemonium ensues. My heart is racing and I am unable to process a logical thought or focus on the crisis at hand. I am typically a calm person, but when something goes missing, so does my mind!!

I think losing things is related to the things I can't remember I have done. Did I unplug the hair iron? Did I close the garage door? The daily tasks that are so automatic, I take care of them without thinking.

I am told, if a person would say out loud what they are doing, they are more likely to remember it. "I am closing the garage door." Might be worth a try!! The concept is similar to taking notes in a class, writing it down helps you to remember it.

On the off chance you are looking for remote control, a survey in 2011 found that 4% of lost remotes are found in the freezer or refrigerator. There are no words....

On your journey today, may you remember everything you need to, may all your lost items be found, and may you take the time to slow down.

MARCH 6th

LIVING in a town that is home to a major university is a unique experience. Beginning in late August, the town literally explodes with the influx of about 25,000 undergraduate students. The campus is about 1,700 acres, but many of the University of Iowa buildings are close to or in the heart of the downtown. Every year, there is a shock factor when this happens, after the relative quiet of the summer months, when most of the students and faculty are gone.

There are so many positives to having the University here, B1G Ten sports, Broadway shows, big-name acts at Hancher and one of the largest teaching and highly ranked hospitals in the country. I love it, and can't imagine not having these adventures in my backyard

Now we come to the "however," section of the program. Making and keeping friends in a university town can be difficult. I like to compare it to the people mover at the airport, some of the University people you meet come in on the people mover, jump off and stay for a while, then jump back on the mover and disappear out of your life. This has been very hard for me sometimes. I am a collector of friends, and once someone is in my life, I have trouble letting go. The exception to that is if they become a negative influence.

I have had to accept the fact that some friends are only there for a few chapters of my story before they are written out of the plot. I learned to treasure those chapters and wish them well on the rest of their journey. My tribe is an ever-changing blend of people.

> Call it a clan, call it a network, call it a tribe, call it a family. Whatever you call it, whoever you are, you need one.
>
> — JANE HOWARD, JOURNALIST

MARCH 7th

> I am the vine, and my Father is the gardener. He cuts off every branch in me that bears no fruit, while every branch that does bear fruit he prunes so that it will be even more fruitful.
>
> — John 15:1-2

I love to write, which is why, hopefully, these daily essays have become a book that you are reading. I thought the bible verse from John was appropriate because my talents and abilities come from God.

Words are the fruit of the brain. They give life to feelings and thoughts. Hopefully, we use our words carefully, and prune the unkind and mean, thoughtless words from our vocabulary. Unfortunately, I think the vocabulary of the general population has been shrinking. We have such a garden of beautiful, descriptive words...words with more specificity that we could use. Choices...we are always reminded, and remind our children and students to make good choices. Articulate carefully and make good word choices. Make your writing or speaking a banquet of delicious words for your reader or listener.

I love vocabulary, love the word vocabulary and love learning new vocabulary. Hmmm...maybe I need to learn some new words that mean vocabulary. How about terminology, language, nomenclature, and phraseology?

MARCH 8th

Are you ready to celebrate International Women's Day? One special day to recognize the worth and achievements of women. I know, one day is not enough, and hopefully women are celebrated many ways and many days by those in their lives.

I have been so inspired by women I have followed or encountered in my life; politicians, authors, athletes, the women in my circle. I have also been inspired by men, but today is about me, us, she, her. I want to share a few quotes from women whose careers I have followed and admired.

> "If you want something said, ask a man; if you want something done, ask a woman.
>
> — Margaret Thatcher a/k/a the Iron Lady, former British Prime Minister.

> "I firmly believe you never should spend time being the former anything.
>
> — Condoleezza Rice, former Secretary of State, USA

(Sorry, Ms, Rice, but I had to use the word "former" in your title.)

I am guessing most of you reading this, along with me, don't have aspirations that equal the accomplishments of those two women.

However, what you accomplish in your life is just as important. Hopefully, my granddaughters are reading this, and I say to them:

Dream big, figure it out and make it happen. All my life I have wanted to write a book, have kept files and notes, and by golly, I have done it! Never give up, never let the naysayers talk you out of your dreams.

On your journey, remember what Eleanor Roosevelt said, "The future belongs to those who believe in the beauty of their dreams." Adventures, daydreams, sweet dreams, outrageous dreams, are all yours for the taking.

MARCH 9th

When traveling, it is so much fun to see the interesting names that places have, many have names that are reason enough to stop and visit!! Here are a few I hope you will enjoy, in no particular order. Feel free to toss them into conversation when appropriate!!

- Dripping Springs, Texas (Very evocative, paints a picture.)
- Hot Coffee, Mississippi (Seems self-explanatory!)
- Normal, Illinois (I don't think so, oxymoron??)
- Two Egg, Florida (Look this one up, has a great story behind it!)
- Why, Arizona
- Cheesequake, New Jersey (Strawberry please, 5.6 on the Richter.)
- What Cheer, Iowa
- Screamer, Alabama
- Hell, Michigan
- Truth or Consequences, New Mexico
- Boring, Oregon (Sorry for these residents.)
- Accident, Maryland

I am sure these towns all have a story about the origin of their town name. Some I do know, but others I sure am curious about!! We also have some very descriptive names for locations in this country. Mountains come to mind: Smoky Mountains, Blue Ridge Mountains, Rocky Mountains. I have visited all of these mountain ranges and the names do justice to the sight!

I came across the name of a town in Wales, that I have to share with you. Llanfairpwllgwyngyllgogerychwyrndroblllantysiliogogogoch. I have not tried to pronounce this, as I do not want to harm myself. The meaning of this is "St. Mary's church in the hollow of the white hazel near to the rapid whirlpool of Llantysilio of the red cave." Next time you take a road trip, write down the interesting names you come across!

MARCH 10th

In my recent phase of reading historical fiction, I remembered a book from my childhood. I adored this book and the story it told. It is fiction but based on events that happened in 1940.

The book is "Snow Treasure," written by Marie McSwigan. The story takes place in a small Norwegian village. The Nazis have parachuted in and taken the village and its' citizens captive. The villagers are trying to save gold bricks from the Bank of Norway, sneaking it past the Nazi soldiers. The plan was to be executed by a group of children, loading their sleds with the gold, and sledding it down the mountain to safety.

In June, 1940, a Norwegian freighter reached Baltimore, Maryland with a cargo of nine million dollars in gold bullion!

Amazing story of the bravery and courage of these children and the citizens who organized it. Hard to imagine asking children to risk their lives to help their country, but it has happened in war times in many places. I love stories of resistance during World War II. It shows the spirit, patriotism and moral courage of these people. It makes me ask myself if I would be brave enough to participate. I hope the answer is yes.

Even though this is a book meant for 10-13 year olds, if you haven't read it, I think it's a story worth reading.

> Courage is resistance to fear, mastery of fear, not absence of fear.
>
> — Mark Twain

On your journey, don't let fear of any kind be the voice you listen to. Drown it out with the knowledge that it can be overcome and don't let it keep you from living your dreams.

MARCH 11th

> The universe buries strange jewels deep within us all, and then stands back to see if we can find them. The hunt to uncover those jewels-that's creative living.
>
> — From the book "Big Magic" by Elizabeth Gilbert

Live with passion, find the jewels hidden within yourself, you will never regret the journey. Do something you have always wanted to do. Do something that scares you. Do something that excites you. Take a class, teach a class. Make a list that is wild and crazy of anything and everything you would like to do. Then pick one and make it happen.

Here are a few off the wall ideas to get you started:

- Be a mentor
- Learn to tap dance
- Play the banjo
- Throw a tomahawk
- Knit a scarf
- Write a book (or a journal)
- Take a photography/cooking/language class
- Plan an adventure-big or small, love them all
- Use a hot glue gun (no permit necessary)
- Find a hobby that is YOU

Writing this book is the largest jewel I have found within myself. This is a passion, a dream, a vision and I dug deep and found it. I have loved every moment of this process, and am already having regrets about finishing it. I will have to find another jewel, and I look forward to this. Uncover your jewels (do not take this too literally, you know who you are). Live life in the front row! Rush out in the rain and get soaked by the sky! (This you can take literally, your neighbors will love it!)

MARCH 12th

Happy Birthday to the Girl Scouts!! This organization is over 100 years old today!! Happy Birthday to my grandson, Josh! He is not over 100 years old!!

In 1912, Juliette Gordon Lowe started this group with 18 girls in her backyard in Savannah, Georgia. Her vision for this was an organization that would prepare girls for their future with courage, confidence and character. I was a girl member in grade school, and in later years served in many volunteer capacities including troop leader, and board member. As a girl I wasn't particularly musical or athletic, but I found a place where I could be a star. I was very good at selling cookies.

The other day, I went to Redbox to rent a movie. This is kind of a big deal, as I am fairly new to this adventure. What did I find, as I pulled up in front of the Redbox?? On a cold, windy day, there was a pair of sisters accompanied by their dad at a table selling Girl Scout Cookies!!

Genius marketing!! Who can pass up cookies to go with their movie rental.

Selling cookies is just one of the activities that teach the girls real life skills. They set goals, make a budget, take orders, and decide how the troop will spend the money they make. Not a bad lesson, and they have fun doing it!!

Did I buy cookies at the Redbox? You betcha!! I also always buy if they knock on my door and make their pitch. Cold calls are tough, and if they have the initiative to do this, I am going to buy. Remind me not to include my address here.....

MARCH 13th

THIS PAGE LEFT INTENTIONALLY BLANK, because some days are just like that. Write your own reflections today, because I got nothing!!

MARCH 14th

May I be the first to wish you a happy and joyous Pi Day? I hope for you all things that are mathematically and algebraically rewarding.

This day is a celebration of mathematics and in particular the Greek letter Pi which is a symbol used to represent a constant: the ratio of the circumference of a circle to its' diameter, approximately 3.14. Hence, the holiday on 3-14 every year.

Those of you who haven't fallen asleep or run from the room screaming, thanks for living through that scary trip back to middle school math!!

I am guessing that many of you are wondering how to celebrate this holiday. I have a very simple answer for you: PIE!! A group of my friends (yes they are teachers) started a few years ago going out for pie, or making pie and getting together.

Any kind of pie qualifies, and since Pi is a never-ending number, there are no limitations on how many slices of pie you enjoy. Go big or go home!!

One year, I helped to organize an event at the middle school where I am a guest teacher. On March 14th, we brought all 400+ students out to the football field and formed a giant Pi symbol, which loosely looks like a long division symbol. It was like herding cats and then expecting them to stay in one place. We got it done, and the local newspaper published a picture of our Pi symbol.

I believe we can find something to celebrate every single day. It doesn't have to be big and flashy but have some fun, look for unusual days to celebrate!! Love, laugh and live life large!!

MARCH 15th

The ides of March, NCAA basketball tournament: March Madness, and hair products. The anniversary of the day Julius Caesar was assassinated college basketball and yes, hair products. Sorry, some days it is just how my mind works. I was thinking about my hair products and the term March Madness seemed to apply.

As any month in a Heartland winter can be, March can be blustery, windy, cold and bleak. I was preparing myself for the day, in my usual slapdash way, minimal makeup, a little attention to the hair, and then lots of "product" as they say in the hair styling biz. The first product I apply to my hair after it is dry and flat-ironed is something called "WindBlown." I used it to give my hair some volume and that faux messy look. As I pondered the name of this product, I laughed out loud. I am spending money on a product to make my hair look a little wind tossed when I can step outside and get the look for free.

In my defense, Windblown has a light hairspray in it to keep the wickedly sexy mussed look in place. The windblown look that March winds provide also provide a look. However, the look one achieves in this manner resembles someone using an electric hand mixer on your hair. It is not the same. It's a look, but not the effect I am going for.

Hair products do have delightful names. Here are a few others by Redken, that by name seem to me to have nothing to do with hair! "Rewind" makes me think of watching a movie, "Rough Paste" is something a auto body shop might use, "Velvet Gelatine" seems like a lovely soft dessert served at a fine dining establishment. Another one that I actually use is called "Wax Blast" which could be used in a car wash.

Inner beauty is great, but a good hair day is fabulous...

MARCH 16th

Children are the living messages we send to a time we will not see.

— Unknown

Decades ago, on a hot, sultry summer day in Iowa; a thirteen year old girl remembered then, as I do now, the many special times a little girl spent with her Grandpa.

As far back as I can remember, and even before that, we were the best of friends. He would often drive the thirty miles to pick me up to spend a week or a weekend with him and Grandma. A visit to the pretty little town where they lived (and where I was born) was not complete until we had visited the 92 Cafe. Grandpa always took me to the cafe whether I was in town for a week or just for Sunday dinner. He wanted to show off his favorite (and only!) granddaughter to his friends. I would be dancing out of my shoes with excitement when we went. We would sit on red leather topped chrome stools that would spin around. Grandpa would have coffee, and I would have chocolate milk.

The memories of those times are so vivid, that even today when someone opens a pack of Juicy Fruit gum, I think of him. He would always have a pack of Juicy Fruit in his pocket for me. He never forgot, and in those days, it was a heady experience to have a whole pack of gum at one time!

What was special about Grandpa? Chocolate milk and Juicy Fruit days.

Eating a piece of cake in a bowl with milk poured over it, or his special fried pumpkin blossoms. His great love of music and Bing Crosby imitations. A thousand other things that expressed his love of life and his family.

So in sharing this story, I would like to say treasure the small moments because they become powerful memories that you store in your heart forever. Happy Birthday Grandpa!

MARCH 17th

LATELY, I have seen the phrase "be kind," all over the place. It is on t-shirts, coffee mugs, Facebook posts, and school bulletin boards. The Oxford Dictionary defines the word kindness as follows: "the quality of being friendly, generous and considerate." For my own definition, I would add taking that extra step, giving someone a helping hand without being asked, and being respectful.

There is an Emily Dickinson poem that I have always been fond of. This poem was written in 1864 and published in 1929.

If I can stop one heart from breaking,
I shall not live in vain.
If I can ease one life the aching,
Or cool one pain,
Or help one fainting robin
Unto his nest again,
I shall not live in vain.

The cost of kindness is nothing, but the value of kindness can't be measured in any quantitative way. It is like so many human emotions, love, happiness, pain, and heartbreak. Only those experiencing the emotion or the kindness received can measure it in their heart, soul and mind. I say this all the time, so if I am repeating myself in this book of musings, I apologize. Take a moment to be kind. There are countless ways to show kindness that take so little time and effort but mean so much to the recipient.

Lord, let me be a blessing to at least one person I meet today. Let our interaction make their world a little brighter and their load a little lighter. Help me show kindness and respect to all and let your light shine through me. Amen

MARCH 18th

TODAY WAS a pajama kind of day. No place to go, no one to see, just me, myself and I. I had a to-do list, and the stars must have been aligned because after my coffee I hit the ground running. That coffee must have had some special powers today because I was on fire!!

My thought process goes like this: why shower and change to get all grubby again cleaning the old homestead? It also keeps me from ditching the to-do list and going to get coffee or run unnecessary errands. I do know myself and my tricks to avoid chores!!

An additional advantage to pajama day is that when I need a break, I am already dressed for serious napping. You have no idea how much time that saves, just stop, drop and nap. I am all about doing things efficiently and napping is no exception.

Today was a very productive and fruitful pajama day, which if I am honest, isn't always the case. But today was a win! Around dinner time, I do start to feel a little guilty about still being in my pajamas...but I can overcome the guilt pretty quickly...after all, it's almost bedtime!

On your journey, today, give yourself permission to have a pajama day, or a nap whenever you see the need!!

MARCH 19th

I HAVE BEEN THINKING about jam, jelly, and preserves. (Yes, my world is rather small some days!) What in the world is the difference between these tasty toppings for toast or the iconic peanut butter and jelly sandwich? Growing up, it was all jelly for us, at least that's what we called it!

Being the curious type, and once I get hold of something, my mind has a death grip on it until I get the answer. I am relentless, like a terrier who has latched onto your pant leg. So, I sallied forth to seek answers. Maybe many of you know the difference, but for those that want to join my clue-less club, I will share what I learned!! All of these delectable toppings are made from fruit in some form, mixed with sugar and pectin. The form of the fruit is what differentiates the end product.

Jelly is made from fruit juice. Jam is made from fruit pulp, which is less stiff and easier to spread. Preserves are chunks of fruit in syrup or jam. So when a recipe calls for a specific type, usually jam or preserves, probably don't want to use jelly. Preserves and jam are required to contain at least 45% fruit.

I haven't forgotten marmalade, it is a word used specifically for citrus preserves, like orange marmalade. It sounds like you are taking your game up a level, if you have toast and marmalade for breakfast.

On your journey today, I hope you don't find yourself in a jam. It has happened to me often. Just try to preserve your dignity and get on with your day.

MARCH 20th

THE WRITING of this book took place in a variety of locales. Home, school, coffee shops, trips to Florida, North Carolina, New York, and Europe all spoke to me and gave me different sorts of inspiration. I found that writing in new places and different spaces helped me cultivate new ideas, and tweak some of the old ones.

Coffee shops are the cliched venue for writers, frustrated writers, and those who would aspire to be a writer. There are many marvelous reasons for writing in a coffee shop. First of all, deep in the Heartland is an incredible bookstore and cafe called Prairie Lights. It has been the inspiration for many writers.

Coffee tastes so much better than at home and there are so many possibilities. Plus, they usually have tasty treats in the bakery case. People watching opportunities are everywhere, along with the possibility of some casual conversation. Lingering is allowed and they don't accuse you of loitering….usually...

Perhaps, the best part of writing at a coffee shop is being able to stare into space, mutter to yourself, and make faces without anyone thinking you are strange. If someone you know happens to be there, they already know you are strange so all is good.

Writing is not for everyone. I find so much satisfaction and joy in the act of writing, and remain ever hopeful my readers will feel some of the same joy in the reading of it.

Channeling Coco Chanel as I prolong my stay at Prairie Lights: "In order to be irreplaceable one must always be different." Embrace your differences and those of others, find your passion and practice it daily.

MARCH 21st

My grandmother, Celia (and don't call her Cecilia by mistake, that is a game loser) was a very good cook and hostess. We spent Christmas and Easter at her house every year, as well as many, many Sundays for dinner. Her house smelled divine upon entry, and there was no doubt there would be a wonderful meal awaiting us. Nothing competes with Grandma's home cooking.

She had white dishes, with ornate raised design around the inside rim. Huge collection, coffee cups, bowls, platter, the whole nine yards so to speak. I thought those dishes were very special, one of a kind set. Setting the table with those was an honor. When those dishes were coming out, it was going to be a feast!!

The entree for the holiday dinners was hamloaf. Many of you may not have had this, but as kids we thought this was some treat!! Here is her recipe for this:

2# fresh ham (no fat) ground, 1# cured ham ground, 2 eggs beaten, 1 handful of oatmeal, 1 c finely crushed saltines, ¼ tsp pepper, 1 can tomato soup

Mix everything except soup. Form loaf. Bake 1 hour @ 350 degrees in a pan with water in it. Cover with tomato soup and bake ½ hour longer.

I have made this since she died, and it was good, but not like hers. As a side note, I found out years after she was gone, the white dishes I admired and coveted, were ones obtained through a gas station promotion. Beauty is in the eye of the beholder as they say.

MARCH 22nd

I KNOW you will find this hard to believe, but I am not a big fan of going to the dentist. I am, however, a big fan of my dentist, whom I have known for years. He is a very nice man and a good dentist but I don't enjoy the process. Two hands, seven dental instruments, a rubber dam and a wedge in my mouth is not my idea of a good time. But, I had a cracked filling that needed fixing. How bad can that be? Silly me, silly question, tempting the universe.

I settled into the dental chair, ready for the sounds and sights I knew would soon come…. The sting of the novocaine shot, the buzzing of the drill, the high pitched whine, the whoosh of the vacuum attachment.

He gave me the first novocaine shot, and we settled in for a chat as I waited for it to work. Nothing happened. He gave me another shot and we chatted some more while we waited. Nothing happened.

Four shots of novocaine and forty minutes after I settled in the chair, I am not numb. (At least not where I am supposed to be) There is a vague tingling in my cheek but I am not numb. I always knew that someday my superpowers would be activated, and glory be, the time has come!!

Unfortunately, the dentist was not impressed and told me he couldn't give me any more novocaine. Evidently, there are some unpleasant side effects if you have too much novocaine at a time. So, looks like I will have to give myself a pep talk and come back. The price one must pay for superpowers is a high one.

MARCH 23rd

In the Heartland, many lives revolve around the planting and harvesting seasons. I am not a farmer but many of my family and friends are part of this noble life. Growing up I was lucky enough to have grandparents and uncles who farmed and I spent many a happy summer vacation on the farm.

I have been thinking about some pairs of words.

Scattering-Gathering

Sowing-Reaping

Planting-Harvesting

Giving-Taking

What you scatter in life is so much more important than what you gather. The seeds of thoughts, actions and interactions throughout your life lay the foundation/roots for what you gather.

Sow seeds of encouragement, reap the bounty of helping someone accomplish a dream. Plant an idea, watch the harvest when the idea comes to fruition.

Plant a crop that is worth harvesting….love, trust, loyalty, commitment.

Give love, take love that is given to you.

When it comes right down to our time here on earth, we're all just walkin' each other home. It is that simple.

On your journey today, take a walk, take a chance, take someone with you to get ice cream….

MARCH 24th

MANY OF MY childhood friends seem to have better memories than I, regarding our growing up years, including high school. Allegedly, some of the stories they tell include my involvement in particular incidents. I can't disagree with them, because I honestly don't remember some of that. I do have some specific memories of elementary school that I will share today before I forget those!!

I attended Longfellow Elementary School, situated in an older, historic neighborhood. Loved every minute there, and still regard it fondly, as well as lifetime friends I met there.

I remember the excitement of wearing my Brownie dress and beanie on Girl Scout meeting days, crying when Joey Briggs chased me at recess in the 3rd grade and kissed me, and wearing pants under our dresses to walk to school in cold weather.

I remember in 6th grade, our population consisted of about 38 boys and 12 girls. There was one class of all boys, (that teacher deserved a medal) and our class with "half and half." I remember Mrs. Griffith reading aloud to us "The Trumpeter of Krakow," which I waited for with excited anticipation every day.

I remember heading home one day in 2nd grade with my tin lunchbox. The 6th- grade safety patrol stopped me at the corner and told me it wasn't time to go home, it was only lunchtime. I was adamant it was time to go home. This very wise 6th grader told me to look in my lunch box and see if my lunch was there. It was, and I went back to school!!

I remember fondly, the boys and girls of Longfellow and the days we shared there. I am so very thankful that many of them are still part of my life.

MARCH 25th

My hometown in the Heartland is Iowa City, Iowa. Iowa City is the home of the University of Iowa, and the internationally renowned Iowa Writers Workshop. In this rural state, we have an oasis of education and cultural events. Broadway musicals, and the Joffrey Ballet to name a couple of regular events.

Iowa City has also been named a UNESCO City of Literature. The University of Iowa has been a hotbed of wrestling championships and domination of the sport. What in the world connects these two seemingly unrelated topics??

There was an interesting alignment of the stars evidently, as Iowa City recently hosted an international writing conference and an international wrestling tournament...on the same weekend. I was not surprised by this turn of events, but it did jumpstart my thinking. What possible scenarios could occur with these two groups of people?

I envisioned writers and wrestlers, sharing a beer or cocktail at one of our local purveyors of adult beverages. The conversation would be wide ranging. Talk of the Oxford comma, conjunctions, Pulitzer prizes, pins, takedowns, riding time and Olympics would abound.

I don't know if any of these two diverse groups collided or colluded anywhere that weekend, but if so, it would be very interesting.

I came across a quote which could apply to writers and wrestlers. Maybe they're not so different after all. "Hard work beats talent, when talent doesn't work hard." Tim Notke, Movie Director

MARCH 26th

I TRY NOT to have regrets about my life. I made choices, as we all do. Each choice determined the next part of the path for my life. Having said this, I do have some regrets about choices I didn't make, or didn't even understand were options. Sigh.....things I wished I would have asked my grandparents and great-grandparents about their lives.

My great-grandmother was born in the 1880s. She lived through the aftermath of the Civil War, The Great War (WWI), WWII and so much more. Lifestyle and technology changes exploded in the almost one hundred years she lived. When I was in elementary school, she was still cooking and baking with a wood-fired stove. I was amazed at how she could judge how much wood to use to keep the right temperature, especially for baking!! She made clothes for me by hand or with a treadle sewing machine.

Here are a few of the hundreds of questions I should have asked:

- What was your daily life like growing up?
- How far did you go in school? What was a school day like?
- What was your life like during WWI/WWII?
- Describe how the Depression affected you.
- Did your family have a Victory Garden during WWII?
- Did any of your family members serve in the military?
- What was your wedding like? How did you meet Grandpa?
- Describe your parents for me.

Moral of the story: If you are young enough to have grandparents, ask them lots of questions. They will love telling you about their life, and you will be richer for the experience. Grandparents are the links in the chain that connect one generation to another, don't miss out on the chance to find out about the family that came before you.

MARCH 27th

TODAY I HAVE a confession to make. My name is Lori, and I might have a slight love affair (some might call it a problem...) with my electronics. Laptop, iPad, iPhone, Kindle, Amazon Echo, Fitbit. Yes, I have them all. If there were more, I would buy them. I use them for a variety of purposes; email, Facebook, reading, research, writing, entertainment....and wait for it....this will surprise you....computer games. They are a great time filler at doctor appointments, watching TV and exercising my brain. Yes, I went there. I like to think the games I choose are educational, help my brain stay active, and in general keep my razor-sharp wit and conversation at its peak. Honestly, I really don't care, I love the games!!!

I do play a lot of word games, and one of my favorites is SpellTower.

If you like words/crosswords, give this one a try. It does have its challenges. Much to my dismay, I have discovered that "womp" is not an accepted word while playing this game, neither is "relked." I hate it when the rules stifle my extensive, imaginary vocabulary. Those are just two of my words that were rejected, but I am out there trying to find answers that will further my score. Nothing ventured nothing gained as the saying goes.

Maybe I could start a support/brain exercise group for people of my age that love their gadgets and screen time. I would need to make sure there were enough outlets for everyone who might need to get "recharged!"

On your journey today, use all your words, take joy in life's small gifts, and think hard about what you are willing to do in exchange for an hour of your life.

MARCH 28th

TODAY'S intellectual essay will be about toilet paper. Yes, I said toilet paper. Our lives are so full of choices these days, in every aspect of our daily life. Purchasing toilet paper has become more time consuming than I deem necessary. So many choices, so little time...Charmin, Northern, White Cloud, Scott, Soft 'N Gentle, Velvet, Kleenex, Kirkland, and Coronet. There are more, but in the interest of time and your ability to process this highly technical information, I will not list them all!!

Single rolls, double rolls, mega rolls. 12=24, 24=36. Seriously???? Then there is the ultra soft, ultra strong, ultra cheap, quilted, ultra plush, fast dissolving....somebody rescue me now!! I do not bring my graph paper and calculator to the grocery store when I shop. It should be simpler to choose, this is a basic need. I don't need all the choices. My modus operandi has developed into a grab and toss a package into my cart.

As long as I am on this subject, I find it mildly hysterical when I see TV ads for toilet paper. Isn't everyone buying this? They don't make the Sears Catalog anymore. (Some of you are too young to understand, for folks my age, it is an urban legend, and for your older folks, well, sorry.) I understand that they are trying to persuade you to buy their particular brand of heaven in a roll of toilet paper, but I still think it is amusing!

When you get the said toilet paper to your home, we have the age-old debate, does the paper roll over or under? If you picked under, you are wrong. The original patent for toilet paper diagram shows the paper rolling over the top of the roll, not from beneath the bottom. So with all due deference, respect and eternal gratitude to the inventor, let us stick with the plan!!

MARCH 29th

I AM SITTING at Barnes and Noble today, with my requisite coffee drink. Today it is just plain old American black coffee...well maybe I added some cream…. some sweetener….and a dash of cinnamon... It was amazing to watch, the barista just poured it from the spigot on the coffee maker! No blending, whipping, icing, frapping, laying on of the hands or whipped cream to make a frothy (translate expensive) concoction!! It has been a rough week, and I am just content to be in my happy place, surrounded by books and spending quality time with my laptop.

I have been attempting to come to my "office" at least once a week to write. I usually am very productive, the people watching is great, and I am surrounded by millions of words, written through the ages by many great authors, and some not so great.

Last week when I arrived, I was a few minutes early, as were some other patrons. We were waiting outside the door, waiting for the staff to unlock the castle gate and welcome us to the kingdom. There was a man standing behind me as we waited to enter. As the doors opened, the man budged me out of the way, and literally raced to the coffee shop to claim a table. All the tables were empty since they had just opened. He was on a mission or had been practicing his wind sprints and couldn't stop himself.

He then races around the store, gathering enormous piles of books to stack on his table. He skims through each one for a few minutes. When they are done, he piles the books on the waste receptacle, where patrons deposit trays, dirty dishes etc. As a bibliophile, I find this strange and rather unkind treatment for the books. Not sure about his mission, but have observed him perform this ritual several times. People are unique, and so much fun to watch!

MARCH 30th

CHILDREN ARE a special gift from God. They come to us in a variety of shapes, sizes, unique personalities and abilities. It is a glorious grab bag of blessings. No child is perfect, but some children are differently abled and need special assistance to manage their journey here on earth.

I just read a touching book called "Angel Unaware," by Dale Evans Rogers. The book is the story of her daughter with famous cowboy Roy Rogers, Robin was born with Down's Syndrome. Doctors informed the parents that Robin probably wouldn't live for more than two years because of a heart condition. They suggested Robin be placed in a "home" with other children like her. Robin's parents decided they would take her home, love her and cherish whatever time they had.

The story is told through Robin's point of view from heaven. She was born in 1950, and at that time, Down's Syndrome children were rarely seen in the general public. Families placed them in an institution or hid them away at home. This book, and Robin's story helped to change that. The world has become bigger and better because of our changed views as a society, and the inclusion of our less abled members.

I have a grandson with Down's Syndrome. He was a delightful toddler and has grown into a caring and special young man. His life has been fraught with different medical conditions, physical and mental that he has had to fight through. He has changed many lives that he has touched.

On your journey today, take a moment to appreciate all the children in our world. Let's all work to make it a place for children to be loved, to thrive, to blossom and to contribute, each in their own way.

MARCH 31st

Oh, joyful day!! A new baby has arrived and the happy parents are going to reveal the special name they have chosen for this little person. They have been reading baby name books, writing down names they hear on tv, and politely ignoring suggestions from family. (No, Mom, we are not naming the baby Bertha.) This act of naming is much easier in the United States than in many other countries. We don't have a lot of standards, hence the names, Indiana, Blue Ivy, Bronx and Apple.

In Germany, the name of the child must be gender specific, must not be named after an object or product, and not negatively impact the future well-being of the child. Sorry, but the name North West is not going to make the cut here.

Denmark has a "Law on Personal Names." Parents can choose from a pre-approved list. Again, the name must match the gender. It is possible to apply for a different name by getting it approved by your church, then paying a fee and applying for government approval. Cross your fingers!! Too bad Bruce and Demi, Scout and Rumer didn't make the cut...back to the drawing board!

Just two of the countries that have very specific naming laws. Fascinating, curious, and surprising. I am rather in favor of the "not embarrass the child in the future" clause. Parents may think they are clever and give their child an unusual name. Unfortunately, they are not the ones who will be teased on the playground throughout their school years!

Names are important and part of our identity for a lifetime.

> Words have meaning and names have power.
>
> — Unknown

APRIL 1st

AHHH.....THE first day of April, a harbinger of spring....and the day that can ignite terror in the hearts and minds of parents and teachers.... April Fools Day!! A day where pranks are allowed, expected, maybe even encouraged!

This may be hard to believe, but I am not a good April 1st prankster. It seems such a natural holiday for me, since it involves being a fool... I am much better at pranks on random days on unsuspecting victims,

I do have a good prank for today. Call in sick to someplace you don't work. I find this hysterically funny, let me know how it works out! Hint: This might work more effectively if you choose a business with lots of employees!!

A seemingly unlikely source of pranks over the years has been the BBC (British Broadcasting Corporation). In 1957, they reported on the spaghetti harvest in Switzerland, which evidently was a bumper crop that year. The report also included the fact that the spaghetti growers had bred the crop to grow to a uniform length. Many viewers called in to find out how to grow their own spaghetti. Who would think the BBC would pull this off??

On your journey today, be alert, be careful, check for "Kick Me" signs on your back, and be "prankful" for the lightheartedness of this day.

APRIL 2nd

I FIND it amusing when journalists or others state that celebrities are just people like us. Let me see if I can find the similarities in my life and that of a "celebrity," in the categories of travel, living arrangements, friends, and security.

Travel: When I vacation: Road trip, or airplane flight. Airplane flight consists of a seat in economy class squeezed in with the other peasants, hoping to get a cup of water and 5 peanuts. Celebrities travel in first class where their every whim is satisfied, even before they know what they want; or they travel in a private jet. Seems the same to me.

Living arrangements: I have a townhouse that I purchased brand new a few years ago. I staff my own house, sometimes not satisfactorily, but good help is hard to find. Celebrities have multiple multi-million dollar homes fully staffed. Seems the same to me.

Friends/Entourage: I am blessed with a large group of friends. Sometimes we burst onto the scene in a flurry of "look at me," but normally we are just having lunch, shopping or road tripping. Celebrities have an entourage which may or may not include "friends," but probably is comprised mostly of people they pay to work for them. Agents, publicists, managers, and other famous people appearing somewhere for the paparazzi to see. As this book goes to print, I have not been invited to host any award shows or receive any awards. Seems the same to me.

Security: If they are talking about the Social kind, I am almost eligible. Celebrities have their own armed security and bodyguards. I have had interactions with armed security, but that's another story. Seems the same to me.

APRIL 3rd

As I have mentioned, I am a lover of words, a wordsmith by self-proclamation...which makes it even funnier when I so articulately say something like: The eggs aren't done, they are too liquidy. Really, wordsmith?? That's the best you've got??

I like legitimate words that are funny, at least my wacky sense of humor finds them so, and I AM easily entertained. Here are some of my favorite funny words, in no particular order.

Gobsmacked	Pantaloons
Carbuncle	Canoodle
Bazinga	Warble
Finagle	Scootch
Cheeky	Persnickety
Prestidigitation	Dither
Imp	Skosh

There are many more funny words in our language, but just wanted to give you a wee sample! When I was growing up, two particular words were in vogue, and we felt really cool saying them and being able to spell them: supercalifragilisticexpialidocious and antidisestablishmentarianism. Throw those in your conversation on your next lunch break or happy hour. On your journey today, spice up your conversation with some new words, read a couple of the pages in the dictionary and have an extra sprinkles kind of day.

APRIL 4th

April 4th in the Heartland can be a cold rainy day or a lovely spring day, depending on the whims of Mother Nature. I don't know what the actual weather was on this date in 1968 in Memphis, but figuratively it was a dark and stormy night. Martin Luther King Jr. was assassinated on this date many years ago. I was in Memphis a few years ago and visited the remaining facade of the motel balcony where he was standing when he was shot. A small insignificant place to look at, but a place where history was made and the world was changed.

Dr. King was a Baptist minister, a leader with a strong voice in the Civil Rights Movement in the 1960s. His famous "I Have a Dream" speech inspired a generation. He was a bright light and a peaceful voice in our country that was silenced too soon.

One of my favorite quotes of his is as follows: "I have decided to stick with love. Hate is too great a burden to bear."

I wanted to honor Dr. King today on the anniversary of his death. So let us do something today to make our little corners of the world better. Small acts of kindness and service can make a significant difference in the lives of others. You may never know the ripple effect of your actions, but dropping that one small stone in the water could change someone's life.

Dr. King said: "Faith is taking the first step even when you don't see the whole staircase." Take that first step.

APRIL 5th

SIGH...ANOTHER change, another good-bye. A few years ago I moved into a brand new townhouse. I love the space, the accouterments, the location. I was lucky enough to enjoy these years with a soybean field in my backyard. But all good things must come to an end, or so I have heard.

I did know that it was probably only a matter of time that in this new development area that eventually the soybean field would go. New townhouses, probably similar to mine will be built there. Lovely for this growing community, but a tear might sneak out of my eye and roll down my cheek.

I loved watching the change of seasons pass through this soybean field, planting, growing, harvesting and a beautiful view. The Iowa girl in me relished this piece of "farm" right in my backyard. I could view all the activity from my couch, looking out through my deck doors, or sitting out on the deck. I mean, after all, there isn't much on TV these days. Gave me a little farm "cred" to be able to comment on how the beans were doing at any particular time during the season. I will take any help I can get to appear that I actually know what I am talking about. I will miss my connection with this soybean field.

Farming is a noble profession and not for the faint of heart or those afraid of hard work. "And on the Eighth day, God looked down on his paradise and said, 'I need a caretaker.' So God made a farmer." This is a small piece of the 1978 speech by Paul Harvey. Look it up if you haven't heard it, it is amazing. As it should be.

On your journey, find your connection to nature and revel in it.

APRIL 6th

WELL, it might be spring, but I am certainly no spring chicken...This is not a recent development, depending on your definition of "old," I have achieved that status...awhile ago. Every decade I optimistically declare whatever my age is to be the new "40." I might need to raise the bar on that one of these days.

Now that we have established how young I am not, I'd like to share with you my thoughts about cosmetics. I didn't wear much makeup as a young woman, and even well into my adult years. Thanks to three generations of women before me, my complexion didn't need much help. It is different today. I can find lots of flaws to cover, conceal, or hide. Foundation makeup is not cheap and they sell it in those tiny tubes or bottles. Really? Why don't they sell it in quart or gallon cans? Maybe I could substitute spackling putty, it comes in huge buckets at Menards or Home Depot, and I already have a putty knife. A cost savings idea, I am thinking.

Along this same topic, I am thinking of writing to the Surgeon General demanding that warning labels be put on magnifying mirrors. My word, that's a shock first thing every morning! Of course, if I didn't use the magnifying mirror, maybe I wouldn't see all the flaws and wouldn't need the huge bucket of spackling putty. Seems like a chicken or the egg conundrum to me. However, there is the welfare of the general public and small children that have to be considered if I am wandering around sans makeup.

The bottom line is that I have earned every wrinkle, laugh line, sun damaged spots and the yielding to gravity that is inevitable. They are part of the journey of my life and I will celebrate each and every one.

APRIL 7th

Time you enjoyed wasting is not wasted time.

— T.S. Eliot, poet, essayist, playwright.

I have lived in the Heartland my entire life, and I am still surprised when April shows her pretty little face. I always feel that April should feel like spring on day one. Tulips, daffodils, and crocus should start to poke their green sprouts up through the soil. The sun should be starting to warm our faces and hearts.

The surprise is that April can be a cold, dreary, rainy month, particularly the first half. We are so ready at this time for it to be spring, but unfortunately, we can't just wish it into existence.

I actually love a rainy day. If there are no appointments, obligations or places to go, it is so cozy to stay in. Listen to the rain, read a good book, or curl up for a nap. Sometimes I spend the rainy day doing a lot of nothing. If I do say so myself, I do it very well. I have experience at this. It's on my resume. The hardest thing about doing nothing is knowing when you are finished. It can take awhile. Sometimes it can take me a few days to finish the nothing.

So to continue with more wise words from T.S. Elliot, "Do not follow where the path may lead. Go instead where there is no path and leave a trail." I am pretty sure he didn't mean for one to blaze the trail by being good at doing nothing. But, if you have a talent, seems a shame not to use it...

APRIL 8th

Breaking news: update on my novocaine adventure...so the two weeks evaporated as time has a tendency to do. It is time for the return visit for some more revelry and mirth. The thought of this appointment had been dancing around in the back of my mind like a bad tango. It is much more daunting, anticipating this visit, wondering what will transpire...what with my newly acquired superpowers and all.

I was seated in the dental chair, waiting for my dentist to make an entrance. When he walked in, he quietly commented to his assistant, "Well, she came back." I countered with, "I have nerves of steel, I am not afraid of needles, and of course there are the superpowers."

The first shot of septocaine (stepping it up due to my superpowers) was administered. We waited. Nothing. He called in another dentist who gave me a second shot and tried to massage the septocaine into going into the gum where it was supposed to go. We waited. Nothing. Next step, one of partner/owner dentists was called in to consult. He suggested changing to septocaine, which had already been done. He then made some recommendations for the placement of two more shots in different places. Shots administered. We waited. Glory Hallelujah! I am feeling tingling and numbness in all the right places. The necessary work proceeded.

In case you were wondering, they don't charge you for the extra numbing products, nor do they give you a discount for the inconvenience, pain, suffering and emotional trauma.

I don't like to brag, but it did take three dentists and four shots of septocaine to take me down. I am clearly a force to be reckoned with.

APRIL 9th

Many of us have big tasks, projects, or jobs that we want to accomplish. It can seem too big a mountain to climb, an impossibility, or a fool's errand. A woman in California had a dream, an impossible dream. She can teach us a large life lesson by her actions to make the dream come to fruition.

Author Jaroldeen Edwards tells the story in her book, "Things I Wish I'd Known Sooner." She was taken on a drive on the Rim of the World Highway, California SR 18 in the San Bernadino Mountains. There she saw an amazing sight. Acres and acres of daffodils blooming on the mountainside in many shades of golds and yellows. Near the home that was on the property, there was a sign that read "Answers to the Questions I Know You Are Asking." The first answer, "One Woman, Two Hands, Two Feet and Very Little Brain." The second answer, "One at a time." The final answer, "Started in 1958." This amazing and tenacious woman, Gene Bauer, planted over a million daffodil bulbs, one at a time.

"The Daffodil Principle," is a spectacular story and the journey of accomplishment for this woman. She changed the world around her for the better, one flower bulb at a time. I am stunned whenever I stop to really think about this. She didn't give up after a few years when some of the bulbs didn't bloom, challenges slowed her. She just kept planting.

I like to think I have written this book following her principle. I have chipped away at the task, one word, one paragraph and one page at a time. I can only hope that you, my readers, have gained some enjoyment from reading it. The bulbs on the mountain encourage us, give us hope and teach us that the biggest changes can happen if only one tiny action at a time.

APRIL 10th

I MAY HAVE MENTIONED BEFORE, I am a list maker. I love lists. Even more, I love crossing things off of lists. There are so many types of lists one can incorporate into daily life. Grocery lists, honey-do lists, daily to-do lists, bucket lists, I could go on...Today is about a new kind of list: Things I am not going to do today!

Not Happening Today List

1. Cleaning floor mats in the car
2. Sweeping garage floor
3. Scrubbing shower(s)
4. Mopping bathroom floor
5. Making calls to service providers with call center reps who don't speak English.
6. Exercising (this makes the not happening list often)
7. Read "War and Peace"
8. Run tedious errands
9. Organize my closet
10. Making dinner

Now that is a serious list, it will take the better part of the day to not do all those things. Sigh, what fun it will be at the end of the day to check off all the things I managed not to do, as I sip an adult beverage and contemplate life.

On your journey, some days need to be not for accomplishing the routine tasks of our lives, but for actually living them. I give you permission to take the day off and live like somebody left the gate open.

APRIL 11th

Dontcha just love a song that tells a story? I know I do. Most genres in today's music don't tell much of a story, or at least one I can relate to. First of all, one must be able to understand the words to know if there is a story in there!! A good song is like a well-written short story to me. In the world of country music, probably most songs tell a story or have a message to deliver. Granted, sometimes it might be boy loses girl, boy gets dog and pickup truck, girl marries someone else. I am exaggerating of course, which I know is a huge surprise that I might do that.

Here are some of my favorite short stories, told in song. Elvis Presley's hit "In the Ghetto," written by Mac Davis, singer/songwriter which was a billboard hit in 1969. Mr. Davis wrote the song, remembering friends he had as a boy. He didn't understand at the time why his friends had to live in such a bad and dangerous part of town. Elvis shared those feelings and the song brings me to tears everytime I hear it. Take a look or listen to the lyrics and feel the pain they evoke.

"The Dance," written by Tony Arata and performed by Garth Brooks, is another story that rings true for me. The premise is that an experience/relationship ended in pain, and "Our lives are better left to chance, I could have missed the pain but I'd have had to miss the dance."

True words that make my heart glad and sad simultaneously.

Life is a story, sometimes short, sometimes a novel. We get to write some of our own lyrics, and others are written for us. Write your story passionately, don't sleep through the good parts, and share your lyrics with the world, so we can all sing along.

APRIL 12th

Happy Grilled Cheese Day!! Yes, there is a special day to celebrate the grilled cheese sandwich in all of its' splendour!! Americans have been enjoying this classic comfort food since about the 1920's when sliced bread became readily available (thanks to the Iowan who invented the bread slicing machine, Otto Rohwedder) along with American cheese.

Who hasn't enjoyed this with a bowl of tomato soup as a child growing up?

The British call it a cheese toastie and use cheddar cheese. They have the cutest names for things!!! The French of course have been serving the croque monsieurs in cafes since the early 1900's. It is baked or fried with ham and cheese. Or you could sample a croque madame, which includes a fried egg on top….So many choices, so little time.

I have enjoyed ordering a "grown-up" or "gourmet" grilled cheese while eating out. This version usually includes several kind of cheese, (that doesn't include American!) bacon (need I say anymore?) and sometimes tomatoes. Obviously this can be made in your own kitchen, but just doesn't have quite the cachet as when someone makes it for you, and it costs $15…

Growing up, our grilled cheese was made with Velveeta and happily dipped in ketchup. Those were the days, for sure!! I am not a big fan of Velveeta in sandwiches today, but use it in dips and soup as it melts nicely. My grandpa used to cut a slice of Velveeta cheese, serve it on wax paper with a dollop of ketchup on it, eating it with a fork as a snack. As a young child this seemed pretty cool to me, I had never seen anyone else do this. I was easily impressed, still am!!

Enjoy a version of a grilled cheese sandwich today and enjoy the simplicity of this childhood comfort food.

APRIL 13th

ONCE UPON A TIME, in a galaxy far far away, a young lady married her Prince Charming and became his princess. Thirteen was their lucky number, so on this day many years ago, in a land of palm trees, sunshine and oceans they married. They had a wonderful life together, with many adventures. They made memories with their family, and their grandchildren were their pot of gold at the end of the rainbow. Alas, not all fairy tales have a happy ending. The Prince was called to go live in Heaven, and the Princess was left alone. She was very lonely, but she worked at keeping the Prince's memory alive with their grandchildren. She made many more happy memories with them and reminded them of the other happy times in the past. I was that Princess.

This date in history, also happens to be the birthday of one of my favorite Presidents. President Thomas Jefferson, chief author of the Declaration of Independence, gentleman farmer, and inventor. Jefferson was very creative with his ideas for gadgets. If you haven't visited his home in Monticello, in Virginia, put it on your bucket list. The estate is splendid and you will see some of his inventions, that were used in his daily life.

So, whether a President, Prince or Princess, this day could be a lucky day for you as well. President Jefferson said, "I'm a great believer in luck, and I find the harder I work, the more I have of it."

On your journey today, work hard, honor the past, make some memories along the way and maybe you'll find a spot of luck as well. (Oh, did I mention your income taxes are due in two days??) Wishing you love and luck on this day and every day of your life.

APRIL 14th

I HAVE CONFESSED to many things in this book, including leading a secret life as an Anglophile. This includes not only my fascination with British royalty, but some of the interesting words used in England, Scotland and Ireland that I think we should adopt here. I have been trying to work them into my conversation. Generally, I get strange looks from people, but that is not an unusual occurrence for me. Thought I would share some of the fun words today!!

My very favorite is the Scottish word "Tartle." Pardon my tartle. Tartle is the act of hesitating during an introduction because you have forgotten someone's name. Feel free to work this in whenever the opportunity arises! Dreich means drab, depressing weather.

England has so many words I love. Cookies are biscuits. A brolly or a bumbershoot is an umbrella. Chuffed means pleased or satisfied. Love this word, seems so descriptive, rhymes with puffed (up with pride).

If something is not clockwise, it is anti-clockwise. Plonk is a cheap wine, again the word seems apt for the definition.

So, speaking of England….their "Daylight Savings Time," is called British Summer Time or BTS for short. It covers the last Sunday of March through the last Sunday of October. Similar to ours, but yet I wonder….Who goes out to StoneHenge and other henge sites and moves those stones forward an hour? It would be a definite tourist attraction, rather like the changing of the guard at Buckingham Palace, but only occurring twice a year. Let me know if you see tickets on sale for that.

On your journey today, I hope you don't suffer a tartle, drink any plonk or leave your brolly at home. Whatever the day brings, embrace the possibilities and don't let anyone rain on your parade!

APRIL 15th

I HAVE WRITTEN various stories about travel; memories, misadventures, and bucket list wishes. Today I am thinking about places I want to visit, stay, and revel in. I want to drink them in, savor the tastes, smells and landscape. I want to learn about the people who live in these places and experience their daily lives. I have seen these places in pictures or on travel shows, and the beauty I have seen is almost more than I can take in and process appropriately. Have I piqued your curiosity adequately? Okay, fasten your seatbelts and let's go!

In the Netherlands, in the province of Holland, thirty minutes from the capital of Amsterdam, something exciting waits to be seen. The Keukenhof, the world's largest flower exhibition is said to be a glorious sight, and is famous for the many tulips there. The tulips bloom from the end of March to the middle of May, with the best vistas happening in mid-April. I long to see acres of fields of tulips in all their glorious colors. A feast for the senses awaits!! Of course, there are other sights to see, windmills, canals, the Van Gogh Museum, and the house Anne Frank was hidden in during WWII.

The lavender fields in the area of Provence, France are another sight in which to revel!! The scent, the beauty of the purple plants known for certain medicinal properties would be another glorious sight to behold. The rolling hills, olive groves and pine forests in the area would be another attraction. Do you think they would let me roll around in the lavender? I wonder if you can buy a special ticket for that.

Travel and visiting unique spots are food for the mind and soul. Travel is knowledge attained and perspective broadened.

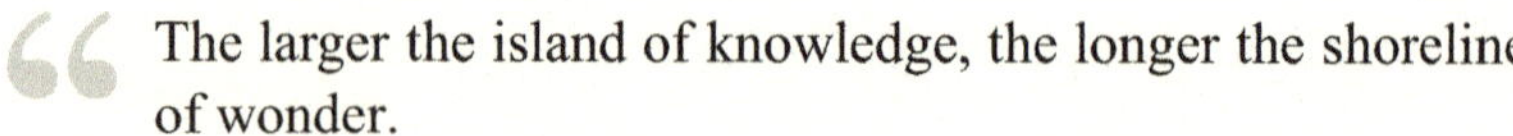

> The larger the island of knowledge, the longer the shoreline of wonder.
>
> — RALPH SOCKMAN, PASTOR & NBC RADIO PERSONALITY

(Notice I didn't mention once that your Federal income taxes are due today?)

APRIL 16th

As some of you reading this know from experience, I like to poke a little fun at myself. Granted, it is pretty easy to do because I have a lot of material. Between gravity storm, crazy ideas, failed projects and ER visits, I never lack for a story. I tell you these things to introduce you to a favorite quote of mine, from Gilda Radner. Things go wrong in life, so be prepared.

"I wanted a perfect ending...Now that I've learned the hard way, that some poems don't rhyme and some stories don't have a clear beginning, middle, and end. Life is about not knowing, having to change, taking the moment and making the best of it, without knowing what's going to happen next. Delicious ambiguity." Ms. Radner was a hilarious comedienne who was taken from us too soon, by ovarian cancer at the age of 42. Local connection, she was married to Gene Wilder, a University of Iowa graduate. Wilder is a famous actor/director/entertainer.

So in honor of Gilda, buy the ticket and take the ride, even though you don't know what the outcome will be. Embrace change. Make change. (And I don't mean two tens for a twenty...) Eat the cake. Buy the shoes. (Especially buy the shoes.) May your journey be filled with happiness and the ability to roll with life's punches. May you fully experience the delicious ambiguity of life.

APRIL 17th

> Writers spend three years arranging 26 letters of the alphabet. It's enough to make you lose your mind day by day.
>
> — Richard Price, an American novelist and screenwriter.

So now you know the secret behind some of my rambling and zany ideas! Really quite amazing when you think about it, all the nuances, emotions, ideas and communication that we accomplish with just the 26 letters. In fact, writing about this is scaring me. This book isn't done yet, and I only have 26 letters to finish it. Yikes!

On that note, today's featured letter is the letter "G." Lots of grandiose and grilliant (brilliant, but I wanted a "G" word...I am a writer, I can do that.) words to choose from. Here are some of my favorites:

Glisten	Gleaned	Gleamed
Glint	Gadzooks	Gloaming
Gallant	Giggly	Grace
Grand	Gazebo	Gewgaws

I enjoy all of these glorious words! Gloaming is probably my favorite. I have seen it used in books set in Ireland and Scotland. It is also used in the musical Brigadoon, I believe. It is such a descriptive, romantic word for that time of the day when the day is slowly, subtly sliding into the night.

APRIL 18th

In 1960 there was a song by the Shirelle's with these lyrics: "Mama said there'll be days like this, there'll be days like this my mama said." They were right, she did and there are!! Days, that the best thing about them is when they're over!! I might have a few personal examples to share…

Pinterest has great ideas for cooking, quilting, hairstyles and a plethora of other subjects. There should be a warning label on these ideas for the naive believers. Needing to take a salad to a Christmas party, I saw a recipe for Greek Salad on a Stick. In my mind, I could see everyone taking a skewer of my cleverly arranged marinated cheese chunks, tomatoes etc. The reality was, nothing would go on the skewer without being decimated. All my planning was for naught. I threw it all in a bowl and we had Greek Salad in a bowl.

Sometimes I have laundry issues. The hangers with clips on them to hang pants, will not survive a round in the washing machine. This was one of the more unique objects I accidentally laundered. I never check pockets, so it can be a regular treasure trove when the laundry is done. I am really good at laundering money. Literally….

One more recent example, I am almost out the door to school when I make contact with the wrought iron baker's rack in my kitchen, with my little toe. It immediately turns a black shade of purple, the pain is overwhelming, and I can't get my shoe on to leave. As the day progressed, the bruising to form a perfect isosceles triangle across my foot. Do not try this at home. It was not as much fun as it sounds, even with the math angle!!

APRIL 19th

MUCH TO MY DELIGHT, a few years ago we spent a week in Boston. I enjoy Revolutionary War history, so what place could be more perfect? The history here is pervasive, everywhere you turn, you run smack dab into it. We started with the Freedom Trail, which is a 2.5-mile trail that walks you by sixteen historic sites. The path is marked by red bricks, so it is very easy to follow. We did parts of the trail on different days, but you can easily do it in one day.

Some of the places the trail takes you to are Boston Commons, Paul Revere House, Bunker Hill, Old North Church, and many other places you have read about in your middle school American History class. The Granary Burying Ground is the final resting place of Paul Revere, Samuel Adams and John Hancock to name a few. The bar across the street from the Granary has a huge banner advertising: "The only place in the world you can have a Sam Adams with Sam Adams."

The John F. Kennedy Presidential Library and Museum was everything you would expect and more. A wonderful monument and legacy for a President, father, brother, and husband taken too soon.

We had been warned before we left that Bostonians were snooty. We found exactly the opposite. People could not have been more helpful as we stumbled around the city, sometimes finding ourselves a little misplaced. A city streets worker couldn't answer our question one day, so he called his boss, got directions and offered to walk us to our destination. That's what I call Yankee hospitality!

So much history to revel in. New experiences challenge us, teach us, and help us to see the world from a different perspective. If you happen to go to Boston, don't miss out on the chance to have a beer with Sam.

APRIL 20th

I AM TAKING a wild guess here, but I am pretty sure most of you have some type of bucket list, life list whether it is written or unwritten. A list of things you want to do before...well, we don't have to go all the way there.

I have had numerous lists. In the past few years, I have crossed many things off. So, I thought I would write not only a new list of things I want to do but also a list of some things I never want to do. The never do list was pretty fun!!

Things I hope to do before...well, you know...

1. Visit Scotland, Wales and Ireland.
2. Publish a book...oops...check.
3. Live in a loft for a month in New York City or Boston.
4. Have a screen porch with a porch swing.
5. See the Northern Lights.
6. See the Pearl Harbor Memorial in Hawaii.
7. Visit the NE states, Maine, Vermont etc in the autumn.
8. Visit the lavender fields & Monet's gardens in France.

Things I never want to do...ever...

1. Bungee jump.
2. Snow ski.
3. Go to an all-day wrestling tournament.
4. Own a pet bird
5. Wear a bikini (that ship sailed so long ago, Columbus was on it)
6. Step on a jellyfish.
7. Grow a mullet.

APRIL 21st

LEFT TO MY OWN DEVICES, totally without adult supervision, I began to think. That alone, should scare most of the people who know me. I promise that today's musings are quite calm and ordinary. Hoping you will participate in this exercise after today's reading! I decided to write a description of how I see myself. Some of these attributes (good and bad) will not surprise you as you have been reading my ramblings. Here we go.....I am a woman of a "certain age." (This is how we say, " I am old" these days.) I am the tail end of the baby boomers, and here are some characteristics that define who I am today.

- Raised by my biological mother and adopted by her husband, my dad. I have 2 younger brothers that I was raised with. I have 3 half sisters and a half brother that I don't really know.
- Converted southpaw, fighting the leftie impulses my entire life!
- Bookworm since the day I learned to read, if the pile of books on my nightstand is less than 10-12, I worry I will run out of things to read. Thank you, Kindle for filling in the gap!!
- First generation college student.
- Impulsive and hyperactive, I used to describe myself as the Energizer Bunny on steroids. Now it is more like the Energizer Elephant on caffeine
- I am an organizer, social butterfly, event planner, list maker and really good at going out to lunch with people.
- In my life, I have cycled through various creative endeavors, including embroidery, counted cross stitch, scrapbooking, knitting and quilting.

I hope you will take some time soon, to take inventory of who you are. Write it down, reflect, and embrace the road you traveled to become the person you are today.

APRIL 22nd

> The heavens declare the glory of God, the skies proclaim the work of His hands.
>
> — Psalm 19:1

Happy Earth Day!! Earth Day is not an official national holiday, but when have I ever let that keep me from celebrating something, anything?? The first Earth Day was created in 1970 by Senator Gaylord Wilson of Wisconsin. He believed the concerns of the environment were not being addressed by the media or the government. Hence, Earth Day to raise awareness.

Here in the Heartland, the Earth is very important, as many here work the land and it is their livelihood. They are knowledgeable and good caretakers of the land.

Earth Day is a good day to volunteer to help in your community. Clean trash out of a creek, a park, a ditch or your neighborhood. Reclaim, recycle, reuse, be aware of how your actions impact the Earth. Take a walk in the country, on the walking trail, or anywhere and appreciate the natural beauty in which we live.

Traveling across this beautiful nation of ours, the sights and sounds of God's handiwork are everywhere, and they are glorious. The hills of Tennessee, the majesty of the Grand Canyon, the ocean in North Carolina, the rolling hills and prairie in the Heartland are all a sight to behold. From sea to shining sea, from mountaintops to flower filled valleys, from the prairie to the forest, from the giant Sequoias to the aspens, we are indeed blessed.

> And into the forest I go, to lose my mind and find my soul.
>
> — John Muir

Muir was largely responsible for the creation of Yosemite and Sequoia National Parks. So, go and let nature refresh and give you peace.

APRIL 23rd

WELCOME TO WORLD BOOK NIGHT!! Although it seems like the USA version has fizzled out, I am planning to celebrate (surprise, surprise) with the United Kingdom event. In the UK it is a celebration of reading and books. One of the goals is to get books into the hands of those who may not normally read. Books are donated to care centers, homeless shelters and hospitals to name a few. Individuals are encouraged to give books, new or used to someone they know to pique their interest in reading.

What is not to like about this?? A night celebrating books and reading, that is almost as good as Christmas for me! I love getting and receiving books. A book is the gift that keeps on giving, long after the book has been read. The reader is forever changed in ways small or large just by reading.

Start an adventure tonight. Read that bestseller that's been sitting on your nightstand for oh so many months? Pick up a magazine about your hobbies or interests. Read a popular young adult book, it may open your eyes. Reread a favorite book from your past, indulge in some nostalgia. Read some historical fiction, there are some great books in this genre.

Groucho Marx said, "I find television educating. Every time somebody turns on the set, I go into the other room and read a book." Well said, Groucho!!

Read, Enjoy, Repeat….as often as you can, it's a prescription for a more interesting life.

APRIL 24th

Today is another little known holiday that you can add to your collection of annual celebrations. April 24th is Poem in Your Pocket Day. Share your favorite poem or poems. Leave copies of poems around town, wherever your day takes you. Coffee shops, windshields, tucked in the canned goods at the grocery store, under the salt and pepper at the diner are all good spots. If you go there, leave a poem there. Be creative and have fun.

Another way to celebrate today is to write an original poem. There are so many ways to write a poem. Limericks are short, rhyming, usually humorous and often naughty. Haiku is the shortest form of poetry, very structured in form, but up to the author how or if to use punctuation or capitalization. They contain three lines, with five syllables in the first and third line, and seven in the second. Remember having to write these in high school English class? Here is an original haiku from me to you:

> Pen in hand I write
> for you the lovers of prose
> to read at leisure.

Okay, I never pretended to be a poet, but it was fun, used some math and gave it my best effort. Success and adventure lie just outside of your comfort zone. Read, write and hide some poetry today!

APRIL 25th

The Circles of Women around us weave invisible nets of love that carry us when we're weak and sing with us when we're strong.

— SARK, American author and illustrator.

How lucky are we, as women to be part of this sisterhood? I have been blessed with many circles of women that celebrated with me when life has bestowed blessings upon me and cried with me when life has dealt me injurious blows. These women showed up on my doorstep. They show up when I call for help, and they show up when they know I have the need but not the will to ask.

A few years ago I reconnected with a good friend from high school and college days. We had resumed our friendship and were possibly headed for something more. One day when he was helping me with yard work, he had a heart attack. He subsequently died in the hospital a week later without ever regaining consciousness. These women showed up at the hospital every day. They sat with me, prayed with me and fed me. They lifted me up in their arms and in their hearts.

I was moving in a month. My ability to focus and be productive was non-existent. Two of these women showed up on my doorstep one night with pizza and the statement that they had come to pack up my kitchen. They ignored my protests that I would get it done, and proceeded to pack my entire kitchen, which of course, turned out to be more hours of work than I had imagined. They continued to show up and show up and show up.

I have many stories about the strong, caring women in my life. These women live in my heart and will always be part of my life. We laugh together, cry together, pray together and have built a circle of strength together. May you be so blessed as to have your own circle.

APRIL 26th

I LIKE TRYING to think outside the box. Sometimes, I want to open the box and see what's inside. This was the case several nights ago. I was shopping at my favorite Heartland grocery store, Hy-Vee. There was a special display designed to catch the curious shopper's eye with something called a Mealtime Kit. It promised to be ready in thirty minutes. I purchased the Chicken Cavatappi with vegetables. All ingredients were included except a few household staples: olive oil, salt, and pepper.

Saturday night, let's make a real meal. Opened the box and was quite surprised at how nice the ingredients looked. Bright red cherry tomatoes, asparagus, pasta, spice packets, and two chicken breasts were included. The directions were very clear and we had a great time preparing something different, that was clearly the real deal. The ingredients were simple, yet the meal was delicious.

The best part of the meal was the interaction of cooking together. There was lots of laughter and a great meal at the end of it. Much more fun than ordering in or going out to eat. Granted, we cook together other times, but not often enough. It is very satisfying to dine on food that we prepared. The special moments in life are often disguised as small moments until you reflect on them. The kit gave us the motivation that night and made us vow to cook together more often.

On your journey, skip the tried and true and do something new. Make up the rules as you go. There is no right or wrong with what you choose. This quote by Anne Lamott, novelist and non-fiction writer sums it up: "Don't look at your feet to see if you are doing it right. Just dance!"

APRIL 27th

HAPPY ARBOR DAY!! Actually, Arbor Day is celebrated the last Friday in April in most states, not on a specific date. Arbor Day originated in Nebraska City, Nebraska in 1872. It is a day to celebrate trees...no I am not kidding...trees are a great thing to celebrate. I have had many trees in my life and I am grateful for them all. Nebraska even made it a state holiday...close the government, let the kiddos out of school and get crazy over trees.

The objective of Arbor Day is to plant trees, educate people about trees and the importance of trees in our life. In 1872 when the holiday started, Nebraska was a treeless plain the state wanted to change that.

Even though I am having a little fun with it, I love trees and love the idea of planting trees as a legacy for those generations to come. I grew up in a house that had the oldest and largest ginkgo tree in the county. Even today, I will run into an acquaintance, and they will say, "Oh, you lived in the house with the ginkgo tree." Everyone knew our house and my brothers and I enjoyed a lot of fame and notoriety from that tree. (Well, it might not all have been the tree...) It was part of our identity. It was and is a magnificent specimen of a tree.

A quote from Nelson Henderson, author, sums it up nicely: "The true meaning of life is to plant trees under whose shade you do not expect to sit." A beautiful gift indeed.

APRIL 28th

ALPHA, Bravo, Charlie, Delta, Echo, Foxtrot, Golf, Hotel, India, Juliet, Kilo, Lima, Mike, November, Oscar, Papa, Romeo, Sierra, Tango, Uniform, Victor, Whiskey, X-ray, Yankee, Zulu.

I know many of you will recognize this as the NATO Phonetic Alphabet. I have always been fascinated by uses of language, military jargon, symbols, secret codes and the like.

This spelling alphabet came about in the 1920s and was first used for aviation communication. It is the most widely used radiotelephone alphabet. I was always inventing secret languages and codes when I was a kid so that probably explains why I am still intrigued by different ways of messaging. I think I am pretty cool when a customer service representative asks me to repeat or spell something, and I do the whole, "No, that's d as in Delta." Does knowing this alphabet mean I am bilingual?

I would love to know who chose the words...Romeo...Golf...Whiskey, very fascinating.

On your journey today, whatever language you use, speak from the heart, mean what you say, and stand by your words.

APRIL 29th

I HAVE writer's block and my heart just stopped. It suddenly became real to me, I am writing a book. Me. Who do I think I am? Living in a Unesco City of Literacy, home to the internationally renowned Iowa Writers Workshop throwing my words out there alongside those of famous authors who have attended school, taught or written here. I speak of Kurt Vonnegut, Tennessee Williams, (Does the title "A Streetcar Named Desire" ring a bell?) Jane Smiley, and Flannery O'Connor to name a few. I may have been in the sun too long. What was I thinking?

My heart is in my throat, as I think of others reading my frivolous observations and stories. I mean, we are not talking Pulitzer Prize material here. Strangers are going to read words that mean something to me, and it is out of my control how they will react to them. I feel very vulnerable. It would be easier not to do this. But, I am going to take a deep breath, and follow my dream. I will take courage from the words of William Faulkner: "You cannot swim for new horizons until you have courage to lose sight of the shore." So, swim I must, the shoreline has just faded away into darkness and my eye is on the horizon.

My dream has always been to write a book. Clearly this is not the next great American novel, nor is it meant to be. These are personal stories, observations, and tomfoolery intended to make the reader think, laugh and reflect. If I can provide a smile, a reprieve from life's challenges or evoke a favorite memory, I will consider this a success.

APRIL 30th

There are so many things to love about road trips. Quality time, hours and hours of time with your loved ones. Endless gas station bathrooms and fast food lunches abound. Throw in a rest area that's closed, when you really need one! I really do love road trips, lots of good conversation and no distractions. If we are driving long days, we will listen to an audiobook for a few hours here and there to pass the time. Finally, the age-old pastime of looking at license plates of the passing cars to see where they are from, and if they have an interesting slogan.

Here are a few of some current or former license plate slogans:

- Alaska-The Last Frontier (Very appropriate)
- California-Eureka, The Golden State
- Connecticut-Still Revolutionary (Love, love this one)
- Delaware-The First State (Hard to argue with that)
- Idaho-Great Potatoes-Tasty Destinations (Another personal favorite)
- Iowa-No writing on our new plates, did we run out of words??
- Kansas-As big as you think (I find this one a wee bit strange)
- Kentucky-Unbridled Spirit (Love this for a horse crazy state)
- Nebraska-Honestly, it's not for everyone (No argument here)
- New Mexico-Land of Enchantment (Simply lovely)
- Oregon-We Love Dreamers
- South Carolina-While I Breathe, I Hope
- West Virginia-Wild and Wonderful
- Wyoming-Forever West (yes you are not only west, but wonderful)

There you have it, my selection for most interesting or strange. Color me wildly disappointed in Iowa. So many brilliant and creative minds in this state, surely we can come up with actual words to describe this beautiful land. Try your hand at writing one for Iowa, or any state! Enjoy your next road trip and don't forget to read the license plates!

MAY 1st

May Day!! Do you remember making May baskets and leaving them on doorsteps in your neighborhood?? That was so much fun and I loved doing that. We would pick some violets, add some candy and place in a construction paper basket that we had made ourselves. Simpler times, simpler joys. This day is traditionally recognized, at least in the Heartland, as the true beginning of spring. April can be a cold and rainy month, but we can usually count on May!

"April showers bring May flowers," as the children's ditty goes. I love the blooming of the flowers. I do miss, the flowers that were more common in yesteryear gardens. I still see them sometimes on farms where there is a huge flower garden. Here are some of them:

- Bachelor's Button
- Poppies
- Hollyhocks
- Iris
- Larkspurs (Nancy Drew book, "The Password to Larkspur Lane.")
- Dahlias
- Heliotrope (smells like vanilla)
- Four o'clocks (guess when they open every day)
- Gladiolus
- Peony (my very favorite)

We could take some advice from flowers. This quote from an unknown source gives one something to think about: "A flower does not think of competing with the flower next to it. It just blooms."

On your journey today, just bloom.

MAY 2nd

Today is the anniversary of the day the German Army signed an unconditional surrender in 1945 ending WWII. The heroes of this war inspire me. The young men who stormed the beach at Normandy, the resistance movement in the occupied countries made up of everyday people who risked their lives every day to help their Jewish friends and their homeland. I am humbled when I read their stories and I salute their bravery. They give me hope.

To mark this day, I am sharing some books that take place in this era. They are historical fiction based on actual events or in one case a biographical account. It is so compelling to read about the human struggle to overcome tyranny on a daily basis. The strength and courage of the human spirit in the face of adversity is unparalleled.

"The Lilac Girls," tells the stories of 3 very different women, based on a real-life heroine in New York City.

"We Were the Lucky Ones" is about a family in occupied Poland, and the ways the war affected each of them. It was written by a daughter of one of the sons in the story.

"Beneath a Scarlet Sky" is about a family in Italy and their acts of bravery, sacrifice, and resistance.

"The German Girl," tells the story about a young German girl and her family who fled Germany, seeking refuge during the war.

On your journey, today, rejoice in the courage of these heroes, give thanks for the positive change they made in the world, and look to them as an example of how many small actions can help change the world for the better.

MAY 3rd

As you are reading this collection of my random thoughts, I thought maybe I would explain what led me to writing it. I have always wanted to write a book, and for years have kept a file of ideas, sayings and thoughts. The book was always going to happen "someday," as the saying goes, but someday never came. The spark that lit the fire came in the shape of a Christmas gift from my special someone. It was a book about creative writing, with thoughts from some well-known authors, and writing exercises/prompts from each. I started doing the exercises and was hooked.

So, I started writing this, and a dear friend said to me: "What a legacy this will be for your grandkids." Those words fanned the flame and then I no longer had a choice. Besides being a legacy to my grandkids, it hopefully will do something else. I hope it gives them a sense of their grandmother as a person. Someone who has been young, silly, in love, heartbroken, faced challenges with grace and humor and is a survivor.

So, here are a few quotes for them, and for you my reader that represent how I have tried to live my life.

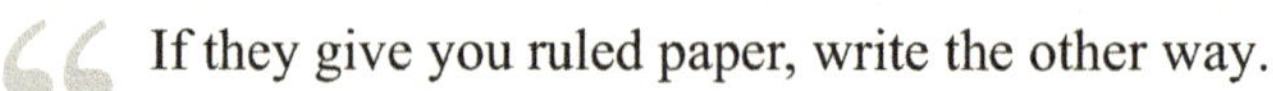

> If they give you ruled paper, write the other way.
>
> — Juan Ramon Jimenez

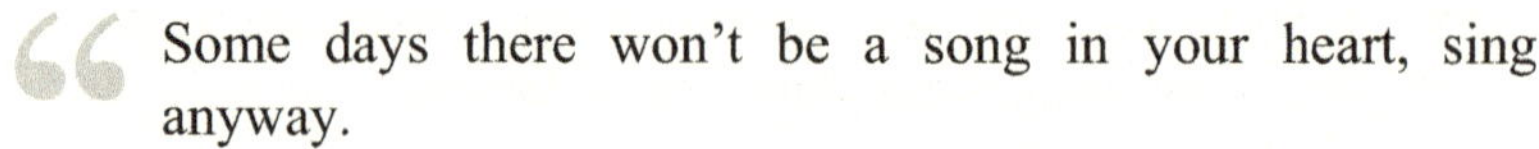

> Some days there won't be a song in your heart, sing anyway.
>
> — Emery Austin

> You miss 100% of the shots you don't take.
>
> — Hockey legend Wayne Gretzky

MAY 4th

Planning a trip? Get out the atlas and the fun will begin....if you can find your atlas...this has been a problem for me the last eight months or so. I purchased one of the large, and I do mean large, United States Atlas by Rand McNally. Nice spiral binding so it will lay flat while you plot and plan your things to do and places to go. I used it lovingly and often.

Time has passed, as it has a way of doing. Time to use the atlas again. I looked all the logical (?) places that I would have stored it. Not there. Looked all the illogical places that I might have placed it. Not there. It is not anywhere. Keep in mind, it is not that small of an object. Failing to find an earring is one thing, but a large atlas, really?

After several weeks of searching, being frustrated, missing my atlas, I gave in and purchased another atlas. I decided on the smaller version this time, as it was more portable. Used it, liked it, I had moved on. I still secretly mourned the loss of my first atlas, but life must go on.

I was dusting one day, (shock) and lo and behold, I came across the large atlas. It wasn't in plain sight, but it was somewhere that I should have found it much sooner if I dusted more often. Busted again. Sigh....So we laughed about it, and I was happy to see my old friend.

I decided a few days later to retrieve the small atlas and have them room together, made sense to me. I looked in all the logical places, (does this sound familiar?) and could not find the small atlas. I looked everywhere. This one is smaller and could hide more easily. It has remained hidden, and its' location remains unknown to me. I still know where the large atlas is, I think. If I always can find one of them, I guess I am good. Other than the lingering question in the back of my mind...

MAY 5th

New York City, the city that never sleeps. Neither did we.. (Much) I loved spending time in the Big Apple and hope to return sooner rather than later. Times Square is just as crazy busy at midnight as it is at midday. Stores and restaurants are open, and there are people everywhere. I love the energy of this city!!

One of the touristy sights we wanted to see was the Empire State Building. We had become very comfortable with walking around the city, walking as much as 11-12 miles a day. On the day planned to see this iconic sight, we started out on our walk to get there.

We reached the correct street, we know we are in the right block, but where the heck is it? I mean, this is one big, famous, iconic building. 102 stories tall… Seriously, where is it??? After puzzling about our locale for a few minutes, we asked a passerby. We had walked right by it, several times!!

There is no hoopla out front, just a very discreet sign on the door that says "Empire State Building." From street level, it didn't look any different than all the other buildings around it!! We very much enjoyed seeing the view and all the spots made famous by movies such as, "An Affair to Remember," and "Sleepless in Seattle." We did not see King Kong swinging from the building and batting down planes….thank goodness. Unbelievably this building is open every day until 2:00 A.M,

As "they" say, sometimes what you are looking for is right in front of you. Turned out to be literally true for us on this day! On your journey, take a careful look around you, don't overlook the obvious and enjoy the view.

MAY 6th

A LONG TIME AGO, when I read an obituary that included a phrase something like this, John Doe died after a 5 year battle with cancer. I asked myself several questions. How is that possible? How did they do that? How did they survive that? It seemed a mountain too high for anyone to climb.

Unfortunately, I was going to find out. When my late husband was diagnosed with cancer which had a very dismal prognosis, the learning began. We just lived. every day. New routines became "normal." Tests, doctor appointments, chemo and radiation time were part of our days and weeks. The house got cleaned, meals were prepared and laundry was washed. Life went on. A day at a time. We laughed, we cried and we lived. We went on a marvelous family vacation to Lake of the Ozarks. We surprised our Florida grandchildren on Christmas Day. We mowed the yard and shoveled the snow. Life went on.

We talked about very serious things. One day, after an appointment with particularly bad news, I was washing dishes and crying. I said to my husband, "We should have so much more time." His reply to me, "But look what we packed into the time we had." He was so strong and brave. Life went on.

A day at a time, and then those days add up….to years if you are lucky. We had the gift of two years after the diagnosis. Thanks to an amazing doctor who discovered it early. It could have only been six months which is the norm for most people with this type of cancer, including TV anchor Peter Jennings. It was a hard day at our house when he died. He had been diagnosed at about the same time as my husband. Dr. Gwen Beck of the University of Iowa Hospitals and Clinics was and is our hero! She is still my personal physician today, and I will never forget what she gave us.

MAY 7th

I THINK of my great-grandparents often, with great fondness, and wish I would have been older and smarter before they left us. Oh, the conversations I would have had with them.

My great-grandmother, born in the late 1800s was a tough, hard working woman. Her name was Ora. Much to my delight and that of my brothers, her sisters were named: Cora and Nora. We thought that was hysterical. Of course, at that age, we thought lots of things were hysterical. Easily entertained were we!! Not as much hilarity with the last two sisters who were named Ruby and Pearl, a couple of gems, those two.

Ora had a wood cook stove for much of the time when I was a child. It was so fascinating to me how she knew how much wood to put in, and could make the most marvelous cookies, brownies etc in that thing. She was also a quilter and a seamstress. I wish that she knew that I have become a quilter, she would love that.

She came to have a television and watched it in her later years. She became a soap opera fan. The stories she would tell us about those drinking, philandering ne'er do wells she saw were told with a sad shaking of her head about the depths of depravity she had witnessed. The thing was, she thought the characters were real and they were really drinking alcohol, playing fast and loose with morality, and not people we would want to associate with.

I learned a lot from her and in my mind can still hear her giving me advice, and of course, doting on me. It's wonderful to have someone in your life who thinks you are the cat's pajamas. Take note of those people in your life and wring out every ounce of your time with them like it was a soaking wet washcloth.

MAY 8th

What do you do with old memories in the form of pictures? I sorted some old pictures last night….and I do mean old...circa high school and college days. I was overcome with nostalgia and a little bit of longing for the girl I was back in the day. It's a little bit like missing an old friend. I was much the person I am now, with less wisdom, and the worries of the universe had not caught up with me yet.

As the song lyrics written by Mary Hopkins tell us, "Those were the days my friend. We thought they'd never end. We'd sing and dance forever and a day. We'd live the life we choose, we'd fight and never lose, for we were young and sure to have our way."

As we all learn, those days do end. Life changes, our abilities change, and the things we think are important change. For one thing, strawberry wine is no longer at the top of our grocery list, and parties don't have to wait until our parents are out of town. Not to mention any names, but you know who you are…. Those memories, however, are priceless, and the person we were back then had a great influence on who we are today. Enjoy the memories and share the stories with those who helped you live them!!

Today's journey is a blank page waiting to be filled...Hope you make some memories, and take a moment to remember days gone by and the friends who were with you back in the day.

MAY 9th

TODAY IS A DAY TO REMEMBER...It is Lost Sock Memorial Day. Who has not been touched by this event that occurs too frequently? Most of our lives have been affected by the lost sock, usually many times over our lifetime. It is not known what causes socks, who enter the laundry as a pair, to depart the laundry as a single. The real mystery is after I dispose of the single sock, several weeks later the other one will turn up.

How can you celebrate lost socks to commemorate this day? I might have some ideas for you...

- Dispose of the single mingle socks in your drawer.
- Use the single socks as cleaning rags.
- Turn them into sock puppets. (A little stuffing, ribbon around the "neck" and a magic marker/button face)
- Don't wear socks and save a life today.
- Shop for sandals instead of socks.
- Search the washer, dryer, behind the dryer...anywhere you suspect socks may be hiding out.
- Expand that single sock puppet into a family of puppets.
- Create a skit using your sock puppet family.
- Engage in a minute of silence for all your lost socks, and indeed all the lost socks everywhere.

Hoping this silliness will put a smile on your face, in spite of this annoying occurrence where socks go AWOL!! On your journey today, don't sweat the small stuff, enjoy the important stuff, and stuff a sock puppet.

MAY 10th

THINKING of writing my own obituary. I can start with the month and day, just don't know the year. My maternal grandmother and my mother both died on the same day, May 10th, 14 years apart. It seems reasonable to think if this is some bizarre family tradition, I will end my journey on earth on this day. What to say about me when I'm gone....Let me give it a shot.

.....In addition to the previous information about her careers and community involvement, what would Lori like us to remember about her?

She cared about her family and was head over heels about her grandchildren. She was a fun Grandma, and nothing was too crazy or silly if her grandkids wanted to do it. One of her granddaughters wrote this to her in a card when she graduated from high school: "I wouldn't have had nearly as interesting a childhood without you in it". She held this comment close to her heart for the rest of her years.

She was known for her shenanigans, some of which involved gravity storms and slight injuries to her person and more to her dignity, but that didn't slow her down. She was known to repeat a quote she read somewhere, "If it weren't for law enforcement and gravity, I'd be unstoppable."

We are certain that she has passed through the heavenly gates, is busily looking for a bookstore, a quilting group, a coffee shop, and a tribe of girlfriends to have adventures with.

She hopes that at her wake, there will be more laughter than tears, stories that reveal who she was to each storyteller, and her family to carry on her legacy of laughter and love.

MAY 11th

Several years ago, I had the great honor and privilege of hearing retired four-star General Colin Powell give an informal talk at a conference I attended. This patriot and American statesman also served as Secretary of State, and National Security Advisor. This man is the epic portrait of the American Dream. Born and raised in Harlem, son of Jamaican immigrants, he achieved immeasurable success serving in some of the most powerful positions in the world.

As you might guess, General Powell was charismatic, personable, very informal and spoke to our minds, spirits, and dreams. Here are General Colin Powell's rules:

1. It ain't as bad as you think. It will look better in the morning.
2. Get mad, then get over it.
3. Avoid having your ego so close to your position, that when your position falls, your ego goes with it.
4. It can be done.
5. Be careful what you choose. You may get it.
6. Don't let adverse facts stand in the way of a good decision.
7. You can't make someone else's choices. You shouldn't let someone else make yours.
8. Check small things.
9. Share credit.
10. Remain calm. Be kind.
11. Have a vision. Be demanding.
12. Don't take counsel of your fears or naysayers.
13. Perpetual optimism is a force multiplier.

Great advice from an extraordinary man. He has served this great nation with honor and dignity and is a role model for all. On your journey today, take heed of his 13 rules, remember dreams are achievable, service to your country and mankind is admirable.

MAY 12th

On a recent trip to Europe, our first stop was in the spectacular city of Prague, The Czech Republic. Prague was fortunate to escape the bombing that occurred in Europe during WWII, so it remains as it was for many hundreds of years. Fell in love with the city and the people.

Of course, during one of our adventures where we lacked adult supervision, we spent some hours exploring (translation, some walking in circles or aimlessly as none of the streets in Prague are straight). We are in a neighborhood that is off the tourist path, and decide that it is time for lunch.

It's always wonderful when traveling to sample the local cuisine. We always prefer to eat where the locals gather. So when we spotted a restaurant that looked like a local place, we wandered in. The name of the restaurant was La Casa Blu. Yes, that's right, we decided to have Mexican food in the Czech Republic.

Watching other patrons enter for lunch, it was clear this was a favorite for lunch breaks of workers from other businesses in the area. Time to order. The Mexican entrees on the menu were in Czech, of course. My Spanish is not going to help us here.

I was able to identify a taco dish, while Verne ordered a burger. He spoke English, the waitress answered in Czech. Tacos with sweet and sour pork, and some sides for me were delicious. Verne's burger was not hamburger but chunks of meat on a bun. The star of the show was his side dish….it was an enormous dish of lettuce (I think maybe a whole head of lettuce gave its life for this meal), with boiled potato halves beautifully placed. Very interesting Czech take on Mexican food. Right country, wrong food. That is us!!

MAY 13th

After my recent adventure series at the dentist, I thought it would be fun to share something I saw while in Florida. Walking around on a very pleasant, sunny day, minding my own business. (Yes, I can do that…)

I was not, repeat not thinking about dentists, it is a happy way to live life.

When what to my wondering eyes should appear, but a sign that said "Serenity Dental Spa!" First of all, the whole thing is an oxymoron in my opinion. I would never associate serenity with anything dental. So, to feed my curiosity I had to investigate this anomaly!!

My research turned up the following information. This dental "oasis" has massage chairs, big screen TV with Netflix in every exam room. They have Pandora and other music options. They provide filtered water for drinking.

Serenity also boasts of state of the art dental equipment. Does this mean that I won't have 6 hands and 17 instruments in my mouth for hours??? I might be exaggerating a wee bit, but that is what it seems like! Did they do away with the infamous, devious rubber dam?? One can only dream.

This seems too good to be true, I think they need to offer adult beverages and guarantee no pain for the patient!!

I will apologize in advance to the dentists I know, but this quote from a legend made me laugh out loud.

> Happiness is your dentist telling you it won't hurt and then having him catch his hand in the drill.
>
> — Johnny Carson

MAY 14th

Carole King....the music of my growing past....On a trip to New York City we went to see the Broadway musical "Beautiful," the story of her life. It was eye opening and life changing for me!! I was unaware of the many hit songs she had written or co-written for other artists.

The staging and music was astonishing, spectacular and beyond anything I had imagined. When the show was over, I remained in my seat. With the last notes of music hanging in the air, I sat motionless, spellbound, and trying to absorb every song and moment of this play so I would have it forever.

Some songs she wrote for others before she started recording, "Up on the Roof," "Locomotion." and "Go Away Little Girl," which was a hit for two artists, 1962 and 1971. She is a unique talent.

I can still see the album I owned of "Tapestry," in my mind, which came out in 1971. (The album not my mind) Still in high school, embracing the "hippie" culture that was prevalent in Iowa City. Sweet memories of a time long ago. Bell bottom jeans, leather moccasins, style diva...

I am listening to the cast recording as I write this, savoring the music and moments again. Have you ever had an experience like this? It could be a play, a movie, a book or any event in your life that transformed you in some way. Grab all the gusto life has to offer. New adventures, experiences, love and laughter. Listen to the music of your youth, and replay, relive, remember, rejoice.

> When this old world starts getting me down and people are just too much for me to face, I climb way up to the top of the stairs and all my cares just drift right into space. On the roof it's as peaceful as can be, and there the world below can't bother me...up on the roof.
>
> — Written by Carole King and recorded by The Drifters

MAY 15th

Substitute teaching has become a "retirement" career for me. Many perfect things about it!! I can choose when or whether to work. I have made lots of friends, and I love working with middle school age kids...most of the time.

5th graders are a delightful bunch for the most part. One day, our classroom work was a poetry exercise that had to do with color and emotions. For example, what color makes you happy? They were all working away, chattering and giggling. I was walking around the class and I heard one of the girls say, "Is diamond a color?" Yes, my dear, many women do believe diamond is not only a color but their favorite color. She is a girl with wisdom beyond her years.

The other overwhelming fact about 5th graders is the noise level. Their "quiet" would wake the dead. Their silent reading time is accompanied by talking. They don't have "indoor" voices! A room full of these children is a cacophony like no other. When I leave school after a day of this age level I literally can hear the silence, it is as thick as cotton. I relish and savor every moment of it!! But a world without the laughter, cries of delight and chatter of children, would be a very quiet place, but oh so colorless and bleak.

On your journey today, find something to giggle about, find your inner child and let it out to play, and find delight in the simple things.

MAY 16th

I AM BACK to sharing alphabet soup with you!! Add crackers if you need to!! There is a song that has four, count 'em four of my favorite words that begin with "B." Any guesses what the song is? Many of you are too young to know the song, but it's a classic!!

The song is "Bewitched, Bothered and Bewildered," lyrics by Lorenz Hart. What?? That's only 3 "B" words you say? Well hold on to your seats, let me give you an excerpt from the lyrics!!

"I'm wild again, beguiled again, a whimpering, simpering child again. Bewitched, bothered and bewildered am I." The song is about someone who is wildly, crazily and probably about to get their heart broken in love. When I hear the lyrics, I feel very attuned to them, especially the bothered and bewildered part....welcome to my world!!

My love of words encompasses all forms of wordplay. Lyrics are often so clever and imaginative, and if they are good, in my humble opinion, they tell a story that is relatable to most of our lives.

I will leave you with a few more "B" words that I am particularly fond of. Bodacious, brimming, bestow, bon vivant. Pick one or pick them all and use them in your conversation today, spoken or written!! Amaze your friends, confuse your enemies and have some fun!!

MAY 17th

Meeting friends for dinner is such a lovely night on the town. I must say, that on occasion, I have had friends cancel meeting up with me for a variety of reasons. Real or an excuse, what are you going to do? At disappointment to be sure, but one must move on.

The award for the most creative reason for being late to meet me for dinner goes to a dear friend who shall remain nameless. (SJH) When I answered the phone, she began to explain. The time old “there’s a squirrel in my bedroom” excuse never gets old. Especially when the squirrel is burrowed in the bed covers. After a couple phone calls and text messages, relaying breaking news, such as the police are coming….no sirens….the police are here; we did eventually meet for dinner about 90 minutes later than planned.

Dinner was hysterical, as she filled me in on the minute by minute account of her squirrel encounter. I was very impressed with the ingenuity of the police officer’s idea to get him out. No, he didn’t shoot him right there in the bed. He merely opened the window! There may have been margaritas involved at that point, my memory is foggy.

Interestingly enough, she has 2 or 3 not small dogs who were not at all bothered by this invader, not barking, chasing or catching said squirrel. A species that they would probably chase furiously out in the back yard.

A night neither one of us will ever forget...On your journey, beware of wild squirrels, they may turn up in the most surprising places! The best part of the story; it is now a legend in the annals of our friendship, and will live forever as we tell, retell and embellish the story.

MAY 18th

So much to love about traveling...at least once you get past the never predictable vagaries and shenanigans of the airlines. Travel is a great equalizer. When one travels, it doesn't matter who you are at home...especially when you are in a country whose mother tongue is unfamiliar to you! It is humbling to ask for help and not be understood. It is also arrogant to assume everyone you encounter will speak English.

Traveling through Germany, everyone speaks English in the larger cities. However, in small towns and villages, not so much!! I went into a clothing boutique in the small city of Meissen, where the world famous handmade porcelain is produced. Neither of the clerks working there spoke any English. As I tried to figure out the size conversion, we smiled, pointed and nodded. I went to the dressing room to try some things for size. When I came out to look in the mirror, they both exclaimed, "Tres chic!" Enter France…

I paid for the items and said "Dahnke," at the exact moment she said, "Thank you." We both laughed as I turned to leave. She quickly came after me to give me the receipt, I smiled and said, "Thank you." as she said, "Dahnke." Again, laughter to complete the task!

I felt very cosmopolitan, purchasing clothes in a village in Germany, speaking English, German and French to complete the transaction. I surely will always remember this adventure every time I wear my "tres chic" clothing!!

Learning some German as we traveled was so satisfying to my brain. I highly recommend taking an adult ed class in another language just to keep those brain cells firing at top speed!!

MAY 19th

TODAY'S SELF wishes I had written down all the hysterically funny stories that occurred during my banking career. There were more early in my career as a consumer loan officer, in fact some doozies. Here are a couple that I can remember.

One day a man was at my desk applying for a loan. I interviewed him about his work, income, and debts. I looked at his credit report and did the loan work up. As occasionally happened, he did not qualify to borrow the money, and I regretfully and politely explained the reasons to him. He was angry and not afraid to tell me so before he left.

I was still at my desk about 10 minutes later when he stormed back into our offices. My immediate thought was literally, "He went to his car and got a gun." Well, he had a weapon, but it wasn't a gun. He took his shoe off and pounded it on my desk to emphasize the barrage of words he had for me. It's funny now, but there was an element of fear at the time!! Security came and escorted him out of the building.

Another good story involved a college age man, also applying for a loan. He had little to no income to tell me about. I was quizzing him to see if there was more income. Finally, he leaned across the desk conspiratorially, and said, "Well, I make fake ID's and sell them." I was dumbfounded, flabbergasted and amazed all at the same time. I calmly explained to him that sources of income that were against the law could not be considered as a basis for a loan. Bring me a W2 or a pay stub, and we're in business! Color him surprised. Ah, the innocence of youth.

Working with the public is interesting, never boring, and very fulfilling when you are able to help people achieve goals and dreams. And of course, there are the stories….

MAY 20th

MANY OF YOU have probably figured out by this point, that I can do some crazy things, usually not on purpose. This incident I am about to tell you about may have been one of my most "blonde" moments. No offense, but I can say that because I am blonde, most of the time....

The shampoo and conditioner that I normally use are in dark red, pleasantly shaped bottles. They seem to work well on my hair, and I have used this particular brand for a number of years. Did I mention that the bottles look identical?

So, just going about my daily routine with my morning ritual shower, shampooing etc. I thought I noticed a difference in the shampoo, but often products do change things up, so I didn't give it a second thought, or seventh as it turned out.

It was about a week after that initial thought, that something just didn't seem right. So one morning, before I got in the shower, I took a closer look at the bottles, with my glasses on and without water in my eyes. My findings showed that for about a week, that would be seven days, seven consecutive days that I had been shampooing, and conditioning my hair using the two bottles which turned out to be both conditioner. No wonder the shampoo didn't lather much. My hair was sure soft, silky and very conditioned though. I have always been honest about the fact that I am not a rocket scientist. Every once in awhile I like to prove it.

It is said one learns from mistakes. I clearly have had a full life of learning!! On your journey, embrace your mistakes, laugh at them, then move on and be a positive force in your little corner of the world.

MAY 21st

I LOVE A GOOD RANDOM, fun or interesting fact. It is especially enjoyable if I can actually remember them, and casually toss them into conversation. Knowledge is a great thing!!

Here is a list of some fun facts for your day, provided with the following caution: These facts are deemed reliable but the veracity of them is not guaranteed by the author!

- 40,000 Americans are injured by toilets every year. Frankly, with my history, can't believe I haven't fallen victim to one of these.
- Almost is the longest word in the English language with all the letters in alphabetical order.
- No square piece of paper can be folded more than 7 times in half. Most of you have stopped reading now and are looking for paper.
- The #hashtag key is called an octotroph.
- Grapes will explode if you put them in the microwave. (Do NOT try this at home)
- The many colors of Fruit Loops all taste the same. NO!! Say it isn't so!
- Men are more than 6 times more likely to be struck by lightning.
- The average person walks the equivalent of 3 times around the world in their lifetime. Try to get that on your Fitbit!

Now you know one of the many fun things I do when I have too much time on my hands, and no adult supervision.

On your journey, remember therapy is expensive, bubble wrap is cheap.

May laughter and love find you today and always.

MAY 22nd

I AM sure many of you like to bring home souvenirs when you travel, as do I. This quest for souvenirs has turned into a more interactive event for me when I travel now. I like to take pictures with police officers wherever I go. (And for you cynics, no, it's not because I would ever do anything to warrant an encounter with the police.)

This hobby has turned into some very memorable encounters. I usually just walk up to them, thank them for their service to their community and ask if we can take a picture together. I have never been turned down, although the young policeman in Prague, Czech Republic wasn't so sure about it, but he cooperated. He did not smile though, very stoic.

Here is an incomplete list of police officer pictures I have acquired (and I'm still on the hunt!):

- Kansas City-Mounted policeman on the biggest horse I have ever seen
- Memphis- Motorcycle police on Beale Street
- Las Vegas- Two young bicycle cops
- New York City- Mounted policewoman, and a patrol cop
- San Juan, Puerto Rico- Policewoman in a patrol car
- Prague, Czech Republic-Policeman on foot

Boston is a memory I will never forget...sorry police officers, but the firemen outdid you on this one!! We were in the Italian neighborhood, and I spotted a firehouse and decided to go in. I explained to the young fireman I was from out of town and thanked him for his service to the citizens of Boston. Then I asked for the requisite picture. He responded by calling the whole department out to take a photo with me.

Sincerely thank the people who serve your community, it will be a special moment for both sides. Give some love, it creates smiles, goodwill and turns an ordinary day into something special. Try it!!

MAY 23rd

Are you a mystery lover?? Not the mysteries of the universe unanswerable questions, like where in the heck did I hide my keys, or why in the world did I agree to do this, but murder, kidnapping, and general mayhem. If you like the hard-boiled detective variety, this may not suit, but open the box, expand your boundaries and give this series a whirl!!

James Patterson has written books too numerous to mention. I am a fan of a particular series, The Women's Murder Club. I find it exciting, when I stumble across a new series, so much to look forward to, so hoping to share this excitement with you! There are 17 books in this series right now, and guessing more to come. The book titles all include a number, so easy to read this series in order!! For example, "1st to Die," "2nd Chances," and "3rd Degree" are the first three titles.

The protagonist is Lindsay Boxer, a detective with the San Francisco Police Department. The other three members of the club are a district attorney, a reporter and the Chief Medical Examiner for the county. There are other recurring characters in all the books.

The stories are mysteries for the group to solve. Murder, romance, chaos, and criminals abound. The stories change from book to book, featuring one or more of the four women and their situations.

> Every solution to every problem is simple, It's the distance between the two where the mystery lies.
>
> — Derek Landry

Buy the ticket, take the ride, go the distance, solve the mystery!!

Wishing you happy reading, whatever you choose!

MAY 24th

Good Morning!! I thought it would be fun to learn a new phrase today….in eleven different languages. You just never know when you might need this, and I like to be prepared (former Girl Scout). I sometimes need to say this phrase in my everyday life, not just when I am traveling…..I am lost. Yes, that is the phrase, I am lost.

- Latin: Perditus sum
- Spanish: Estoy perdido
- German: Ich bin veloren
- French: Je suis perdo
- Czech: Jsem ztraceny
- Iowa: You don't have to say it here, we will know and will give you a ride, ask you to dinner and give you a Scotcharoo.
- Scottish Gaelic: Tha mi air chall
- Italian: Mi sono perso
- British: Pardon me, chap. I am lost. (said with attitude)
- Portuguese: Eu estou perdido.
- California: Hey dude, like, where am I?

I am sure I could continue this, and insult other places, but this seems like enough for one lesson. Don't you feel more prepared to travel now?

A Czech proverb tells us: "You live a new life for every language you speak. If you know only one language, you live only once." Even if we can't learn a new language and be fluent, we can learn some words and phrases.

On your journey today, challenge your brain!! Learn how to say hello in several languages….or where is the water closet, that definitely could come in handy!!

MAY 25th

TODAY'S THOUGHTS may be uncomfortable for some. For others, I hope it will validate their feelings, and help in some small way. If this happens to you, many will not want to speak of it with you, so I feel the need to talk about it openly. I am talking about widowhood. Losing your spouse is one of the hardest challenges life will hand you.

I knew my husband was going to die, every day for two years, I knew he was going to die. Knowing the inevitable doesn't make the outcome easier to bear. The first loss is their physical presence. In the blink of an eye, they are just not there. No matter how sick they were, whether they were at home or in the hospital, they were still part of your physical life. You could still care for them, talk to them, cry with them and love them.

Another loss is the fact that there is nobody in the world who knew and loved you as they did. A piece of yourself is gone. You lose the shared memories that were yours alone...the "remember when" moments. The loss of identity is also connected with this. You are no longer a wife. One of your roles in life is gone.

Hunting and searching for a new "normal" will become your job. Some will think you should "move on" more quickly. They are wrong. Everybody's journey of grief is different and moves at different speeds. Whatever you are feeling is normal. If the grief overwhelms you, seek help. Start with your doctor. It's not being weak if you need a helping hand.

Grief is like the ocean, it comes in waves, ebbing and flowing. Sometimes the water is calm, sometimes it is overwhelming. All we can do is learn to swim.

— VICKI HARRISON

MAY 26th

THE HISTORY of the bugle song known as "Taps" has a variety of purported sources. I am not a historian so that is not my battle to fight. What I do know about "Taps" is that it is a 24 note melancholy song traditionally played on a single bugle. It is typically played at flag ceremonies, military graveside services and other types of memorials.

As a Girl Scout, we sang this song to end our meetings, or if we were camping, around the campfire to signify the end of the night. It evokes very strong memories for me as those times still hold a magical place in my heart.

One day, the subject of this song came up and a friend was astonished that there were actually words to it! I was astonished that he didn't know that. I think the words are beautiful and more people should know them….hence...may I present some of the lyrics to "Taps," copyright to Pennsylvania Military College.

Verse 1: "Day is done, gone the sun,
From the lake, from the hills, from the sky.
All is well, safely rest, God is nigh.

Verse 3: Thanks and praise for our days,
Neath the sun, neath the stars, neath the sky.
As we go, this we know, God is nigh.

Verse 5: While the light fades from sight,
And the stars gleaming rays softly send,
To Thy hands, we our souls God commend."

I will leave it to you to find Verses 2 and 4!!

MAY 27th

MEMPHIS....GRACELAND....BEALE Street....Sun Studios....and all that is Elvis!! After many years of being an Elvis fan, a dear friend offered to accompany me to Memphis for a long weekend. She was not particularly an Elvis fan, she rocks to Jimmy Buffett, but knew this was a bucket list kind of trip for me.

Memphis has much to offer, and we had a wonderful time. Beale Street is so much fun, music venues everywhere, indoors, outdoors. There is live music every day/night pretty much anywhere you turn.

Graceland was more than I expected, and I loved seeing the iconic home of Elvis and all that entails.

We decided to take a walking tour of downtown Memphis to get some history and see as much as we could. Enter, the legendary Rooster.

Rooster was a red-head, local Memphian (no not amphibian) and could sell grass seed in the Sahara Desert. All the shop owners and carriage drivers knew him by name. He was very knowledgeable and we learned a great deal about Memphis.

However, our 90 minute tour had turned into a two hour tour and there seemed to be no end in sight. We couldn't shake Rooster!! We needed to walk back to our hotel and then go to a scheduled tour at the Gibson Guitar Factory. He paused to take a breath, we grabbed our chance, tipped and thanked him. End of tour. One would think. No chance!! Rooster just kept walking with us as we headed to our hotel, and kept talking, introducing us to folks along the way. I was contemplating calling 911 because it seemed we were trapped.

We made our escape and still laugh about the tour and our friend Rooster!

MAY 28th

Small moments, powerful memories. As I may have mentioned, a time or seven, my grandchildren are the world to me. I am saddened, however, by the fact that my late husband, their beloved Grandpa, had to leave us too soon. He was cheated of much of their growing up years, and they were cheated of the fun, inventions, and wisdom he could have added to their lives.

Small moments, powerful memories. My oldest grandson happens to be an individual with Down syndrome, who is a thoughtful, kind young man who processes information and events to a far greater degree than I think we know.

Small moments, powerful memories. As a child, he would come to visit, walk in the front door and head directly for the kitchen, where Grandpa had an old Ritz Cracker tin, filled with, of course Ritz crackers. They had a mutual love of that tasty, buttery cracker. Ritz crackers were their thing! It has been quite a number of years since Grandpa has been here to share Ritz crackers with Tyler. But Tyler has not forgotten. He beams at Christmas when he receives a box of Ritz as one of his presents! It is at holiday gatherings, or Pagliai's Pizza parties, that he will come sit by me in a quiet moment. He will usually say something about not wanting to make me sad, and then he will talk about Grandpa. Sometimes he will say, "Grandma, I miss your husband." Tyler is all about relationships!!

Small moments, powerful memories. On your journey, treasure what may seem like an insignificant moment. We never know the impact they will have in the future. Tyler's grandpa used to say to me about the grandchildren, "They may not remember what they do here, but they will remember the way we made them feel."

MAY 29th

I HAVE BELONGED to many clubs in my life, but have had a new experience in the last few years, after joining a dance club. We had taken a couple of sets of dance lessons when friends invited us to be guests at their dance club. It was held at a very lovely hotel and consisted of a happy hour, a lovely dinner and then a live band for dancing. After an enjoyable evening and a few adult beverages, we agreed to pay the membership fee and become members.

It is not an overwhelming commitment. There are four dances a year, summers off. The dances are held in different locales and are sometimes themed. Dressy attire is always appropriate, but there are guests there in every conceivable kind of clothing. The people watching is top notch!!

As our time in the club went on, we started to notice some surprising characteristics of our fellow club members. We knew quite a few people when we joined, so we felt like we belonged immediately. We were not the "newbies" that stood out from the crowd Well, we may sometimes stand out from the crowd, but that is another story. The most interesting fact we uncovered, is that many of the members don't dance!! I should have known, that as easily as we were accepted, the membership bar was not set very high! So, the pressure is off, if you don't feel like dancing, you don't have to!! We do enjoy the dancing and socializing, and I would still attend if I broke my leg.

We are amateur dancers in a club where there are some very skilled couples. We have shed our insecurities, we dance like nobody is watching, we laugh more than should be allowed on the dance floor, and some of our best moves are a surprise even to us. Just trying to grab hold of all of the opportunities presented to us to live our life to the fullest. Hoping you will do the same!

MAY 30th

WHEN I DECIDED to start a part-time retirement career as a guest teacher, there was a waiting period before I got my license. During that time, I could work as a para-educator in another teacher's classroom. My sister-in-law Julie, was teaching Kindergarten and had been for many years. I was able to help in her class several times which was so much fun for many reasons, and she was an incredible teacher.

Recess duty was always the opportunity for interesting things to happen. The most important thing I learned having recess duty for the kindergarten during winter, is you really only need to know three sentences.

1. Get off the ice!
2. Put the snow down!
3. Give him/her their hat back!

I loved my time with these adorable sprites. They were eager to help, do their work and share their love. After my first day, children would tell me they loved me when they left for the day. They also found it rolling on the floor funny, that there were two Mrs. Lacinas in their classroom.

My mother passed away during this time period. My sister-in-law had the class make pictures and thoughts for me on construction paper. The pictures were heartfelt and loving. My favorite was from the boy who drew pictures of two stick figures playing catch, with a sun shining in a blue sky. His caption read, "Don't be too sad. There are other mothers in heaven for her to play with." I think of this often and marvel at the compassion and love of little children. They are tiny people with the biggest hearts you will ever find.

MAY 31st

I OFTEN THINK about the paths in life that I did not choose, for lack of knowledge, finances, and Iowa middle-class life. So just for fun, here is a different life I could have chosen and who knows what the outcome would have been!!

I would have blossomed and thrived at a small private college. Dorm life, living away from home, seeds to plant for lifetime friendships with four years to nourish and grow them, smaller classes and professors who knew and cared about me. I think this would have provided an amazing environment for me. However, I needed to pay for my own college education and living in Iowa City, many of us just glided into the University of Iowa without much thought for anywhere else. I am thankful to have graduated from this prestigious university, but it was a long and hard road.

Post college, I would have looked for a job in Boston or New York City to have the big city experience. It would have been the perfect time to move, no relationships, commitments or anything to tie me to Iowa.

What an adventure that would have been!! Or would it? I will never know but enjoy thinking about it.

I am pretty sure, barring a great love affair with a Yankee, I would have moved back to Iowa City, to return to the perfect place to live, raise a family and be part of a community. Maybe I would have brought my big city experience to a job at the University of Iowa!

But.....and this is a big but....(pardon the visual image I may be evoking), if I had not done exactly what I did, in the exact place and time back then, I wouldn't be where I am now. Now is a pretty sweet place to be for me. Count your blessings every day, for what you have, not what might have been.

JUNE 1st

PHYSICAL FITNESS....I think that was a gym class in elementary school. I remember having to do the Presidential Fitness Challenge during those years. It is a vague memory, not unpleasant but not evoking outbursts of joy in remembering it. I never dreamed then, that as an adult, along with millions of others, I would be "counting my steps." It has been a craze sweeping the country and perhaps the world.

I own a Fitbit, the cheapie Zip version. There are many fancier, smarter and sophisticated Fitbit devices, as well as other products.

Note to self: The Fitbit Device works better at counting your steps if you actually wear it instead of leaving it on your dresser, on the nightstand, in Florida when you return to Iowa....Live and learn... It is motivational for me to see my step count, have goals and try to beat my own records. My Fitbit friends, whose steps I can see must be fastening theirs onto a six-year-old or a ceiling fan at night, based on their number of steps. (Yes, some sour grapes here!!) It does annoy me slightly that it counts nothing when I am on a 20-mile bike ride....just sayin'.....

There is a definite health benefit from these gadgets. I recently saw a story on a news program about a girl and her SmartWatch. The alarm went off indicating her heartbeat was extraordinarily high. She was taken to the hospital immediately, and long story short, it most likely saved her life. It was indeed a very smart watch!! Food for thought if looking for some kind of fitness device!!

On your journey today, take a hike, take a bike, and whatever you do, do it with gusto!!

JUNE 2nd

It has often been said that we have two seasons in the Heartland; Winter and Road Construction. This year seems particularly annoying as almost every major street, route, highway, pedestrian mall that I traverse is closed, dangerous, detoured, a traffic nightmare or all of the above!!

There are so many things to love about road construction, (insert sarcasm font!), but I have a few favorites. The top of the list is the signs that say, "Men Working." Isn't it funny that they have to post a sign so we know that is what they are doing? Or are they posting it as an attraction, because it's an unusual sight? It is especially humorous when after the sign, there are 4 men gathered around a hole looking into it, while another man is "working" on it. Oxymoron on display.

We must not forget the orange barrels or pointed cones (we affectionately call them road corn.) that are lined up for miles, with no sign of any work having been done, planned to be done, or ever going to be done. Let's just have one lane for a long stretch of this busy, busy highway, because we can.

Then, the joyous moment when you see the most magical words in the universe: "End Road Work."

On your journey, today, take a walk, take a ride on a bike trail, stay off the roads, and watch out for orange cones unless you see them at Dairy Queen!!

JUNE 3rd

ADVERTISEMENTS ARE PROLIFIC, often annoying and we can't seem to escape them. They talk to us on television, catch our eye when billboards appear as we are driving and make us turn multiple magazine pages to get past them to the stuff we really want to read. So, now that I have vented a bit, I have to admit, some are clever, funny, unbelievable and offer us a chance to purchase things we didn't know existed and certainly didn't know our life was not complete without said gadgety thingamajig time saving gizmo!!

I saw an advertisement for a candle, meant to comfort someone who is homesick. There are "scents" available from a variety of large metropolitan areas. I am a little skeptical, and pretty certain that I would not want a candle that smelled like Dallas, Detroit, Chicago or Sacramento, no matter how homesick I was. Now, if you give me a candle that smells like fresh mown grass, peonies in full bloom or the cold crisp smell of an autumn day, sign me up!!

Who thinks of these ideas? Was this idea the brainchild of a group of people sitting around a conference table trying to think of a way to sell more candles? Were they getting paid a great deal of money? Who signed off on this epic idea, destined to fail?? Just my opinion, but one wonders how these things come to be. At least I do...and now I've made you think about it!!

Will Rogers put it this way: "Advertising is the art of convincing people to spend money they don't have for something they don't need."

JUNE 4th

TRAVELING HAS BECOME a big part of my life in my "leisure" years. I do have a love/hate relationship with it!! I love going to new places, seeing the sights of the world and enjoying the adventures that travel brings. The anticipation and excitement of planning the trip, and counting down the days until departure time arrives. So, what is not to like about this, you might ask? I have one word for you: PACKING. It is not a four letter word, but maybe should be.

I admit often and openly that I am not a good packer. I second guess myself, as to what I should bring, how much I should bring, what suitcase to use, which carry-on, how many carry-ons...get the picture??

Road trips are much easier when it comes to packing. We have a nice sized SUV, so as I like to say, I can bring anything I want. Which drives fear into the heart of my gentleman friend as he contemplates loading my whole wardrobe into the car.

I might be exaggerating a little bit, but this is mostly non-fiction!! If the space is available, why let it go to waste???

Plane travel, much trickier. There is a limit on how much you can bring, so the choices take on a much greater importance...translate that to anxiety and stress for the not so able packer!! We will not talk about the time that I allegedly brought 7 pairs of shoes to Las Vegas for a long weekend. Women reading this will totally understand the whole shoe conundrum. Someday, maybe I will solve the packing puzzle, until then I will stumble along in my haphazard way.

So packing issues aside, travel is a wonderful thing. It educates, opens your mind to new ideas, opens your eyes to new sights and broadens your world view. Memories for a lifetime are created. Someone once said, "Wander often, wonder always." Trips can be for a day, a week, a month, it doesn't matter, travel is travel!!

On your journey today, plan to travel, plan a trip, plan an adventure!! Let the world be your playground. Work pays the bills, but adventures feed your soul! "Live in the sunshine, swim in the sea, drink in the wild air." Ralph Waldo Emerson

JUNE 5th

High School Class Reunions….where do I begin?? I have been the organizer (a/k/a herder of lost sheep) for my high school class for the last 25-30 years. Hard to remember when it happened….please make it stop!! I do actually enjoy trying to keep track of the 275 or so people I graduated with, and the pleading, begging, cajoling and threatening to get them all in the same place every 5 years. It is not for the faint of heart.

There are many, including those who live locally that do not attend for a variety of reasons, real or imagined. All I can say to those people and to you, the more the years pass, the more fun it is. There are no other people that have the same frame of reference as you during those formative years!! Everyone who attends is genuinely glad to see the people from that time in their life.

The one puzzling thing to me, is why does everyone look so much older than me? It reminds me of my Grandmother. She had received an invitation to her 60th class reunion, (a very small class of around 15). I offered to take her so she could attend. She looked at me with dismay, and said, "Why would I want to go see all those old people?" Point taken, Grandma!!

Kurt Vonnegut, well-known author, and instructor at the Iowa Writers Workshop nailed it with this remark: "True terror is to wake up one morning and discover that your high school class is running the country."

As we used to sing in Girl Scouts, "Make new friends, but keep the old. One is silver and the other gold." Treasure your friendships, their value is immeasurable.

JUNE 6th

I WOULD BE REMISS if I did not acknowledge the significance of this day in our history. Today is the anniversary of D-Day, when the Allied Invasion of Normandy took place.

160,000 troops from America, the United Kingdom, and 10 other countries landed on a stretch of French coastline, becoming the largest seaborne invasion in history. 13,000 Americans parachuted behind enemy lines. These heroes were very young men, some only nineteen or early twenties. The mission they were able to successfully complete was historic, unbelievable and changed the world. They definitely deserve the title of "The Greatest Generation."

Some iconic songs were written during this wartime inspired by the stories of love, loss and war. One of my all-time favorites, "I'll Be Seeing You" performed by Bing Crosby haunts me every time I listen to it. Here are a few more that some of you will recognize from movies and oldies!!

- "Boogie Woogie Bugle Boy"
- "Sentimental Journey"
- "Love Letters (straight from the heart)"
- "Don't Sit Under the Apple Tree"
- "Chattanooga Choo Choo"
- "On the Sunny Side of the Street"
- "You Are My Sunshine"

Music is a narrative of the life and times in which it was created. Looking back, it gives you such a feel for what people were thinking and doing." On your journey today, give thanks for the brave individuals who pulled off the impossible and shaped the world for a future generation.

JUNE 7th

THERE ARE times I rush unthinkingly through my daily routine of work, errands, activities and what not. When I take my time to notice my surroundings, I marvel and wonder at God's handiwork. I have some favorite song lyrics that express so well my feelings about life and the spectacular world we live in.

> Look at those evening shadows, casting a peaceful light. The sun is disappearing, it's a beautiful sight. Moments caught forever by the Master's touch, a lasting reminder to us. You only paint the picture once, you only get one chance. Take the time to do your best while the brush is in your hand. Make sure it's just right before the colors dry. You can't change it once it's done, you only paint the picture once.
>
> — "YOU ONLY PAINT THE PICTURE ONCE" — SONG BY LEGENDARY GROUP ALABAMA

It's your life, your story to write, your picture to paint. Be thoughtful, be present and in the moment. Give the world the gift of your very best self. Make memories, they are more valuable than any material possession. They will travel with you in your heart and mind everywhere you go. No luggage fees, no TSA regulations, no limits. They are yours for all eternity. Treasure them, share them and keep making more, your heart has an endless capacity for holding memories.

JUNE 8th

The two most important days in your life are the day you are born and the day you find out why.

— Mark Twain

Wise words indeed from the legendary Mark Twain. I hope that all of you reading this have reached that point in your life where you know why you were born. We all have a purpose and a passion to pursue. Each of you is unique and amazing. There is no one else like you. (I am not sure why, when people say that to me, they seem relieved about it and somehow it doesn't feel like a compliment!!)

I am not sure if I have recognized the purpose of my existence in the larger sense. There are certainly days and moments where I feel the world is a better place because I am here, and God has given me the tools to work and keep seeking that purpose.

Every life you touch, every talent and gift you share with the world changes things in ways you will never know. I believe there is a plan and we are all important parts of the whole. Nothing would be the same without you. Your life experiences and the way you have reacted and adapted to them are part of your uniqueness.

You, Lord are our Father. We are the clay, you are the potter. We are all the work of your hand.

— Isaiah 64:8

On your journey, today, give the world the best version of yourself, rejoice in who you are, and give thanks for your blessings.

JUNE 9th

Fifteen years ago, I received a cancer diagnosis. It came as a complete shock to me, as I am sure it does to everyone. I have always been very faithful about my annual physical and "female" checkups. I am alive today, because of that. During the exam, my doctor felt something that shouldn't be there. She assumed it was a cyst, but it needed to be checked out. She scheduled me for a colonoscopy, telling me, that the growth might be able to be removed during that process.

After the colonoscopy, the physician told me they couldn't remove it and I would need surgery, regardless of the biopsy results. I went to see the surgeon alone, assuming it was a routine, annoying, but necessary surgery. It was the beginning of summer and I asked him if the surgery could be postponed until fall, as we had travel plans for the summer. He gave me the strangest look, and said, "I don't think so, we don't wait when it's cancer." That was how I found out. The gastroenterologist hadn't bothered to call me with the biopsy results. The surgeon felt horrible as he assumed I had been told. I left there shaken and scared.

Nevertheless, I had the surgery, two hospital stays, several procedures, three rounds of chemotherapy and six weeks of daily radiation therapy. Thanks to my gynecologist, my cancer was found before the manifestation of symptoms, which I was told by the oncologist rarely happens.

Thanks to my family, friends, and faith, I had lots of company on this journey. Thankful to the one who paints the sunsets in the sky that he still had plans for me on my earthly journey. I never asked him, why me? To quote Corrie ten Boom, "When a train goes through a tunnel and it gets dark, you don't throw away the ticket and jump off. You sit still and trust the engineer." I trusted the engineer. I am a survivor.

JUNE 10th

SUMMER....THE word evokes a myriad of memories of days of yore and the freedom we had when I was young. (Yes, hard to believe but I was once young.) The long hot days of summer that were never long enough for the neighborhood gang!!

On many a summer day, we explored the city on our bicycles, not coming home until dinner. Our moms would pack us a sandwich, then we would ride to Clover Farm, the little grocery on Summit Street for the "extras." My choice was always strawberry pop and a banana split. The banana split was a cake like treat with banana filling. Then we were off!

College Street Park was often the dining destination. Lots of shade, lots of room to run and be children. No cell phones, no watches,no reason to be worried, just time to sprawl in the grass, play tag and jump off the swings!! Home by dinner time to tell of the adventures.

Evenings were often spent playing kickball at Longfellow School. We lived right next door, very nice to have our own playground!! Play till dark, or a little later if Mom forgot to ring the bell. Several of the moms had bells to ring when we needed to come home, and we all knew which one was ours.

My memories of these times evoke sadness as well. Today's children can't have the freedom we had to just be kids. It would not be safe for them to roam the way we did. In addition, there are way too many "organized" sports, lessons, and activities for children today. Starting at a very young age, they need a daily calendar and a personal assistant to keep track of their schedule. No time for dreaming, imagining and lying in the grass looking at clouds. Those were the days, my friends.

On your journey, remember a simpler time, and do some cloud watching.

JUNE 11th

It's summertime, clothing is more casual. Shorts, t-shirts, flip-flops are the expected uniform. For those connoisseurs of witty clothing, I thought I would share some funny t-shirt slogans I have seen.

- Sorry, I'm late, I didn't want to come. (This could come in handy)
- Celery is 95% water and 100% not pizza. (So true!)
- Wine-a hug in a glass. (No explanation necessary)
- Yes, Officer, I saw the speed limit. I just didn't see you. (Oops)
- Does this shirt make me look bald? (If you have to ask….)
- Wake up. Be Awesome. Repeat. (Words to live by!)
- Exercise?? I thought you said extra fries. (Exactly)
- Iowa: 75% Vowels, 100% Awesome. (Had to include this!)
- What rhymes with Friday? Vodka

Many would say that women of a certain age shouldn't wear t-shirts with funny sayings, or even t-shirts at all. They are probably right, but I might be a woman of a certain age, and I am mightily tempted once in a while by a clever shirt. Tony Robbins said, "The only limit to your impact is your imagination and commitment." And maybe your clever t-shirt….

On your journey today, laugh at the rules, live in the moment, and if you can't wear a clever t-shirt, give one as a gift!!

JUNE 12th

Mindfulness....taking it slow......quality not quantity......savoring......Sitting on the porch looking at Lake Cayuga, one of the Finger Lakes in upstate New York. It feels good, it feels right, it feels refreshing to mind and body. There is a movement making its way slowly across the country (slowly) which is appropriate. The first mention I heard of it, was from a friend in New Jersey, he was talking about a "Slow Stitching" movement. He is a quilter among other things, as am I. Sometimes we are in such a hurry to finish a project, we stop enjoying the process of making a beautiful item. Why do we do that?

So let's apply that to other things that we do, supposedly for enjoyment. Planning a vacation... scheduling an itinerary that has no time for spontaneous adventures or happenstance things we stumble upon. Racing from one destination to another so that we can do more things but have less time to enjoy them. Does this seem wrong to you?

It sure does, even to this Type A personality.

Take a breath, slow down your walk, your hike, your kayak adventure.

Squeeze every ounce of beauty and enjoyment out of the moment. Engage all your senses in the pursuit of a quality moment. Forget about how much can be done, quality over quantity never disappoints.

Not just today, but on your life's journey, slow down, inhale, exhale, relax. Do less, be more.

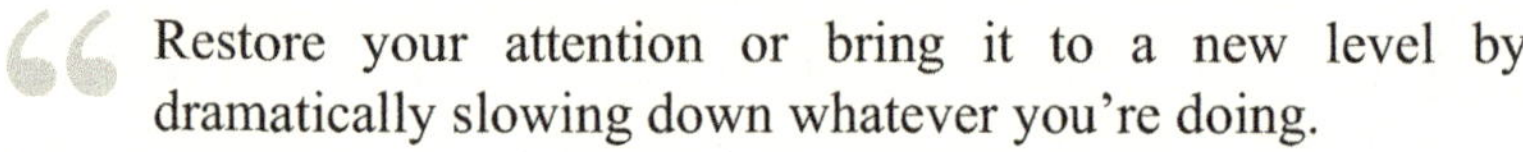

> Restore your attention or bring it to a new level by dramatically slowing down whatever you're doing.
>
> — Sharon Salzberg, Author

JUNE 13th

HAS IT BEEN A MONTH ALREADY??? Okay, time for another letter du jour.

(Just be glad there are only 12 months, not 26!) This month I am thinking about the Letter "K." Most words that begin with K have a nice crisp edge to them.

Here are some of my favorites for you to think about:

Keen	Knickerbocker	Kowtow
Kooky	Kerchief	Knuckled (not a crispy one)
Kindred	Kerplunk	Klutz
Kolache	Kitten	Kaffeklatsch
Kickstand	Kibitzed	Kaleidoscope

That is a list of some great words!! Three that I think are so very descriptive are kowtow, kaffeklatsch and kibitzed. He kowtowed to the women as they kibitzed at the kaffeklatsch.

June is certainly a keen month to kerplunk in the pool, eat a kolache or adopt a kitten. I did leave out something that begins with K that is very yummy, Krispy Kreme Donuts, now there is a word with some kick!!

The purpose of these "Letter" days is to make me think, and share with you great words that maybe aren't used as much as they used to be. Communication is so important in our lives, and using specific words, fun words, silly words is an opportunity for us all to stretch our vocabulary limits a bit!! Now if my pants would stretch a little more after the Krispy Kremes….

JUNE 14th

"YOU'RE A GRAND OLD FLAG, you're a high flying flag, and forever in peace may you wave. You're the emblem of the land that I love, the home of the free and the brave." A patriotic march by none other than George M. Cohan. The musical movie "Yankee Doodle Dandy" was a biography of his life. The music is of course by Mr. Cohan. He wrote many other songs you would probably recognize, including "Yankee Doodle Boy,' "Over There," and a personal favorite, "Give My Regards to Broadway."

Happy Flag Day!! Hope you enjoyed these iconic lyrics to one of my favorite patriotic songs. The tune is jaunty, the words are clever and it makes me want to march around waving a flag and looking for a parade!! (It is not true that I do this regularly, no matter what you may have heard.)

On June 14, 1777, the Second Continental Congress adopted the flag. Over the years there were local and state celebrations on this, the birthday of the flag. In 1949 Congress designated this day as National Flag Day. It is not an official federal holiday but is celebrated nevertheless in a variety of ways in many locales.

On your journey, today, display your flag, and honor the red, white and blue. Celebrate this day, this flag, and this nation.

JUNE 15th

ENTREPRENEURS OF THE HEARTLAND-TAKE HEED!! These ideas are free for the taking, you can thank me later. I have noticed a lack of variety in the market of mobile food. In this age, where convenience is everything, there is money to be made in this area.

Remember the sound of the ice cream truck roaming through the neighborhood and the excitement as it got closer and closer to your house? There aren't enough ice cream trucks anymore, but you could start there and move on to bigger things!!

The first idea is a roaming coffee truck. If there was a coffee truck in the area, adults would be pushing and shoving to order that special coffee. Money to be made, and you could make a latte people happy, (Groan) Make the rounds of the neighborhoods, the workplaces, the library and you would be very popular. Caffeinate your town!!

The second idea is a taco truck. Imagine, mariachi music playing, the taco truck is on the move, Lunch, a quick snack, a round of tacos for happy hour, the possibilities are endless!! Beef tacos, chicken tacos, shrimp tacos, dessert tacos. Never actually seen a dessert taco, but why not?

I am sure the coffee truck and the taco truck exist in large metropolitan areas, but let's bring them to the Heartland!!

> I'm just a girl standing in front of a salad, asking it to be 3 tacos, 2 margaritas and an order of queso.
>
> — UNKNOWN

JUNE 16th

Cell phone etiquette or protocol is a much overlooked subject. I believe a class on etiquette should be required to own and use a cell phone in public. This class could also cover non-cell phone conversations in public places. Take a class, pass a test, get a license to buy a cell phone!

Here is a note to people in public places in close proximity to others: we do not want to hear about your dog's (or any other pet's) vomiting in graphic detail...Nor do we want to hear about your relatives who are in jail, in trouble, fighting with you, using drugs, the neighbors or the government. Also, we don't want to hear your personal (and I do mean personal) health, sex or marriage problems.

I have heard so many conversations that I did not want or need to hear while in doctor's offices, restaurants and around the swimming pool at the hotel. Many of these conversations are taking place on said person's cell phone. Just because you are looking down and huddled with your cell phone, trust me, we can still hear you. And we don't want to…

Read a book, go to a movie, take a class or find a hobby and talk about that...seriously.

JUNE 17th

A FEW YEARS AGO (OKAY, maybe decades ago....) Nancy Drew was the fictional heroine of my youth. As an avid reader, once I found this series, couldn't wait to read them all. I haunted garage sales to find used ones, and probably got a new one once in awhile for a birthday or Christmas gift. "The Hidden Staircase," "Password to Larkspur Lane," "The Clue of the Broken Locket," "The Secret of the Old Clock," and "The Secret to Red Gate Farm," to name a few of the 56 original volumes written by Carolyn Keene. The interesting thing is Nancy was created by the same man who created the Hardy Boys as the female counterpart to them.

These books were a pretty easy read, nice mystery to solve, and not too scary for a young girl. I wanted to be Nancy. Who wouldn't? She had a powder blue convertible, and a lawyer father that gave her free rein to travel around and solve her mysteries. Then, the icing on the cake; she had an occasional boyfriend named Ned, who was very handsome, and was only around when she wanted him to be. I am seeing nothing wrong with this picture.

Simpler books for a simpler time. It's hard for me to judge if these books have stood the test of time. Reading them as an adult is not the same. Regardless, Nancy Drew was a young woman ahead of her time!! She went on adventures with her girlfriends, solved a few mysteries along the way and had a lot of freedom for a young woman in that time period.

Think about your favorite books as a grade-schooler. I think it will bring back some fond memories. Throwing out some characters from the past: Bobbsey Twins, The Happy Hollisters, Hardy Boys, Pollyanna. As a little bit older, "The Island of the Blue Dolphin," (loved that book!), "A Wrinkle in Time," "The Trumpeter of Krakow," to name a few.

Thanks for indulging me in this trip down memory lane!! Hope it conjured up some memories for some of you as well. On you journey today, indulge yourself by visiting some fond memories of the past, and make some new memories for the future.

JUNE 18th

Music acts like a magic key, to which the most tightly closed heart opens.

— Maria Augusta von Trapp

So many emotions are evoked by music. I will hear a song from the past and it is like a warm breeze on a summer day. It takes me to another place and time.

If each decade of your life was represented by a song, what would be the song(s)? I came up with some songs for my life, which is not an easy feat. A decade is a long time, and your position on the gameboard of life can change dramatically during that time. I chose songs that had memories for me.

- 1960's: "Dock of the Bay" (or should I say reservoir?) Otis Redding; "Brown Eyed Girl" Van Morrison; "Stop in the Name of Love" The Supremes
- 1970's: "American Pie" Don McLean; "Dream On" Oakridge Boys
- 1980's: "Looking for Love" Johnny Lee; "It's Still Rock and Roll to Me" Billy Joel
- 1990's: "Strawberry Wine" Deanna Carter; "I Will Always Love You" Whitney Houston
- 2000's: "I Hope You Dance" Lee Ann Womack; "Bless the Broken Road" Rascal Flatt

On your journey, today, turn up the music of your life and dance the day away!

JUNE 19th

WHAT IS AN URBAN LEGEND? To me, it is a modern version of folklore!! It is defined as a humorous or scary story, passed from person to person as if it were true. Iowa certainly has its' share of urban legends, many specific to a "haunted" place. For those not from the Heartland, I wanted to lay to rest an urban legend, that has no basis in reality, no matter how cool it sounds!!

Cow Tipping is an activity where one sneaks up on a sleeping, or unsuspecting bovine creature and tips it over for entertainment. There are several problems with this. The first is, cows do not sleep standing up, and what fun would there be in tipping a cow who is already lying down? The second problem is that cows can weight anywhere from 1,000 pounds to 1,800 pounds. I don't know anyone who could tip over a cow, it would take a group, and still would not be an easy proposition. Personally, having spent some time on farms, I would not want to upset any animal that is the size of a car.

The last issue with cow tipping is really a language/definition misconception. Cow is the word for the mature female of cattle. When you see a group of these animals in a field, they should be referred to as cattle, not cows. I am so sorry to disavow you of the vision of people in Iowa sneaking around farm fields tipping over cows/cattle as a form of entertainment!

If this were a real activity, I am sure PETA would have objections to it. I often wonder, does PETA have an official position on eating animal crackers. Inquiring minds....

Appreciate the beauty of the gentle bovine creatures you encounter, and scrap your plans for cow tipping.

JUNE 20th

IT SEEMS like a good day for oxymorons, I mean really, what day isn't? I am very fond of a good oxymoron, especially when they occur naturally in conversation!! The origin of the word is from the Greek language. If you are not familiar with the word, it is a figure of speech that uses contradictory terms in a phrase.

Examples of oxymorons:

Jumbo shrimp	Only choice	Good grief
Small crowd	Plastic glass	Act naturally
Original copy	Fine mess	Random order
Deafening silence	Found missing	Pretty ugly
Zero tolerance	Active retirement	Objective opinion

Just a few for your reading enjoyment!!! Americans use oxymorons often in their daily language and writing. It is a great way to emphasize your point, make a joke with the self-contradiction.

The word oxymoron is not to be confused with the laundry detergent, Oxiclean. I am not sure the purpose of "Oxi" in the name of this product. Oxys from the Greek means sharp or pointed, while moros means foolish in the word oxymoron.

Have some fun today including some oxymorons in your conversation. Wear your long shorts, buy some authentic replicas, and try to avoid minor disasters.

JUNE 21st

Summer solstice, the longest day of the year….not sure I totally agree, I have had some pretty long days that weren't in the middle of June...but I digress...This is the day we have more hours of sunlight than any other day in the calendar year.

In the Heartland, we have about 15 hours of sunlight. The further north, the more sun. Celebrate in Fairbanks, Alaska for nearly 24 hours of sun!! Another day to do something special and celebrate the extra daylight!!

> Summer is the annual permission slip to be lazy. To do nothing and have it count for something. To lie in the grass and count the stars. To sit on a branch and study the clouds.
>
> — Regina Brett

I like the quote, but personally, me sitting on a branch and looking at the clouds sounds like a gravity storm waiting to happen. I think I will go with the picnic blanket on the grass for my cloud study!! Nothing beats a shady spot on a summer day to enjoy the gloriousness of this season. A picnic basket, a cool beverage, a good book and some good company to while away the summer days. Summer days seem to make time stand still, reminds me of when I was younger, summer always seemed to make you think you had all the time in the world.

On your summer solstice journey, take a moment, take the day, take it in. Green trees, green fields, bursts of summer color, painted by the Master for you to enjoy! If you need that permission slip, let me know!!

JUNE 22nd

DIPLOMACY, compromise, working well with others, all things we need to be able to do as adults out in the world. There was a simpler time when those attributes weren't as necessary. We had other tools and skills we could use to make those tough decisions.

Remember any of the "choosing" rhymes from your childhood?

The first one that came to my mind, was "Eenie, meenie, miney, mo, grab a tiger by the toe if he hollers let him go...." I have a distinct memory of a group of neighborhood kids standing in a circle, each one of us had one foot in the circle to do the choosing. Another favorite of ours was " 1 potato, 2 potato, 3 potato, 4, 5 potato, 6 potato, 7 potato more." Very important decisions were made with these diplomatic models. Who was going to be "it" in a game of tag, for example? The rhymes could be used to choose "it" or "out", depending on how the decision was going to be made.

Some of these choosing rhymes could be converted to jump rope ditties. "Bubble gum, bubble gum in a dish, how many pieces do you wish?" Then count the number of jumps before you missed.

What a great methodology!! Impartial, fun to say, no arguing about the outcome (usually!), what is not to like?? I hope you enjoy these brief forays into the past as much as I do. Looking at the kinds of things we learned as children, to negotiate, manage our own play and group of friends. Parents usually weren't standing over us, we were free to roam, play and make decisions about what to do.

Albert Einstein said, "Play is the highest form of research." Taking his advice to heart, I encourage you to go out and research every day! You might delight in the change in yourself and the world around you.

JUNE 23rd

I THINK OUR HOME PLANET, the earth is a wondrous place. Contrary to my major antipathy towards my Earth Science class my freshman year at college, (hey, it was held at 7:30 A.M. and we looked at slides of rocks) I love living on the third rock from the sun. Volcanoes, mountains, glaciers, oceans, rivers, prairies, and meadows what is not to like?

If you are feeling a little on the chubby side, the circumference of the earth is 24,901 miles. Now that is a waistline!! We are spinning about 1000 miles per hour while we move around the sun at about 67,000 miles per hour. This is where my brain starts to shut down. I can't comprehend this is happening. Gravity must be pretty darn strong,and is yet another subject I don't understand. I have a great deal of experience with gravity storms, and usually come out battered and defeated! Do not mess with gravity, it will not end well for you.

I am overwhelmed by the raw beauty of this place we call home. The vistas are spectacular and extraordinary. The creation of this planet is nothing less than a miracle, created by a Master artist. There are many songs written about the beauty of the earth, and in particular our piece of the rock, America.

A verse from one of my favorite songs: "America the Beautiful."

"O beautiful for spacious skies
For amber waves of grain
For purple mountain majesties
Above thy fruited plain."

That verse paints a beautiful picture for me, and I hope for you. On your journey today, enjoy the outdoors, give thanks for the beauty around you, and don't forget to thank a rock.

JUNE 24th

THE ONE DISAPPOINTMENT I have about writing this book, is that I have to type the manuscript. In my daily world, work, school, list making, letter/card writing, I am a big (understatement) fan of "special" writing instruments. It might actually be an addiction or obsession. I realize that typing this is a necessary task, and I actually do enjoy typing on my laptop. Probably because I was taught to type back in the days when we had typewriters, and a whole semester was spent learning to type without looking at the keyboard, etc. Tests had to be passed-grades were given. But I digress....

I can say the notes for this book were all written with one of my many "special" pens. If a pen doesn't feel a certain way when I write with it, then I can't use it. It is a distraction to me. I also enjoy writing with different colors of ink. It's a way to express my mood!! If you could see one of my travel journals, it is very colorful!!

I know this will be hard to believe, but not everyone understands or is sympathetic to my need for "special" pens. On a road trip early in our relationship, I would like to say my gentleman friend marveled at all the pens I brought along, but pretty sure marveled is not the right word!! I figure it's a small thing, it's legal, and it makes me happy!! The relationship is going strong many years later, so it evidently wasn't a deal breaker!!

On your journey today, color outside the lines, use all the crayons in your box and make it a day to remember.

JUNE 25th

"SURROUND yourself with people who will leap out of the dugout should you ever charge the mound." Baseball aficionados will love this quote, and even if you are not a diehard fan, this quote of unknown origin paints a very vivid picture of the kind of people you want on your team/in your life.

One has to seriously consider at times, "Why is that person in my life?" People change, circumstances change, or we wake up to the realization that someone we considered a friend does not have our best interests at heart. Dixie "Downer," Peter "Passive Aggressive" and "Cry Me a River" Rosie are not the people you want to choose for your team!!

There is no need to be cruel about this, one can gently ease them out of your life because their three strikes are up!! Send them down to the minor leagues and move on.

I know I am being somewhat facetious here, but when people are no longer a positive influence in your life, time to let go.

On your journey today, remember you can't control the negativity around you, but you can choose not to participate in it.

JUNE 26th

CHILDHOOD DAYS in the summer were a delight I did not fully appreciate at the time. Today I long for those seemingly endless days of laughter, play, the neighborhood gang, and freedom. One of the delightful activities available to us was something we simply called "playground." I don't know the actual name of this event, but was a summer weekday activity sponsored by the Parks and Rec Department. It took place all over the city in neighborhood parks. My memory tells me it was from 1:00 PM to 4:00 PM every weekday.

We never knew ahead of time what delights lay in store for us each day at playground. It could be games, arts, crafts, or stories.

There were vigorous and competitive games of 4 square every day. 4 square consisted of, wait for it….4 squares painted on the cement, and a rubber playground ball. There was a server square and then 3 other players. The idea was to bounce the ball back and forth to one another, trying to make someone miss. Hopefully, your skill would allow you to "move up" to the server square.

Another favorite was making lanyards with endless varieties of colorful plastic cord. What we used these for, I have no idea. We didn't have keys or ID cards or anything else that required a lanyard around our neck. Maybe a whistle? Regardless, we loved making them and never turned down the chance to do so on craft day.

This story would not be complete without mention of our masterpiece paintings made by squirting paint on a spinning piece of construction paper. Who doesn't love permission to squirt bottles of paint?

The day typically ended with a visit from the ice cream vendor, usually on a bicycle pulling the cold delights in a freezer cart. Those were indeed the "good old days.".

JUNE 27th

Second chances in life are wonderful gifts. Second chances are everywhere, if we are open to them, and not afraid to take our hands off the handlebars! Second chances are like regrets, it has been said that the only regrets one has, are not the things one did, but the things one didn't do. Take a second chance at life and if you are so lucky, at love.

Second chances at love, are beyond anything I can describe. Love takes different shapes and forms depending on our age and place in life when it happens. Young love is full of drama, romance and fireworks and the beginning to your path in life. Mature love is finding someone that can travel life's path with you. You complete each other. Two puzzle pieces that fit together effortlessly and make you both whole. Mature love can still have romance and fireworks but in the context of two people who already know who they are.

My second chance at love is like the sound of the rain that lulls me to sleep. He is a warm fire on a cold winter night and Christmas morning. He is the song my heart sings. He is the autumn colors painted against a warm blue sky. He not only lets me be who I am destined to be, but prods, encourages and cheers me on. Nothing can separate us, not time, not distance and not even death.

A quote from "Twelfth Night" by William Shakespeare says it nicely; "If music be the food of love, play on." So my advice, if the first verse is over, keep listening.

JUNE 28th

Although I have learned many lessons throughout my lifetime, the learning never stops, nor should it. I enjoy learning new things (most of the time) and believe that continuing to learn keeps the heart, mind and soul young.

However, there are some things I have learned that really aren't educational, just illustrations of my lack of awareness...I prefer that term to others that might be used. I will leave those to your imagination...be nice…

I have 5 or 6 or 13 remote control devices at my home. The majority of them are in my living room. I came to the realization one day in the last several weeks, that no matter how close you get to the DVD player, and how many times you push the buttons, the CD remote will not operate it….even if you change the batteries.

Speaking of batteries, do you ever wonder why there are no "B" batteries? There are AA, AAA, C, and D versions. What happened to B? I did a little research, and indeed at one time there were A and B batteries, but to make a long story short, as devices that needed battery power were changed, updated, the A and B were no longer needed. There are still some uses for B batteries in Europe, but the demand is dwindling.

Batteries, remotes, whatever the challenge, I am game!! As Babe Ruth once said, "Every strike brings me closer to the next home run."

On your journey today, don't be afraid to take a big swing!

JUNE 29th

I HAVE DEBATED about writing this page but decided we all have fears, so I will share my fears. Most are silly, and not so much fears, as situations that make me anxious.

I love watching the goldfinches at my feeder and seeing the colorful cardinals, blue jays and woodpeckers joyfully soaring through the sky. However, I am afraid of larger birds that fly incredibly close to me, so close that I cover my head and duck. Seagulls are a prime source of anxiety when I am at the beach. I will never go into an aviary where the birds are flying free all around you.

I don't know if I really have claustrophobia, but I dislike being in small places. Long airplane flights are stressful. I try to get a seat as near to the front of the plane as I can, so I can deplane as soon as possible. In meetings, theaters, church, I want to sit on the aisle, preferably as close to the exit as possible. I would only be partially kidding if I told you that being in the southern part of Florida makes me a bit anxious. I guess it is because my escape routes are limited!!

Having fears or anxiousness is something we all share. I used to worry about many things, over which I had no control. Someone said to me that 99% of the things you worry about never happen. I remind myself of that frequently. Recognizing what makes you anxious or afraid is three-quarters of the battle. Acknowledge the situation and figure out what will help you deal with it. John Wayne, iconic American actor said, "Courage is being scared to death and saddling up anyway."

Saddle up, take the ride, start the day. Watch out for birds, small enclosed spaces and peninsulas. I won't even mention sneaky cats that crawl up on the sofa back behind your head. That will have to be another page.

JUNE 30th

Do you have a special place to "get away from it all?" Sanctuary, by definition, is a place of safety and refuge, a port in a storm, a haven, and an oasis. I am writing about a place that is a sanctuary for your soul. A place that can shelter your vulnerabilities, your worries, and your cares.

When I arrive at my sanctuary, the day to day drudgery, routines and worries slide off my shoulders like a melting ice cream cone in 90-degree weather. I feel lighter, a sense of calm settles over me and I breathe it in. I feel at peace.

My particular place is a seaside sanctuary in a tiny beach town in North Carolina. A dear friend made this a part of my life about ten years ago; for which I will forever be grateful. At that time in my life, I needed this place desperately. I had been through a rough time and was coming out the other side, but had not arrived at the knowledge that it was okay for me to be happy again. This spot, along with hours of laughter and tears with my friend Pam, started me down the road to finding myself again. I had been lost in grief and didn't know how to come out the other side.

My hope for you is you have a place like this, or will find one in time of need. It is not only the location but the support of people who care about you that makes it special. We shelter our physical selves but need to remember to shelter the spiritual and emotional sides as well.

> You have permission to rest. You are not responsible for fixing everything that is broken. You do not have to try and make everyone happy. For now, take time for you. It's time to replenish.
>
> — Plentiful Earth

JULY 1st

WHEN MY BROTHERS and I were growing up, our parents had a camper on the back of a green GMC truck. Road trips were fun, for the most part, because we got to ride in the camper which allowed for lots of shenanigans. My dad had hooked up an intercom system so we could talk to them in the cab of the pickup. We could play cards at the table, climb into the bunk over the cab and watch out the upper window, and last but not least torment each other. This, of course, led to the injured or insulted sibling to use the intercom to tattle. After a few times of this, my mom would shut off the intercom, and left us to survive on our own. Tough love.

On one of these trips, we went out west, headed to Yellowstone. We were camped in a mountainous, heavily forested area. When we arrived, Dad and Mom would have to go to work to get the camper properly leveled and set up. Being the oldest, I was in charge of my brothers, which even today is no easy task!

I decided we should go on a hike. I have very specific memories of that hike, mostly stayed near the road, but we were having a grand adventure. I think we had all found "walking" sticks and we were living the high life in the wild west.

Evidently, we were gone for a very long time. We returned to the campsite and walked into a beehive of activity. My parents had called for help, thinking we were lost, and the park rangers and other campers were all looking for us. I was bewildered because I knew where we were all the time and got back to the campsite with no problem. I believe after my parents got done being relieved, I was definitely in trouble. Seriously? Just a take charge girl leading her brothers on a walk in bear country as sunset approaches. What could go wrong? As an adult, I shudder thinking about it!

JULY 2nd

RAISE your hand if you listen to compact discs (CDs) in the car, or at home!! I thought so!! I am aware that some younger people may not do this anymore, but who asked them, and who cares??

So here is the question of the day: Why are car manufacturers making new cars without a CD player in them? I am talking about cars that the young are probably not buying because of style and a higher price tag.

No entiendo! I do not understand this.

Retail stores, online merchants such as Amazon are still selling music cds and audio books on cd. Libraries are purchasing new audio books on cd. How does this brain trust in the automobile industry think we are going to play them? The particular car I am talking about can't have one installed aftermarket either. Great customer service, nope, you can't buy one from us, and we've fixed it so you can't add one. Oh, and please fill out our survey and let us know how we're doing...

I know we have witnessed some pretty significant lapses in judgment from this industry. Edsel anyone? I hope this is one of their big OOPS moments that they recognize and change. I think when someone pays between $30,000 and $55,000 for a new car, it should have a CD player along with all the other bells and whistles. If a car can tell you when it's safe to pass, give you directions, park itself and brake for you if you are daydreaming, a CD player doesn't seem like a lot to ask.

When we take long road trips, we always take along some audio books to help break up the drive. We have regressed to using a portable CD player that can be plugged into the car speakers, that uses AA batteries, or more accurately put, eats them like candy. I hold it on my lap. Seriously. Maybe we should get a transistor radio.

JULY 3rd

We are all aging every single day, which is a good thing given the alternative, but I didn't have a grasp on the process until "things" started sneaking up on me. There are some great things that come with aging, but the ones that sneak up on you are not.

In my mind, I have always recognized my age as I got older, but until the side effects started kicking in, I didn't mind very much. I have a young spirit, I am silly and goofy at times, and embrace new adventures in my life.

At a certain point, aging is not graceful, easy or pretty. I am grateful that my health is pretty good. But that first time when you really look at your skin and see the wrinkles and jello-jigglers on your arms and neck. Then there is the matter of your joints. Sitting in the car on a long road trip is no longer a walk in the park. We stop, and I slowly roll myself to the pavement and try to make everything start working again.

Activities take longer and exhaust you more. There are times when your body just fails you in mystical, unexplainable ways.

In spite of all the physical disappointments, I am happy for an active mind, for being able to relate to young people without being an old curmudgeon, for the wisdom gained through years of life experiences, good and bad. I am happy for the number of years I have been granted thus far, and all the many people I have collected along the way. There is a richness to friends and family at this age that didn't exist before. In spite of my age, I still have the energy and enthusiasm for new adventures! Bring them on!! Don't let your age define your activities!!

Madeleine L'Engle said it best, "The great thing about getting older is you don't lose all the other ages you've been."

JULY 4th

HAPPY BIRTHDAY, America!! That sure is a lot of candles, but it looks good on you!! The birth of this country in 1776 is an amazing historical event that changed the face of the world forever. Sometimes I wonder, how in the world did the founding fathers and other patriots pull that off??

I wish for all to have a safe, fun-filled celebration on this special day. As you enjoy this holiday, take time to be thankful for those in our armed forces who will not be at a barbeque, family picnic or fireworks. Instead, they will be standing ever vigilant to defend your freedom. Wear some red, white and blue and let freedom ring for all the world to hear!!

A quote from President Reagan, a man who truly loved this country seems appropriate for this day. "Freedom is never more than one generation away from extinction. We didn't pass it to our children in the bloodstream. It must be fought for, protected and handed on for them to do the same or one day we will spend our sunset years telling our children what it once was like in the United States where men were free."

JULY 5th

I LOVED summer vacations when my grandkids were young, so many opportunities to spend time with them, have adventures and spoil them.

One adventure that I had with Josh and Allison, a brother/sister act, started with a trip to downtown Iowa City. Our ultimate destination was the Museum of Natural History in MacBride Hall at the University of Iowa. But we could make an adventure getting there. We parked at the mall parking ramp and walked through the mall towards our destination. Lo and behold, the mall had escalators which are a huge attraction to children. When you are the grandmother and time is not important, you can let them ride up and down on the escalator as many times as they want...and you ride with them.

One summer, I decided Allison and her cousin Micaila were old enough to learn to quilt. They had chosen fabric in colors and designs they liked, and we were ready to go. So before we started, I was explaining the process, cutting the fabric to the specified dimensions of the pattern, etc. They took it all in, good students as always. Allison was excited and ready to start. Micaila, my little scientist (now a biology major in college) looked at me and said, "So we are going to cut all that fabric up in pieces, and then sew it back together?" Well, when you put it that way, it does seem like an exercise in futility. But she is a good sport, so we began the cutting up and the sewing back together!

Whatever the activity or adventure, one thing is certain, the laughter and love that follow. As Sylvia Earle, Oceanographer said, "There's no greater music than the sound of my grandchildren laughing."

Grandchildren are the song in my heart, the light of my life, and their love makes my world go 'round.

JULY 6th

IN CASE any of you are wondering, I have taken some writing classes to help me with this book. If you are still wondering after reading part of the book, I guess that wasn't money well spent. I took a class at the Iowa Summer Writing Festival that was titled, "Write Funny to Me." Sounded like it could be just the inspiration I was looking for. I could learn some writing techniques, learn to be funnier….assuming I was funny to start with, meet some other writers and have a grand adventure. My writer's heart and ego were very excited about this journey. Point of information: a non-published author probably does have the ego of a published author. No offense intended.

The first day of class, the instructor taught us some great techniques, talked about what makes something funny, and the day flew by. The ten of us in the class were very diverse as far as age, background and writing style. I thought this was interesting and would make for good discussion. It did, and it was, but I wasn't prepared for some of the aspects of this. Homework for the evening was to write a piece no more than 1000 words for the class to critique the next day. It was supposed to be funny. Hence, the name of the class...

One thousand words equals roughly three pages. The writing I had been doing for this book, are much shorter pieces, not very in depth or intellectual, nor are they meant to be. I waded in waist deep and wrote, re-wrote, edited my work for about 5 hours. I was satisfied and thought it was funny.

Day two, we start critiquing the work of all the class members. When they talked about mine, I felt like I had been hit with a bag of cement. It's not that they didn't think it was funny, but wanted me to write in more detail, and develop some of the humor. I understood that, but it is not the kind of writing I am working on. and with the support of a good friend I met during the class moved on. As she said, "It's not Shakespeare for God's sake." That put the whole thing in perspective for me! I agree this is definitely not Shakespeare!!

JULY 7th

"TAKE me out to the ball game, take me out with the crowd! Buy me some peanuts and Cracker Jack, I don't care if I never get back…"

Ahhh, yes, America's favorite pastime, it is baseball season!! We have a lot of teams to root for here in the Heartland. The Cubs and the Cardinals seem to have the most support, but every once in a while you will stumble across a White Sox or Royals fan!!

I confess I am not a die-hard fan. I will occasionally be convinced to watch baseball on TV, and I admit it is a great way to take a nap...Oops, did I say that out loud?? Going to a baseball game is much more interesting and exciting.

I have been in a number of major league parks, (5 to be precise) but was introduced to my first minor league game several years ago. Our local farm team, the Kernels...really? Did they pay someone to come up with that? Not much imagination used, and so not cool. Sounds corny….sorry, couldn't resist. It gets even better. The mascot who is dressed like an ear of corn is called: Mr. Shucks!

The game was fun, so much to watch and listen to, excitement was in the air. We had good seats, the brats were great and the beer was cold. The crack of the bats and the roar of the crowd made for a fun night. However, I'm not done….the best part of the game for me was…..wait for it…..they gave me a wristband that said "Over 21." Took me back to a younger era, plus it was much nicer than the one they gave me at the hospital that said "Fall Risk."

On your journey, today, keep swinging till you hit one out of the park, don't be afraid to steal second and celebrate your victories, large and small!!

JULY 8th

I AM certain that many of you enjoy social media venues for daily interaction with those you know. Facebook is my information highway for all things bright and beautiful that occur in the lives of my friends and family….and for the unwelcome news when bad things happen to good people.

I have been a pretty regular presence, posting "Good Morning from the Heartland" every morning. I would include a snippet of an event or activity, my special weather observations, and more times than I would like to admit, sharing one of my gravity storms or other personal failures!! Many were kind enough to tell me they enjoyed my blathering, others suggested I write a book. So….ignoring the fact that I have always thought about writing a book, even keeping a file of ideas, you can blame my Facebook friends for encouraging me and instigating the writing of this epistle!

Regardless of some negative aspects of Facebook, I think anything that helps people cope, connect, and communicate is worthwhile. If one lonely or sad person is helped by connecting with someone via Facebook or enjoys a joke or a picture, there is healing.

In 1970, Diana Ross sang a song with these lyrics, "Reach out and touch somebody's hand. Make this world a better place if you can…..Take a little time out of your busy day to give encouragement to someone who's lost the way."

On your journey, reach out to those whose lives intersect with yours and make this world a better place. I know you can.

JULY 9th

I CAN'T BELIEVE I forgot to go to the gym today....that's six years in a row. Anybody else have a love-hate relationship with working out? I have tried to commit to Gym, but the relationship just doesn't work for me. Sorry Gym, it's me, not you.

I belonged to a gym for a couple of years and did surprisingly well going at least three times a week. I had a routine I did that a personal trainer set up for me, and I am good at routine. The other factor that helped this to work, was that the gym was 5 minutes from my house.

Just between you and me, though, there were a couple of times when I changed my clothes to go work out, drove to the gym, circled the parking lot and left. It was a drive-by workout. Hey....woman's prerogative to change her mind.

I prefer to take my exercise in the form of games or entertainment. I really enjoy tennis. I can play tennis on a 90-degree day for 90 minutes, and it flies by. I can ride my bicycle on the beautiful Iowa bike trails for miles and miles (well maybe just miles) and love almost every minute of it. I can walk with a friend and chatter away the miles, no problem. But you say workout, I am not available. I mean, it says it right in the word, it's work. Besides the fact that I can pull a muscle putting on my socks.

I took a Holy Yoga class for a while, that was held at a church, not too surprising. It wasn't bad, but my favorite part was the end when you lay on your mat for five minutes, and then say "Namaste. " I also like to play euchre and rummy, but that is not much of a workout, even I will admit. I am well aware of my shortcomings, it's a long list, but I have it alphabetized for convenience. I guess not working out is a part of who I am. I am in the Fitness Protection Program.

JULY 10th

WHAT IF YOU had the opportunity to have dinner with any three people, living or dead? Who would you choose? How would you choose? What questions would you ask? Cook or have catered? The challenges are endless, the possibilities infinite.

I have decided not to overthink this. I spent a few minutes thinking of people I have admired and it just came down to what choices would make the most interesting dinner companions.

Choice #1: Condoleezza Rice, professor, political scientist, accomplished pianist and incidentally, the 66th Secretary of State of the United States of America. She is articulate, thoughtful, brilliant, and a patriot who loves this country. I would ask her what her thoughts are on term limits for Congress, how to mend the great divide in this country and what her policy for domestic harmony would be going forward. I will try not to cry and beg her to run for President.

Choice #2: Elvis Presley, the king of Rock and Roll, accomplished pianist, gospel singer, heartthrob for women of all ages, a voice like no other, and a life that was ended too early. He was awarded 138 gold, platinum and multi-platinum albums and singles. I would ask him to talk about his life and his music. Then of course, I would ask him to sing me some of his ballads, for example, "Can't Help Falling in Love," or "Are You Lonesome Tonight." (This all sounds very serious, but actually I could just sit and look at him…)

Choice #3: President Ronald Reagan, who needs no introduction. He made us proud to be Americans, and was a great patriot. He could work with people from all sides, beliefs and walks of life. I would just like to sit and shoot the breeze with him!! (Also, a man with an Iowa/Heartland connection!!)

JULY 11th

THE SMALL MOMENTS of travel that turn into treasured memories, poignant, romantic, earth shattering, or in my case humorous to hilarious. My very special/significant other/friend/boyfriend/better half, Verne and I were in Dresden, Germany. We had spent almost the entire day walking the city, enjoying the sights and sounds. Color me tired, I have 15,000 steps, can we stop now?

As we made our way back to our river cruise ship, we happened upon an art museum. Verne really wanted to tour and view all the paintings, some by the Masters. I was pretty much on museum overload. We agreed I would spend time in the coffee shop writing, while he enjoyed the fine arts. We are so very good at compromise.

I am already situated in the coffee shop and I see him talking to the lady at the ticket counter and gesturing/pointing to me. She was shaking her head no. I am really curious about what is going on. Verne comes over to me as he prepares to enter the museum to explain what had happened. He wanted to rent an audio device to listen to, and the lady asked him to leave his identification as a deposit. He, being the master negotiator, asked if instead I could be the deposit. The answer of course was an emphatic no!

I couldn't decide whether to be insulted or to giggle about his attempt at humor. I decided on giggling. Thus far, German service people are not as friendly to wacky tourists as were the lovely people in the Czech Republic.

Capture the small moments of your life, store them as treasures, and take them out frequently and marvel at the riches you have gained.

JULY 12th

I HOPE you are ready to celebrate National Simplicity Day!! This little known holiday honors Henry David Thoreau who was born on this day in 1817. (No, I was not a classmate of his, quit asking!) Thoreau was an author, naturalist and philosopher. He is known for his book "Walden," that he wrote while living with nature for two years in a small cabin he built by Walden Pond in Massachusetts. Confession time: I have not read this book, but am now guilt stricken as I write this, so might have to do that!!

Thoreau said, "I went to the woods because I wished to live deliberately, to front only the essential facts of life, and see if I could not learn what it had to teach, and not, when I came to die, discover that I had not lived." Now that's a mouthful. So, translation for me is, I want to try the simple life, live in the woods, with only the bare necessities, learn from it, and not have regrets when I die.

Thoreau was ahead of his time. Today, many in the world are trying to live more simply, decrease their carbon footprint, and do more with less. Living in a cabin by a pond sounds idyllic....as long as it has electricity, internet, cable and indoor plumbing. Color me spoiled, 21st century living is not so bad.

All kidding aside, it is nice to live more simply. Possessions become an obligation and whatever perceived enjoyment they once had can quickly fade. Appointments, ball games, errands can steal our life away.

Celebrate today by enjoying the beauty of the outdoors, take a walk, live in the moment, do things slowly for the pleasure of it-not as a race to get them done. Read a book on a blanket by the river, take a picnic, while away the day as if you have all the time in the world. Breathe.....

JULY 13th

Do you have a favorite president? I have several, ranging from early in our nation's history to presidents I have voted for (and have even met two). I must say however, that I find President Thomas Jefferson to be very intriguing. In addition to being one of the Founding Fathers, and later President, he was a scientist, farmer, inventor and writer.

I visited Jefferson's estate, Monticello, which is located in Charlottesville, Virginia. I loved touring the mansion, which has very interesting design features created by Jefferson, as well as some of his inventions. Jefferson wrote over 20,000 letters in his lifetime, and kept copies of them. He designed a system, that as he wrote, another pen that was connected to his, moved simultaneously and made a copy on another piece of paper. Fascinating to observe. He also invented the steel plow, to replace the wooden version. The steel plow had a longer life, could make deeper furroughs while plowing and make the job easier for the farmer.

In a recessed area near his bed, there was a "horse" with 48 hands projecting to hold his coats and vests. He could turn it with a long stick. He loved to show this particular invention to guests. Is this where the term, "clothes horse" came from?

The history of our country is populated with so many fascinating, ingenious and multi-talented individuals. Everything we are today, was built on the stepping stones laid by these great Americans. Inventions are ongoing, but somehow I don't think the inventors of Silly Putty, Fruit Loops and Deep Fat Fried Oreos quite measure up!!

Albert Einstein said, "I have no special talents. I am only passionately curious." Thank goodness for those passionately curious individuals who add interest and convenience to our lives!!

JULY 14th

Scenery in the Heartland, Grant Wood depicted the gently rolling hills, beautiful green pastures, picturesque farms and farm life. I love this beautiful land, ever changing, yet ever the same.

I have spent quite a bit of time by the ocean in various locales, and the rolling waves at the beach are a little reminiscent of the ripples that move through the fields of corn and beans creating silent waves of green. The oceans and the farm fields both have striations of colors that change from place to place and moment to moment.

I will have to admit, that the roar of the ocean is more pleasing to the ear than the roar of the farm machinery during planting and harvesting!! The other difference is, I don't normally take a book, a towel and a cold drink and stretch out in front of the corn field for a few hours of relaxation. However, there are no sharks and you don't have to be a good swimmer!!

Both places have incredible beauty, and I am blessed to live in one and am able to visit the other!!

> The Lord is my shepherd; I shall not want. He maketh me to lie down in green pastures; He leadeth me beside the still waters.
>
> — Psalm 23:1-2

On your journey, enjoy the beauty of creation around you. Let it refresh your soul, and open your heart and mind.

> O Lord, how great are Your works.
>
> — Psalm 92:5

JULY 15th

HOWEVER DID we manage to live our lives before cell phones? That is a question the current generation will never have to answer because they don't know a world without cell phones. Cell phones can be the bane of our existence, but overall I think they make our lives easier and safer.

Back in the earlier days of cell phones, I had one of those cute little flip phones that were the latest thing. I was visiting my family in Florida, when tragedy struck...I was in the bathroom having accomplished what I went in there to do, turned to flush the toilet and simultaneously my flip phone slid out of my front pocket into the toilet just as I flushed. Of course I tried to catch it, but to no avail.

With consternation on my face, and panic setting in, I had to tell my daughter-in-law what I had done. We jumped into the car and headed to the nearest Verizon Store. I said to the clerk, "I lost my cell phone and need to get a new one." My daughter-in-law quickly corrected me and said, "She flushed it down the toilet." He didn't react, but responded by telling us the first thing he needed to do was to make sure nobody had used it. Really? I told him I didn't care if someone had used it, because if they had they surely needed it more than I.

New cell phone obtained and I am on my way back to Iowa. (Side note, their toilet never overflowed or backed up!!)

Upon returning home, I go to my local Verizon store to tweak some things on the new phone. I said to the young man, "You won't believe what I did." He replied, "Oh, we've heard everything here." With a relieved sigh I said, "So glad to know I am not the only one to flush their phone down the toilet." He looked up and said in a loud voice, "YOU FLUSHED YOUR PHONE DOWN THE TOILET???" Guess they hadn't heard everything after all!! Verizon-0, Lacina-1

JULY 16th

As most people do, I spend a fair amount of time driving hither and yon, here, there and everywhere. Groceries, appointments, miscellaneous errands and aimless driving on the back roads of this beautiful place in which I live. I am in a constant state of bewilderment, amazement and annoyance at the lack of basic driving skills of many people who surely are driving without a license. There is no way they passed a test of any kind, or can you order a license on Amazon now?

Here are some of my favorite examples of cluelessness while driving, a chronic disease with no known cure.

Here we are at the basic four way stop. There are a number of ways the clueless can confuse and create chaos here. The basic premise is that we take turns. If you are there first, you get to go first. If you pull up to the stop sign simultaneously with another driver, the driver to the right has the right of way. Then we come to the failure of one or more of the drivers to use their turn signal. If everyone assumes you are going straight as illustrated by your lack of turn signal, an accident could occur. Surprises like that are not appreciated by the general driving public or pedestrians.

I can see already that I am going to run out of space to expound on tailgating,(not the Football game variety!) parking, driving in snow, and interstate highways!! Let's go with parking. To assist, most parking spaces are marked with lines which are not just suggestions, but rather directions for how and where to park your car.. This seems self-explanatory that it is configured for one car per space, not one car for several spaces.

On your journey today, if you must drive, be alert and on the lookout for those whose driving might be hazardous to your health!

JULY 17th

I LIKE my home to be uncluttered, neat and tidy. Unfortunately, it doesn't always work out that way. Several factors enter into creating the devastation I call home. When life has me on the run, it seems like I run in, sleep, and run out.

A large factor that contributes to my clutter is my quilting room. At this very moment, I have three projects in varying stages of completion, which means fabric, fabric everywhere. I like to think of it as the sign of a creative mind. Every so often, I do have to come up for air, get the quilting projects under control so I can continue. When I was in high school, my room was the typically messy teenage girl room. If I had homework to do or a paper to write, I would have to clean my room before I could start the work. Some might wonder why I let it get to the catastrophic point. I am one of those people. Organized chaos is my middle name.

Writing adds another layer of pandemonium to the circus. I have literally hundreds and hundreds of notecards, resource books, and numerous files spread all over my writing area. It looks like Tornado Lori has been through the room. There is a method to the clutter, and I know where every note and file is. Organized chaos, it's my middle name.

I am a work in progress, just like the quilts and the writing. Gradually trying to simplify, declutter and have less stuff to deal with. I will always have one, three or seventeen projects underway, it is what I do and who I am. Organized chaos, it's my middle name.

If life's clutter gets in your way, take a walk (people always tell me to take a hike, is that the same thing?), take your time to clear your mind, and be thankful that organized chaos is my middle name not yours!!

JULY 18th

MONSTER COOKIES....NOT just for breakfast anymore!! Some many years ago, when my wee small grandchildren, were still wee and small, an event occurred that still makes me smile today.

We were on a rare family vacation at Lake of the Ozarks in Missouri. There were ten of us, including four of our six grandchildren. We had a couple of cabins right on the lake. I had baked some goodies to have on hand, including monster cookies.

The older granddaughter who was with us was very comfortable going in and out of our cabin like it was her own. The younger one not as comfortable just breezing in. So, at one point in the day, they both wander in and Allison was explaining to Micaila how to come in and get cookies. Lo and behold, the lesson took. Later in the day, this little sprite Micaila bursts into our cabin and announces loudly, "I'm here for the cookies!" It was hysterical, heartwarming and so unexpected!!

Monster Cookies

1 Stick butter softened, 1 c +2 T brown sugar, 1 c sugar, 3 eggs, 1 tsp vanilla, ¼ Tsp salt, 2 tsp baking soda, 2 c peanut butter, 4 ½ c oatmeal, 1 c (or more!) M & M's, 1 c semisweet chocolate chips.

Cream butter and sugars. Add eggs, peanut butter, vanilla. Beat well. Add oatmeal, baking soda & salt. Add chocolate chips and M & M's.

Grease cookie sheets, bake 12 minutes more or less, depending on your oven at 350 degrees. (I make them regular sized not monster size)

On your journey, never be afraid to show up and ask for the cookies!! Bake, eat, enjoy, repeat!!

JULY 19th

Is it just my imagination? Is it really more difficult for women to prepare for the day or an evening out than men? I think I can make a case for it…My thoughts on this matter came about one morning as I hurriedly tried to fasten a necklace to complete my ensemble for school. Note: My ensembles for middle school teaching are very basic. Some mornings if I am having a bad hair day, or can't decide what to wear, I look in the mirror, shrug, and think, good enough for middle school students. In many ways we are invisible to them anyway!!

Putting on a necklace is usually the last step, and the most frustrating, as you are ready to make the dash to the door to start your day. Could they make those fasteners any smaller on an object that is fastened behind your neck that you can't see??? I don't think so! Women reading this will understand what I am talking about. In addition to the fastener being microscopic, it is difficult to hold open for very long, as you search blindly for it to hook to the other end.

I better not be hearing laughter here, these are serious issues in the daily life of women. Don't even get me started on choosing an outfit, (men don't have outfits, they have clothes), the right shoes, makeup, the time it takes to heat up a device to fix hair, style the hair and of course the elusive adorning oneself with jewelry.

It is no wonder women are exhausted all the time.

On your journey, take a big drink of today, take a nap and take care of yourself….you deserve it!!

JULY 20th

On a very steamy, sultry summer night, I was looking for entertainment that required no real effort on my part, and would keep me inside where it was cool. Television seemed to be the answer. Generally I am a highly caffeinated version of the Energizer Bunny, but I also have some skill at doing absolutely nothing...I started scrolling through the channel guide, hundreds of channels and choices available for my viewing pleasure....or so it seemed....

Let's just say some of the choices included, "Pitbulls and Parolees," "Hoarders," and "Naked and Afraid." I was afraid alright, although fully clothed. This, my friends, is why we have books!!

I love libraries, books, bookstores, books, did I mention books?? I love to share books that I have enjoyed with others. So, I have a recommendation to share in case you run into a viewing challenge as I did, or if you just love to read, as I do.

The Cobbled Court series by Marie Bostwick is excellent. There are 6 books in this series. It is centered around a quilt shop, opened by a woman who has just gotten divorced, pulls up roots, moves to a different part of the country and goes into business. You don't have to be a quilter to appreciate the stories, but if you are a quilter, all the more enjoyment for you. Try the first one, "A Single Thread," and I think you will be hooked!

On your journey today, explore a new book, a new adventure, a new world.

Books are a uniquely portable magic.

— Stephen King

JULY 21st

"MONDAY'S CHILD is fair of face; Tuesday's child is full of grace; Wednesday's child is full of woe; Thursday's child has far to go; Friday's child is loving and giving; Saturday's child should work for a living. But the child that is born on the Sabbath day is fair and wise, good and gay."

I wonder, how many of my readers, have a set of seven dish towels with that ages old nursery rhyme embroidered on it.... I don't know that I have a complete set, but I have any number of versions of this on linens from grandmothers!!

I hadn't seen this rhyme in its' entirety in a while, so of course the first thing I had to do, was check and see what day of the week the world was graced with my presence. The rhyme was thought to foretell a child's personality based on the week day on which he/she was born.

Looks to me like Wednesday would not be the best day on which to be born!! Woe is me, would be your mantra!!

Scientifically speaking, there is clearly no correlation between your personality and the day of your birth. However, an article in Time magazine written by Jeffrey Kluger in 2017 does show some evidence that the season of your birth may have some effect on your personality. Many external factors can affect the development of the baby in the womb. Seasonal nutrition, viruses, amount of daylight, things which affect the mother, can affect the child she is carrying.

Just a little stroll into the past today, remembering a very old nursery rhyme....Embrace the past for what it has taught us, enhance the present with the gifts you have been given, and plan for the future for yourself and those who follow you.

JULY 22nd

HAVE you ever lived in a ranch or split foyer style of house? If you are around my age, which is undetermined and has not been verified as we go to press, I am guessing you have. There is nothing "wrong" with these types of homes, but I am going to have to blame whomever originally designed these houses for the demise of the neighborhood!

The front porch, which used to be the center of afternoon and evening family activities in nice weather is no more. The parents on the front porch, kiddos riding their bikes up and down the sidewalk or street, a dad playing catch with his daughter, these were the lifeblood of the neighborhood. Families mixed and mingled. They shared their troubles and triumphs, and a kind of extended family was built.

These new-fangled homes were built without front porches. Instead, there might be a deck or patio off the back of the home. The back yard in many cases was fenced in for the dog, or just because. I think this certainly didn't encourage the neighborly interaction of the past.

Sigh....I long for the front porch, a pitcher of iced tea, a porch swing and the cozy conversation of friends from the neighborhood, while the children play under watchful eyes. Or the sweetness of the porch swing, a book and a long lazy afternoon reading and watching the world go by. Even more, I mourn the loss of connections betwen people which will never happen, lifelong friendships that will never have a chance to begin, and the neighborhood feeling like our own small town, inside a bigger city.

My wish for you is some time on the front porch swing, hearing the slam of a wooden screen door, someone to enjoy it with and a little piece of a slower, gentler life.

JULY 23rd

ONOMATOPOEIA-SAY THAT THREE TIMES QUICKLY!! Love this word, it is actually easier to pronounce than it looks. (I say that, at the same time I am chuckling and happy that this is print not video!) Defining it is another matter. I will do my best, having read many definitions of it myself. Onomatopoeia (I never get tired of typing that…) occurs when the pronunciation of the word imitates the thing being described. A synonym for onomatopoeia is echoism.

This is one of those words that examples are the best way to understand it.

Onomatopoeia Word Examples:

Snap	Crackle	Pop	Hissed	Sizzle	Buzz
Beep	Hum	Hiccup	Gurgle	Whoosh	Whizz

Sometimes poets use onomatopoeia for effect. These lines from "Meeting at Night," by Robert Browning are a good example:

Three fields to cross till a farm appears;
A tap at the pane, the quick sharp scratch
And blue spurt of a lighted match.

On your journey today, throw onomatopoeia into a sentence for fun, and have a day that is filled with sizzle, snap, crackle and pop!

JULY 24th

MARK TWAIN, born in a tiny town in the Heartland, became a great American novelist and philosopher. In addition to his writing, he was known for his humor and wit. A Mark Twain quote or two is always good reading, and good for the mind, heart and soul!

> Life is short, break the rules. Forgive quickly, kiss slowly. Love truly. Laugh uncontrollably and never regret anything that makes you smile.

This quote expresses so much of what I am trying to convey in this book. Live your life with laughter and love and have no regrets.

"Don't wait, the time will never be just right." Hit that one out of the park, Mr. Twain. There is always a reason, excuse, obstacle to wait to move forward, make the time right by forging ahead.

I remember fondly from my childhood, the book "Tom Sawyer." I read that book many times and always enjoyed the antics and clever ways of Tom. He was a young boy growing up along the Mississippi River He was one of a kind, and yet he was every boy. He loved the outdoor life, and tried six ways to Sunday to get out of attending school and doing chores. If you never read this book, I highly recommend reading it. If you read it as a young person, re-reading it as an adult will give you different insights into the life and times of Tom, and the world as it was so many years ago.

On your journey, take a seat along the riverbank, toss your troubles into the wind, throw a line in the water, enjoy the feel of the sun on your back, and while away the day. Tom would approve.

JULY 25th

ACCORDING TO THE MAYAN CALENDAR, this day is considered "A Day Out of Time." The Mayan calendar is based on the cycles of the moon, with 13 months having 28 days each, and one extra day...July 25th! Actually seems less awkward than the Gregorian calendar most of us live with.

Over seventy cities in Brazil recognize this as an official holiday. Okay, Brazil, I am in!!

It is to be a day of atonement, forgiveness, celebration of your life and community. I am thinking it could also be called "Time Out Day." (Or maybe that is my Middle School teacher brain kicking in.) Seriously, who doesn't need a day to take a day out of time and contemplate life?

It also makes me think of the Madeleine L'Engle book, "A Wrinkle in Time." (No, I wasn't looking in the mirror, and if I was, it would be called Wrinkles Abound in Time.) Loved this book as a child, have re-read it a number of times. I did not go to see the movie, because I didn't want my images of the book distorted. I have yet to see a movie that is better than the book. Some do a pretty fine job, but the complexity of the author's words don't always translate to the screen.

Hmmmm….a little off topic, but that was a true stream of consciousness with no editing that ran through my mind while writing. Sometimes it's a river, but you have been spared that today.

On your journey today, take a day out of time, take a time out, read a "Wrinkle in Time," throw away your mirror and celebrate with the Brazilians. (No, I did not say celebrate and get a Brazilian.) I might need to stop here. Carpe Diem.

JULY 26th

I WILL NOT KEEP you waiting any longer... here it is....The Letter "H" brought to you by the month of July and Alphabet Fan Clubs everywhere. Keep your seatbelts fastened and your chair in the upright position, and leave the rest to us.

Hoodwinked	Hooligan	Havock
Hope	Hilarity	Hootenanny
Harmony	Hussy	Heart-warming
Hoax	Homage	Hickory

There are some great words in this list that you could easily work into your daily conversation or Facebook posts. I mean, when was the last time you told someone you were hoodwinked by a hooligan on the way to a hootenanny?? Or called someone a hussy??? That word is way underused, and can even be used in polite company!!!

> Each letter has a shape, she told them, one shape in the world and no other, and it is your responsibility to make it perfect.
>
> — KIM EDWARDS

On your journey, insert some interesting words into your conversation. Write a letter and include some words that should never be left unsaid, while there is still time to say them. Or just run around using words randomly to create hilarity and havock!!

JULY 27th

I BAKED a carrot cake this morning, and it has been many years since I have done so. This recipe that I have had forever is pretty basic and fail proof. It might be from Betty Crocker. I do enjoy making things from scratch, but I am a very messy baker/cook. Note to self: Do not clean the counters, vacuum and mop the kitchen floor just because said cake is in the oven. You still have to make the frosting which involves ginormous amounts of powdered sugar....need I say more? I did not wear goggles...but maybe next time.

Sharing the recipe because it is pretty easy, and who doesn't like a "healthy" cake with veggies in it?

Carrot Cake

1 ½ c sugar, 1 c vegetable oil, 3 eggs, 2 c all purpose flour, 2 tsp cinnamon, 1 tsp baking soda, 1 tsp, vanilla, ½ tsp salt, 3 c shredded carrots (5-6 medium), 1 c coarsely chopped walnuts

Frosting: 8 oz. softened cream cheese, ¼ c softened butter, 2-3 tsp. milk, 1 tsp. Vanilla, 4 cups powdered sugar

Beat sugar, oil and eggs on low til blended. Add flour, cinnamon, baking soda, vanilla and salt. Beat on low til blended. Stir in carrots and nuts.

Pour into 13 by 9 greased and lightly floured baking pan, Bake at 350 degrees for 40-45 minutes. Check earlier, my oven had it done it about 38 minutes. Cool for about one hour on baking rack.

Frosting: Beat cream cheese, butter, milk and vanilla until smooth. Add powdered sugar, 1 cup at a time until frosting is smooth. Frost cake. I sprinkled a smidgen of nutmeg over the top. Refrigerate, eat, enjoy, repeat!!

JULY 28th

THERE ARE many things in life that are puzzling to me, even at my advanced years. In fact, things that puzzle me could be a separate book, but not sure I could survive the writing of it!!

Yoga, an ancient discipline from India which involves physical, mental and spiritual components. There are more and more "specialized" types of yoga appearing on the scene. Bikram, Hatha, Ashtanga, Restorative, Hot and Holy Yoga to name a few. I really have no idea what most of them are about and what makes them different. Hot yoga, I think I get that….turn the yoga studio into a hot and humid day in August in the Heartland so you can sweat even more doing your exercise.

I have participated in a Holy Yoga class, and enjoyed it very much. It was held in a church, Christian music played softly in the background and there were spiritual components to the practice.

But now we come to what puzzles me...Goat Yoga….I kid you not….I do not understand the reason or appeal of doing yoga with goats wandering around, butting you, sniffing inappropriate places, and possible relieving themselves. Wow, bet there's a waiting list for that class. But since the door has been opened, why not Cow Yoga, or Pig Yoga or Horse Yoga, let's be all inclusive about our animal yoga.

Sorry, if I have offended any Goat Yoga aficionados, but maybe, try to make some friends and do yoga with them. Leave the goats alone.

So, my friends, on your journey today, make time to do whatever inspires you, refreshes you and brings you peace. Namaste.

JULY 29th

ACCORDING TO MY MOTHER, I started life as a left-handed person. Back in those days, that was considered less than ideal. My mom and my kindergarten teacher conspired (well, that might be a little strong) to change that. They would take the crayon, spoon, or whatever from my poor little left hand and put it in my right hand. Eventually they won out against my instincts, and after all, they happened to be bigger and in charge!!

I have noticed all my life that I do some things differently than my right handed friends. I have always had the instinct to do things left handed, but then become confused when I can't figure it out.

I also have a problem with knowing which direction I am supposed to go, particularly inside buildings. I looked this up, and found out there is something called directional dyslexia. I felt so validated. There was a reason I do goofy things!! I also have a problem with spatial awareness. (Others might say I am clumsy or have a tendency to have gravity storms. They obviously don't have the appropriate amount of empathy for my fragile situation…)

At any rate, I have had a very full and successful life in spite of the traumatic events I underwent as a 4 year old. (Yes, I started kindergarten when I was 4, my mother needed the break.) Just think what I could have accomplished using my left hand….Madame President, anyone?

JULY 30th

A SULTRY, stormy night in July in the Heartland?? Happens some years more often than we would like! The tornado watches promoted by the local television stations are constant it seems, every hot and humid night. They are so common, we start to ignore them. Watches just mean the weather is such that a tornado could form, not that there is one.

The important question is, what do you do when the power goes off on a stormy summer evening? I, for one, am not a fan of the power going off. I find it to be unsettling and unnecessary. So, the first thing I do is look around the neighborhood to make sure that nobody has power, and it is not a Russian cyber attack on me personally. Once I have assured myself of that, I can move on.

So, now what happens? How to entertain myself, safely, without adult supervision? So many things require electricity, including my hobby of quilting. Options are calling people on the phone, texting, reading or playing games on what hopefully is a fully charged iPad. If desperate, I do have a car charger, take a ride, get a charge. It can happen.

Take a moment to think about your agenda when the power goes off.

If you have family or friends around, great time to get out a board game, a deck of cards or start a conversation. Face to face talking is still legal in all 50 states, the last time I checked. It is actually highly encouraged and can be very rewarding!!

The power may be out sometimes on your journey, but no one and nothing can shut off the power within you. Try to relax and enjoy being unplugged for awhile.

JULY 31st

SITTING in Barnes and Noble writing today. I have a date with myself every Monday from 9:00 A.M until whenever I have used up my creativity quota for the day, or until it gets too cold in here, whichever comes first. Today, the cold air blowing on me might send me running out the door, before I run out of writing ideas. We will see.

So many thoughts swim in and out of my mind as I sit, hands poised over the keyboard of my laptop, waiting for inspiration to strike. There are so many people to watch, conversations to eavesdrop on, and so many coffee drinks and treats to choose from. Today's treats are an iced Chai tea and a whole grain bagel, as lunchtime has snuck up on me.

The flavors of the coffee shop pale compared to the flavors of the people who frequent the cafe area and the bookstore. My favorite flavor is the child who is so excited to be here, and can't wait to run over to the children's books section. Today there is the average man who has been browsing in the Science section for over an hour, reading parts of books. Not that I am keeping track or that there is anything wrong with that!

I see students, business people, a farmer in bib overalls, some rather bohemian people, other writers, and then there is me. I wonder what people think when they see me. A non-descript woman of a certain age, sitting alone. Her table is covered with many note cards of various neon colors. At times she is typing furiously, other times she is staring into space, and every once in awhile, she gets up and walks around. Is she a teacher? An overaged college student? Maybe she just comes here to answer her emails and look at Facebook and look important.

It seems to be time to end today's episode before frostbite sets in. I need to bring a wrap next week!! Stay tuned and be well!

AUGUST 1st

AHHHHH.....THE Gershwin brothers were right.....summertime and the livin' is easy. August, the tail end of summer. Hot, slow, lazy summer days abound. Ice cold drinks on the front porch, the fan whirling slowly, moving the air in a mild imitation of a breeze...or you can hibernate inside with the air conditioning cranked up! That doesn't sound nearly as enticing or romantic as the front porch!

August is a month that seems devoid of holidays, but I was happily surprised to find one that spoke to me. August 1st is National Raspberry Cream Pie Day!! Who knew?? August is the most prolific month for raspberry production. (Did you know that the raspberry isn't even a berry?? Raspberries like strawberries belong to the rose family.) Raspberry happens to be my very favorite flavor, so I am going to start taking part in this annual celebration.

I have never had Raspberry Cream Pie, love cream pies but never thought about raspberry as an option. There are lots of recipes out there, to suit any taste and skill level. (Martha Stewart's takes 6+ hours! I don't need a degree in pie making, just a pie!!) Some have a chocolate cookie crust, but the graham cracker crust appeals more to me. Find a version that fits you and try it on!! Have a pie bake-off and try all the different recipes!!

On your journey, there doesn't have to be an official holiday to celebrate each and every day of your life. May all your days be filled with the sweetness of life, and I am pretty sure a little pie never hurt anybody!!

AUGUST 2nd

THE WIND IN MY FACE, hair flowing in the breeze, scenery, the freedom….the sweat running down my face and pretty much everywhere else….. the joy of riding my bicycle. It is a grand adventure, to feel like that carefree kid again, coasting down the hills. The problem at my age is the other side of those hills!

I recently demoted myself from a 21-speed bicycle to a 7-speed bicycle. My former bike was a beauty and a very nice model. Several reasons for the downgrade, but the main reason was I wanted a "girl's" bike. I never used all those 21 speeds anyway!! At my age, and my propensity to gravity storms, I wanted to be able to touch the ground, and dismount more easily.

So….I not only got a girl's bike, I got a girly bike. It is hot pink with multicolored striped fenders, a white basket and a bell with picture of a margarita glass on it. Yes, this is my bike. I love it, and I get lots of smiles and comments when I am speeding around town. When I am pedaling very fast, in my head I hear the background music that plays when Elvira Gulch rides her bike in "The Wizard of Oz." I would love to play that song while I ride. It is called "Miss Gulch's/Witch'sTheme." Interesting related fact for you musicians, it is a seven note, "crippled" variation of "We're Off to See the Wizard."

To reassure my readers, I do obey the traffic laws when I ride in the street (which isn't often, I prefer trails), and I have never texted while bicycling.

On your journey, today, ride a bike, get your legs and your heart pumping and relive the glory days of being a kid. It doesn't get much better than this!!

.

AUGUST 3rd

ONCE AGAIN, I just added to my list of errands today. My to do lists are always fluid, but this is just too much...If we could have a moment of silence....I just killed another spoon in the garbage disposal. I am running very low on spoons and eating my Cheerios with a fork is not working well. I do still have more than one spoon, but the count is dangerously low. I don't think I know anyone else who has to buy new silverware because they have lost all the spoons. More than once...

On the bright side, if you have any recalcitrant spoons and need help getting rid of them, I'm your girl. Or maybe you would just like to get new silverware, whatever the reason I am here to help. In my defense, I don't think I am totally at fault, those spoons seem to like to slide down and hide in the disposal and surprise me when I hit the on switch. There's nothing quite like the grinding metal on metal noise at high volume when this occurs. Fortunately, my garbage disposal must be pretty good, as it still works, in spite of the extra work of trying to grind up spoons.

John Mayer said, "I've realized you can use a fork as a spoon if you use it rapidly enough." Mr. Mayer must be more talented than me (which is not that hard). I would love to watch him eat a bowl of soup with a fork.

Wishing you a wonderful day, adventures, surprises, and plenty of spoons.

AUGUST 4th

I HAVE BEEN THINKING about age, probably because I am the proud owner of lots of it. Don't go kicking my tires, they have a lot of miles on them. I have come up with some ideas to categorize age as I see it.

The Age of Innocence I would define as birth to 9 years old. Changing, growing, lots of milestones, baby to toddler to child.

The Age of the All-Knowing would be the wonderful pre-teen and teenage years, when children question everything you say, and wonder how you ever made it to adulthood without knowing anything.

The Age of Having a Clue can be fun for parents. The "kids" have a job and rent to pay, their boss isn't nice to them, the toilet overflows and they are starting to realize that growing up isn't for sissies, and maybe parents do know something and can add value to your life. Let the phone calls home begin.

The Age of Maturity is when the ones you have raised start to have children and the cycle begins again!! Fun to watch, and as a bonus, you get grandkids!!

The Age of Wisdom comes when you have traveled the road of life, overcome obstacles: death of loved ones, illness, hardship. You have worked hard to provide for your family and your own retirement and the time is nearing to enjoy the fruits of your labor.

The Age of Medicare is time to celebrate folks!! You have crossed the finish line! Time to think about slowing down, enjoying life and doing all of the thing you planned or dreamed of doing "when you had the time."

Well, ladies and gentlemen, the time is now, live those dreams!!

AUGUST 5th

PICTURE THIS: a three-state, 3-day bus trip for 30 some women. This trip was sponsored by quilt shops in Wisconsin, Minnesota, and Iowa, the states we toured. The tour stopped every few hours at a different quilt shop. Games, snacks, and prizes can make for an amusing field trip for grown-up ladies. It is really adult day care on wheels, with refreshments.

Last day of the trip, women are weary, low on cash, and easily annoyed. This day's itinerary, evidently planned by someone without a watch or navigational system, had us eating dinner in Nebraska, leaving at 7:30 p.m. and driving two hours to our hotel in Missouri. Strike one.

We arrive at the hotel. I was first at the front desk with my roomie to get our room assignment. We were told there was a problem with our room and we would have to wait until everyone else had a room. She set our keys to the side. Strike two. We waited...I would like to say patiently, but some of you know me. At 11:30 p.m., approximately two hours after we arrived, the clerk called us back to the front desk. She picked up the keys she had set aside earlier, and handed them to me.. I reminded her that two hours earlier she told us there was a problem with that room. She responded, "No there's not." I responded with the fact those were the very same keys. She said: No they're not." After a few minutes of "discussing," I gave in. Off to the room we go. We put the key in the lock and the door opened, only as far as the chain on the inside would allow. The room is occupied. Yep, that's a problem. Strike three. Back to the front desk, and I tell the clerk, "There's a man in this room." She responds, "No, there's not." Are these the only three words/variations she knows? I am speechless.

We did finally get a room, one that didn't come with a man in it. Customer service in this hotel improved greatly when this clerk went home. No words of cheer to end this page, I am still speechless.

AUGUST 6th

Growing up, one of my brothers had an affinity for aquariums. He accumulated fish with his paper route money. Before we knew it, he had three or four ten gallon aquariums with many different kinds of fish. Neon tetra, black mollies, zebras, angel fish, cardinal tetra and others that I don't remember. He was very good at keeping the fish alive, and was even able to breed the black mollies and sell them to the pet store. If you have paid attention, you might hazard a guess that I might not be quite as good at keeping them alive, based on my reputation for killing plants.

The aquariums were beautiful, relaxing to watch and oh so colorful.

Our cat, Boots thought so too. There may have been a couple of incidents where the lid was left off the aquarium, and Boots was found perching delicately with all four feet on the rim of the aquarium. It seemed no fish were missing after the incidents, but Boots sure did like to watch and stalk.

One summer when he was gone, I was left in charge of the care and feeding of the fish. Things were going along swimmingly for the first few days. The third morning there were several floaters. Hmmm….not a good thing. The next day there were even more floaters. Do these fish have a suicide pact? It took me until the following morning when more floaters made their appearance that I figured it out. In opening the lid to feed them, I inadvertently bumped the heater and turned it on, hence, cooking the fish. I felt terrible about it, but my brother took it well and wasn't too upset with me. Although he may have wandered around the house muttering, "Fish killer," under his breath.

Wishing you a day of calm, watch the fish, nap, meditate, dream.

AUGUST 7th

WHEN DID PURCHASING light bulbs become so complicated? I am not even talking about the various wattages that are required for certain light fixtures. Although, it is becoming harder to figure out appropriate wattages because it seems someone changed the labelling without asking me. I don't care how many lumens there are.

I don't even know what a lumen is. Unless it's a noodle, oh wait that's ramen.

Then there are the different sizes of the same wattage light bulb, plus do you want a "regular" light bulb or the newer curly fry variety?

I don't know, I just need it to not be dark in my house. Is that asking too much?? I even had an employee at Walmart helping me the last time I needed a particular size/wattage of light bulb. As we both stood looking at the ominous "aisle of bulbs" I knew a solution was not to be found.

Let's throw in the next variable, do you want LED, soft light or daylight? I don't know. I just want some light, which is a much bigger subject than light bulbs! I always thought it was funny that there is a store called "Batteries Plus Bulbs." Evidently it has come to that. It is so complicated to acquire light bulbs, there has to be a special store for doing so. I am starting to understand the need. I also discovered that Lowes has a light bulb guide one can study to figure this out. I have a college degree. My major was not light bulbs.

On your journey today, let your inner light shine, stock up on light bulbs and pray for this craziness to stop!!

AUGUST 8th

CONFESSION TIME AGAIN, dear readers!! It pains me to share this with you, but I have been diagnosed with a severe case of tsundoku. It is a rather costly condition, but there is a cure. In case you are not familiar with this "disease," here is the definition courtesy of Manuscriptshop.com. Tsundoku: (a word taken from the Japanese language) buying books and not reading them, letting books pile up unread. If you saw my nightstand, book basket and various stacks here and there, you would concur that I suffer from this malady.

For me, this is not a condition that will last forever. I will eventually read those stacks of books. The fact that they exist will not stop me from buying that next bright shiny book that catches my eye. The prudent approach would be to keep a list as books catch my eye, and purchase them when the aforementioned stack is gone or at least diminished. Prudent may not be a word that friends use to describe me. Hence, the book buying.

In my defense, what is the harm? I will eventually read all the books, I hate to run out of new reading material. If I am confined to my dwelling to weather or lack of social engagements, I can power through quite a lot of reading material. Better safe than sorry, my mom used to say...not sure she was talking about book inventory, but I think it translates.

Dr. Seuss, an expert on many things besides green eggs and ham said it best: "Fill your house with stacks of books, in all the crannies and in all the nooks." Sigh…..what could be better? Perhaps I will think of myself as a curator of a collection of printed words, so much nicer than book hoarder. Take time out of your day today to dive into that book that has been patiently awaiting your attention. Lose yourself in the experience of reading,

AUGUST 9th

ORIGAMI FASCINATES ME. It is the art of paper folding, believed to have originated in Japan in the 6th century. I do not practice origami, I am pretty sure I don't have the patience and precision to do this. I am going to try one of these days. I can just add this to the list of creative things I do, and try to make time to learn!! This would surely be a significant accomplishment, as I failed at putting pizza boxes together as a waitress; and we won't talk about my map folding skills.

The Legend of 1000 Cranes touched me, which is why I am thinking about origami. Traditionally, it was believed if you folded 1000 paper cranes, a wish would come true for you. It has become a symbol of hope and healing for many, in times of illness, despair, and life's challenges.

I can feel the rhythm and rote of folding 1000 cranes. Repetitively doing an act like this can be very comforting, especially when you are creating something. It provides a purpose and sometimes that is all we need to have hope. A ritual, one could share with loved ones, as a bonding and healing act, where the mounting pile of cranes shows your progress.

I also see this as a tool for grieving and working through your emotions. An activity to work at, to have hope and to have purpose. A quote a friend shared recently, was such a perfect description of loss and grief, at least in my case. "Right now, in the moment of loss, you live second to second. And then hour to hour. And some day you will live day to day again." Time, purpose, hope, maybe some origami. Sometimes it is the simplest, most quiet acts that help us heal.

Origami for expanding creativity, to make beautiful objects, for hope, and to heal.....It's a thing of beauty no matter how you view it.

AUGUST 10th

For those of a certain age, we had very little technology growing up, or even as adults until the last fifteen or twenty years. Thinking primarily about the "smart" phone, the iPad, Kindle, electronic tablets and laptops. Within a few seconds, we can "download" games, information, and applications. Applications can help us store, sort, retrieve information. A commonly used type of app is some form of electronic calendar. Theoretically, these apps can help us be more organized, efficient and "smarter."

Hypothetical question: What if you had the capability to download new skills to your brain? Here are a few examples: coping, medical, organizing, painting, dancing, crocheting, singing, cooking, basketball, accounting. The rule is you can only choose 3, which ones would you choose?

If this were real, I would be over the moon!! The first "app" I would download to my brain, would be the ability to sing. I have no desire to be Carrie Underwood or Jennifer Nettles (well, I wouldn't turn it down!). I just want to be able to sing out loud, in public and be confident I am not scaring small children or disturbing the peace. This would add immeasurable joy to my life!

My second choice would be dancing. I have no plans to audition for the Joffrey Ballet "Nutcracker," but would like to have the natural grace and ease of those who can dance.

My final choice would be the ability to sketch a little bit. I am not asking for a lot, but something beyond stick figures. Frankly, I was torn between this and basketball skills, but with my proclivity for gravity storms, thought this was safer!! Hmmm....maybe there's an app for avoiding gravity storms...the world would certainly be safer for me!

AUGUST 11th

My husband died at the age of 65 after a two year battle with small cell lung cancer. He owned a number of neckties, and I was trying to think of a way to use them. There weren't enough to make quilts for kids and grandkids. After many months, I had formed a plan. I made a small quilted wall hanging for everyone and one for myself. This way, they would all have something to keep, but it could be hung in a small space: office, alcoves, dorm rooms or apartments.

I let my family choose the tie they wanted, then I coordinated fabric that complemented the tie, and also had a connection of some kind to my husband. One of the fabrics had constellations on it. He was very interested and knowledgeable about celestial events and the heavens above us. Some of the ties, I tied (well, to be honest, my son-in-law Wes tied them, I had no clue), others I just draped over the top of the wall hanging, and put the tail on the back. I hand-stitched all the ties to the quilted project. To finish it up, I made labels with each person's name, and the phrase, "Forever Tied to Dad/Grandpa."

I have made other memory heirloom items for my family members and for friends. It is something to think about when someone special passes away, and mementos are wanted. My husband was a very beloved dad, grandpa, and husband, and his absence left a big hole in our lives.

> Perhaps they are not stars but rather openings in Heaven where the love of our lost ones pours through and shines down upon us to let us know they are happy.
>
> — Eskimo Proverb

Live every day knowing that those you loved and lost are still living in your heart. For as long as anyone who remembers them is alive, they also live. Talk about them, tell stories, remember the times they were here with you until one day when you meet again.

AUGUST 12th

WHERE THE WILD THINGS GO.....WHERE do they go? We found a beautiful place, where indeed, the wild things go. Specifically, where the wild horses go. These spectacular four-legged visions have a place to call home, a place to be rescued, a place to live free, to gallop like the wind and to be cared for.

The Black Hills Wild Horse Sanctuary, south of Hot Springs, South Dakota is down a small dirt road, literally in the middle of nowhere. Trust me, I have been to nowhere, and can readily recognize it.

13,000 acres for wild horses to be free. It is a magnificent place, full of natural beauty. All of the mustangs here were born in the wild, and are rescues or offspring of horses in the Sanctuary. The population consists of American, Spanish, Choctaw, and Curly mustangs. The horses are kept separate by breed to keep the bloodlines pure.

We took a backcountry tour in a rough and ready vehicle, on the search for the herds. It is a sight that I can't adequately describe when a herd gallops by, or stops to investigate the visitors. They are used to people being around. They are free to run wild, but are cared for if conditions deem that water, hay etc needs to be supplemented.

This is one of the best experiences I have had. Standing in the middle of a field, surrounded by the mustangs that will walk up to you, allow themselves to be petted, nickering, tossing their manes and then they are gone like the wind. It is not the easiest place to get to, but more than worth the effort. I would go back there in a heartbeat, and hope to visit again soon.

> God made the horse from the breath of the wind, the beauty of the earth and the soul of the angel.
>
> — UNKNOWN

AUGUST 13th

I HAVE LEARNED SO MUCH while writing this book. As with any life experience, I have learned lots of random information. I have also learned a great deal about my ability to see this through over the last eighteen months. Meeting deadlines, carving time out of my schedule to dedicate to writing, facing creative blocks and overcoming the doubts about my abilities were all good challenges for me to tackle.

The most amusing thing I discovered during this process, is that there are hundreds and hundreds of books about writing books!! There is a whole section at the bookstore for them. Who knew? If I took the time to read all those books, I wouldn't have time to write my own. Hmmm....maybe that's a trick to trap new authors into reading instead of writing. I giggle every time I think about books about writing books. (I am easily amused)

Even though I am poking fun at what seems a redundancy, I did find a few of these books helpful to me. I used them in different ways, some for inspiration, some for commiseration about the plight of the writer, some for writing exercises, (Unfortunately those did not count as a workout.) and some for fanning the flames of the creative fire as it dwindled.

If you need a permission slip to write, I grant it!! Start a journal, write like nobody will read it, put your feelings and thoughts on paper. Try to write a little every day, there is nothing quite like it for a mini-therapy session! You don't have to write a whole page. Write a sentence, a thought, or an idea. Record your thoughts, feelings, and dreams.... Someday, you might feel like sharing them with the world! Life is full of doors to open, try this one and see what's inside.

AUGUST 14th

I HAVE BEEN TRYING to think of a clever way to share with my readers all of the celebrity connections, and wonderful things about Iowa, who many consider fly-over country. (And we are very okay if they just keep flying over!) What is Iowa all about?

Iowa (the Hawkeye State) is the only state whose east and west borders are 100% formed by water. Iowa is the home of two major universities whose graduates and research have impacted the world. In 1855, the University of Iowa (my alma mater) was the first public university in the United States to admit women on an equal basis with men. Agriculture and Food Production is our leading industry. We are second in the nation in production of wind power-renewable energy is the future! US News recently ranked Iowa #1 as the best overall state in the nation to live in. The ranking was based on a number of factors including health care, quality of life, opportunity, economics, infrastructure and education. Iowa leads the nation with a high school graduation rate of 91.3%.

What celebrities were born in Iowa? Let me tell you about a few of them. President Herbert Hoover and his wife Lou Henry Hoover were born here. John "Duke" Wayne, Andy Williams, and Ashton Kutcher were all born here. Another connection to Iowa was someone who once had a job as a sportscaster, broadcasting University of Iowa football games. Eventually, he got a slightly better job in Washington D.C. That man was President Ronald Reagan.

So thanks for letting me tell you a little bit about my home in the Heartland, and one final word of advice about our state; if you haven't had Iowa sweet corn in the summer, you have no idea what you are missing!

AUGUST 15th

An open letter to Congress:

Hello! Anybody out there?? Writing from the middle of America, what I like to call the Heartland. Born here, grew up here, learned the Midwestern work ethic here. I have some questions I would like to ask. Most have been asked before, but maybe not in this format. Short answers are good, telling the truth is not optional, and this may be a stretch, but honesty always wins the prize. Here we go.

1. In what scenario does it make sense that the political leaders of a country are not governed, regulated by the same rules as the citizens? Healthcare, pensions, ethics, and nepotism come to mind. Who gets to approve their own raises? Congress, that's who!
2. We are required to show a valid ID to rent a hotel room, rent a car, buy alcohol, write a check, open a bank account, be admitted to the hospital, apply for a job, just to mention a few. Why would a valid ID not be required to vote? It is one of the most important responsibilities/privileges given to citizens of this country.
3. Why would you (Congress, specifically) think that two, four, or six years should entitle you to a lifetime pension? Most of us who have chosen you to work for us, work a lifetime for a retirement pension, and sometimes are "downsized" before we can get it.

Signed, a concerned citizen who fears that our public servants are acting more like royalty, and we had to fight that war once before.

AUGUST 16th

Spent a very pleasant summer day visiting Winterset, Iowa which is in Madison County. Yes, that is the home of the covered bridges made famous by the movie, *The Bridges of Madison County,* starring Clint Eastwood and Meryl Streep. We drove Highway 92 from the east side of the state rather than using the interstate. Beautiful drive to what is a very rural county. Locations from the movie are very recognizable.

The bridges are wooden bridges, with sides and a roof, so partially enclosed. The roofs were to protect the structural parts of the bridges from the weather. The oldest bridge was built in 1870, the others in the 1880s. They are very picturesque. The drive around the Winterset area to see them really gives you a glimpse of the backroads of Iowa. (A friend from California likes to tell me that all of the roads in Iowa are backroads. I excuse his delirium because, well, he lives in California.)

Winterset also is the birthplace of Marion Robert Morrison, better known as John "Duke" Wayne. There is a small, but very nice museum dedicated to the Duke, along with the house he was born in. This was well worth the cost of admission. Wayne starred in about 150 movies. Amazing to think about a baby born in Iowa to a pharmacist and his wife, ends up being one of the best-known celebrities in the world. A gentleman, a cowboy, a patriot who gave us hundreds of hours of entertainment over many decades.

I will share one of my longtime favorite John Wayne quotes with you: "Courage is being scared to death, and saddling up anyway."

On your journey, saddle up and take on something new and a little bit scary. The Duke will have your back...

AUGUST 17th

TODAY IS BROUGHT to you by the Letter "F." When I was in school a few years ago (no nasty comments please), this was not a letter we wanted to see on a paper or report card. Nothing good would come of that. Many schools now give number scores instead of letter grades. Somehow getting a 4 doesn't seem the same as an A to me!!

However, the Letter "F" does have some fun, fabulous and fantastic words to claim as their own.

Frisky	Frivolity	Flibbertigibbet
Fancy	Festive	Feisty
Fiery	Fervent	Felicitous
Frolic	Fiction	Fruitful
Flamethrower	Fireplace	Fraction

Flibbertigibbet has to stand out as my favorite in this word grouping. No need to describe a frivolous, flighty, chatty person as such when you can just use one word...and a fine word at that.

Fraction, I threw in to appease my friends who teach math. You're welcome.

When was the last time you described a passionate friend as fervent?

On your journey, find time to freshen your vocabulary with some forgotten words, enjoy some fiction and there's always room for fudgesicles!!

AUGUST 18th

HAVE to love words like lingo, jargon, slang, argot, and patter. All terms to describe a special language for a specific group of people. I thought I would share with you the lingo for a group of people that are inhabitants of countries all over the world. They are a quiet group, but very skilled at what they do. Yes, I am talking about quilters. Quilters come in all ages, shapes, sizes, genders and skill level. But they all share this special language. Since it is no longer deemed "classified," I am free to share it.

Here are a few of their everyday words:

Bolts	Grain	Feed dogs	Charm packs
Jelly Roll	Layer Cake	Fat quarter	Flying geese
Log Cabin	Stash	Basting	Quilt sandwich
Batting	Card Trick	Scrappy	PhD

It is very hard some days to concentrate on sewing, and not think about your next snack or meal when some of these words are being tossed around. I wonder, can you get a fat quarter from eating a jelly roll?

I can poke fun at these men and women, because, yes, I am one of them. The vocabulary seemed strange at first, but now I can rattle off about making a quilt with a layer cake and half of a jelly roll with the best of them!! Quilters are generous people, and most of their quilts are given to family and friends for all occasions, happy and sad.

Quilts are for weddings, to take to chemo, for a fundraiser for a sick colleague, for a new baby, for the homeless shelter. Some are made to preserve memories. Quilting is love and quilts are an everlasting hug for the recipient. Quilts are works of heart.

AUGUST 19th

Directions for reading this page: First, cover the bottom of the page before you begin to read. You will see why later.I love to try interesting or new things. I have heard about this in a number of variations and have used it at a party or two. This version is going to be called: Party Fact or Fiction? The idea is that you make three statements to someone; two that are true and one that is false.

They then have to decide which statement is false.

This is a lot of fun for a gathering of friends. It would be more challenging to try it with your family at a holiday or event A lot more work to fool them!! Prizes could be awarded for the one fooling the most, and for the person guessing correctly the most times.

Here are my three statements: (I will tell you the answers at the bottom of the page, so don't peek!

1. My dream job is to be a talk show host, TV or radio. (I've been told I have the face for radio.)
2. I don't like shopping in big box book stores.
3. I once aspired to be an FBI agent.

It was difficult to think of the three statements, the true and the falsehood. Surprising… Okay, make your assessment of my statements and then scroll down for the reveal….

1. Achingly true
2. False, love all book stores, especially the huge ones!
3. True

AUGUST 20th

IT WAS A SWELTERING, sultry summer day in the Heartland. I was in the family room, simultaneously enjoying the air conditioning and the work I was doing on a quilt for a friend. I was cutting, slicing, pinning, having my way with that fabric. Really on a roll and pleased as a toddler with cake all over his face. But, life can change in a second.

The tool quilters use is called a rotary cutter, looks like a small version of a pizza cutter, but 100 times as sharp. Use with caution and skill. Can anyone guess where I am going with this? One quick slice, didn't even feel it at first but I had sliced through my finger. After trying to stop the bleeding and failing, and upon closer examination, I realized I needed to hold my finger together and get to the ER. Called my niece, wrapped it in a towel and off we went.

I walk up to the desk in the ER, clutching my almost severed finger in a bloody towel. The man behind the desk says: "Can I help you with something?" I was tempted to order a diet Pepsi. He immediately turned me over to a triage nurse who scolded me for wrapping my finger in a dish towel. My response was to tell her it was a clean towel.

I will spare you the details, other than I had to school the resident, that it would work better if she brought her rolling table to the side of the bed of the hand that was cut, instead of working across the bed.

They called it an almost total amputation, cut diagonally through the fingernail on my pointer finger. After much debate about if they could stitch it, and who would stitch it, they sewed it together. Not much fun while it was healing, but can't even tell it was injured now. This is why I am not allowed to use sharp things…

Somedays I am amazed by what I can do, and other days I try to get out of the car with my seatbelt on. This was a seatbelt kinda day.

AUGUST 21st

WHEN WAS the last time you received a postcard in the mail? Have you EVER received a postcard in the mail? Depending on your age, you may not have had the pleasure of this old school greeting. Vacationing family members or friends would choose a picture postcard of their location, jot a few sentences and send it off.

I loved getting postcards in the mail.

They still sell postcards in all the popular vacation spots, but I don't think many people actually send them through the mail. There are beautiful scenes of landscape, wildlife, oceans, architecture and much more. I was thinking about some ways to use these other than send them, and I think I've come up with a couple of good ones.

Keep a travel diary with them for yourself. Buy postcards of sights you see and places you go. Write some reflections about the places you have seen. Be sure to date them. Start a card file and file them in date order. How much fun will it be as you look back through them as the years go on? It will confirm the dates of when you vacationed somewhere, and jog your memory about what you did. I keep a travel journal, but I am going to start doing this the next time I take a trip.

Another version of this idea, is to write them to your children or grandchildren with some personal reflections about them and keep them for the future to give them another way to know you.

I will have no problem with this. I talk to myself already, so I might as well be writing to myself. Then if I forget what I said (wrote), I can look it up!! I will have total recall. Just one more way for me to conquer the world around me.

On your travels, take in the sights, sounds and culture and make a record of them for yourself, and for posterity. I think this will bring you and your family much pleasure for many years.It is never too late to start making memories today to enjoy in your tomorrows.

AUGUST 22nd

SUMMER in the Heartland is a glorious affair. To start with, there are more colors of green than the mind can imagine. Subtle differences exist from lawn, grass, farm fields, trees and other verdant vegetation. Driving anywhere outside of a town or city will provide one with these lovely vignettes. Add in the rolling hills and you've got yourself some magnificent scenery!! The land is gentle and very fertile. We are blessed with rich, black soil.

What else does summer bring to our lives? Fireflies (lightning bugs), fireworks, and the fair!! The Iowa State Fair held in August, is a grand event that puts a punctuation point on the end of our summer. As the ads proclaim: "Nothing can compare to our Iowa State Fair." Eleven days of midway rides, the famous Butter Cow, and other butter sculptures that vary from year to year. Great grandstand entertainment from nationally well known performers. I would be remiss if I didn't mention fair food. Well known for mobile food on a stick and probably fried! To name just a few: Loaded taters on a stick, deep fried Milky Way or Snickers, fried peanut butter and jelly on a stick, and fresh pineapple dipped in funnel cake batter and fried. Give me a Zantac, and make it a double!!

Summer nights around the bonfire with friends and family, enjoying the toasting of marshmallows and making s'mores never gets old. It can also be very hot and humid. Some days, walking outside feels like someone threw a wet towel over your head and face.

If you are not from the Heartland, join us some summer. The natives are friendly, the local food can't be beat, and who doesn't want a turkey leg or corn dog from the State Fair? Don't forget to stop and smell the sweet corn!!

AUGUST 23rd

QUESTIONS for the Universe

- Why is there always room for Jello?
- Can vegetarians eat animal crackers?
- Why is abbreviation such a long word?
- Who wrote the Book of Love?
- What is Victoria's Secret?
- Why would Yankee Doodle put a feather in his cap and call it Macaroni?
- Why can't you put the cart before the horse?
- Why is laughter the best medicine?
- Why does Pi never end?
- Which chair arm in the movie theatre is yours?
- Why aren't there more words that begin with the letter X?
- Does thesaurus have a synonym?

Answers, we need answers!!

AUGUST 24th

To me, this day is a day of great sadness. It is the anniversary of the day that the planet Pluto was demoted in 2006 from a full size planet to a dwarf planet. At the time, I felt that Pluto had served faithfully as a planet for 76 years, shouldn't tenure count for something? When I was in school, I learned there were nine planets and all of their names. I am not going to unlearn that. I forget enough things as it is, I am not going to purposely reject that which I was taught and learned in good faith. Is nothing sacred? I am still not okay with this.

Evidently, the International Astronomical Union changed or formalized the definition of a planet. Okay, who are these people, and is it Pluto's fault the definition was changed? Pluto seems to be a lovely planet and it even has five moons. The moons even have names: Charon, Keberos, Nix, Hydra and Styx. I think if an orbiting body, known as a planet has five moons, that's enough reasons for me to consider Pluto a planet.

This is not the first time the IAU has created controversy in the scientific community. In the 1960's and 1970's, astronauts on thc Apollo Missions would name features at their landing sites. The IAU didn't accept those names. Excuse me, have they been to the moon and seen these things?

So, here's to Pluto!! Long may she orbit! She will always be a planet to me. I am in the market for a bumper sticker that says, "Honk if you think Pluto is a planet." Let me know if you see any.

On your journey today, enlarge your orbit, gravitate to people who add color to your world, and don't forget to wish upon a star.

AUGUST 25th

As I am writing these pages, I often turn to the works of writers I admire for inspiration. Mark Twain is one of those writers. I heard a funny story, that sounds just like him, and also illustrates the irony of writing!

Mark Twain received a telegram from a publisher:

NEED 2 PAGE SHORT STORY TWO DAYS.

Response:

NO CAN DO 2 PAGES TWO DAYS. CAN DO 30 PAGES 2 DAYS. NEED 30 DAYS TO DO 2 PAGES.

This is pretty accurate!! When you have a limited amount of space/words, it can take awhile to hone the piece and convey what you are trying to say!! A longer piece allows more leeway and the ability to include a more detailed description. I thought it was fun to include his honest response to the request.

A quote from "Tom Sawyer" that illustrates Mr. Twain's way with words. "Tom appeared on the sidewalk with a bucket of whitewash and a long-handled brush. He surveyed the fence, and all gladness left him and a deep melancholy settled down upon his spirit. Thirty yards of board fence nine feet high. Life to him seemed hollow, and existence but a burden." Quite an apt description of a boy and a job on a nice Saturday, when so many adventures could be had, but alas, one must paint the fence!!

May your day be filled with adventures, friends, and all things delightful!! I would not want to see the deep melancholy take down your spirit as it did poor Tom!

AUGUST 26th

BACKYARD GARDENS ARE A WONDERFUL THING. I personally am not good at growing things, but so many people in the Heartland grow beautiful food for their families and some as a business. They sell locally grown produce and flowers to local grocery stores, and the Farmer's Markets. Many good options to obtain home grown vegetables without doing it yourself.

We are entering that phase of summer, where it is not safe to leave your home unattended or your car doors unlocked. Our local gardeners have tomatoes and zucchini that they can't use, freeze, or give away fast enough. It is not unusual to come home and find a bag of tomatoes on your doorstep, or zucchini on the front seat of your car.

There is no escape from this phenomenon at work either. The lunchroom tables are groaning from the weight of someone's excess of tomatoes, zucchini and sometimes other identifiable objects that someone has grown. At least at work, it's not your personal obligation to find a use for these things.

Don't get me wrong, there is nothing I love better than a big ol' beefsteak tomato from a friend's garden to use in a BLT or slice as a side dish with dinner. As recipients of this garden largesse, we are very grateful. One thing in Iowa we never get tired of buying or being given, is homegrown Iowa sweet corn. There is nothing like it. Anywhere. Of this I am convinced. The harvesting season of this crop is short, so we enjoy it while we can.

> The kiss of the sun for pardon. The songs of the birds for mirth. One is nearer God's heart in a garden, than anywhere else on earth.
>
> — DOROTHY FRANCES GURNEY

AUGUST 27th

"COLORING OUTSIDE THE LINES" is a phrase I frequently use about myself, and when encouraging others to let loose, be a little unconventional and maybe break some rules. I even use it on my business cards.

There is a real story behind that phrase from when I was a wee small lass. I don't remember exactly how old I was, but somewhere in the vicinity of 4-5 years old. My parents had been renting for a couple years after we moved to Iowa City. The big day had come, they bought their first house and it was time to move.

As per normal for most moving days, it was a chaotic day. Some family was there to help. I was left to my own devices as long as I stayed out of the way. Big mistake. I was not a naughty child normally, so still not sure why this happened. Again, I still can't always be left to my own devices. I get ideas. Things happen.

I was in my new bedroom when my mom came looking for me. The linoleum floor was carpeted with my many doll blankets. I had laid them out covering most of the floor. The problem was what was under them. I had decided to color the linoleum and had covered quite a large area. My mom was beside herself angry with me. First house, little dumpling has colored the floor. It was not in her decorating plans.

My punishment consisted of me having to clean the floor and remove my artwork. I hate it when my creativity is stifled. My parents evidently were unaware of the following quote: "Silence is golden...unless you have kids, then silence is suspicious."

Use your naughty inner child today for good, not evil. Let your creativity run amok, it feels great!!

AUGUST 28th

HERE'S HOPING this day will be an interesting day. One never knows the twists and turns any day will take. It is always interesting to have a little extra spice in your life, if you know what I mean…and since you brought up spices, let's go there!

I love the names and sounds of particular spices and herbs, even if I don't have any practical use for them. Some especially juicy sounding spices, I have no idea what they are used for, but somebody must use them because they keep selling them!!

Tumeric	Tarragon	Saffron
Marjoram	Cilantro	Arrowroot powder

And my favorites: parsley, sage, rosemary, and thyme...or is that in a song? Which brings me to songs with spices or herbs in them. See how my mind works? It can be a nice place to visit but you don't want to live there?

- "Scarborough Fair" has the parsley, sage, rosemary & thyme reference
- "Mellow Yellow" talks about Saffron, but it is a person.
- "Cinnamon Girl"
- "Love Grows (where my Rosemary goes)"
- "Incense and Peppermint"
- "Brown Sugar" by the Rolling Stones (okay, I'm stretching here)
- "A Taste of Honey" featuring Herb (get it?) Alpert

I may have gone as far as I can go with this, certainly farther than you would have liked. Writer's prerogative has to come into play somewhere. There aren't many perks to this job. Actually, there are none. That seems wrong. I may have to look into this. Ahh….but there is the sheer joy of writing, and that is enough for me...in addition to the perplexed look on your face as you read this.

AUGUST 29th

WHILE WRITING THIS BOOK, I may have mentioned, it has helped me to write in different venues for perspective and inspiration. One night I was struggling to produce anything worth your time to read. (Some people might say I still haven't.....but where's their book?) Since I was on house arrest waiting for a repair person I could not venture to the nearest coffee shop to write.

I am a person with some modicum of imagination, (decorum, not so much) so I told Alexa (my electronic imaginary friend) to play some coffee house music. Made myself a nice cup of coffee, charged myself $6.00, added a nice tip and put it on my debit card. The service was excellent and the help was friendly. They don't seem to mind that I have my shoes off and my feet on the coffee table.

This adventure is opening up all kinds of possibilities. Maybe I could put a sign out once in awhile, charge the neighbors for coffee to create some traffic in here. Maybe there's a book on Amazon, "How to Open a Coffee House in your Living Room." I am afraid to search for that on Amazon, in case it does exist!! I know I would be able to buy clever mugs, coffee and additives there. Okay, I couldn't let that rest. I went to Amazon and searched. There were two books on the subject....Scary.

Today's scribbling should give you more insight into the mind of a writer. I couldn't get to the coffee house today, and annoyance or frustration can be great inspiration!!

Seize the day, make it work, laugh at yourself and keep on keepin' on!!

AUGUST 30th

I AM fond of many types of music, and some songs never fail to move me when I hear them. The tune, of course is important, but I am sold on a song usually because of the lyrics. The combination of the two components plus the singer makes the magic happen.

One of my favorite "oldies," is "I'll Be Seeing You." (in all the old familiar places) It was written in 1938 for a Broadway musical and sung by Billie Holiday. Since then it has been covered many times by many different artists, including Frank Sinatra, Rosemary Clooney, and Rod Stewart. Each artist adds their own technique, but the haunting melody and words are timeless.

My favorite verse goes like this: (Be thankful there is no audio clip of me singing this)

> "I'll find you in the morning sun
> And when the night is new.
> I'll be looking at the moon,
> But I'll be seeing you."

Songs can motivate, inspire, unearth memories, make us smile, make us cry. What would we do with the music of our lives? Here is another song excerpt that is a favorite of mine: "I see trees of green, red roses too. I see them bloom for me and you and I think to myself, what a wonderful world…" "It's a Wonderful World," most notably performed by the inimitable Louis Armstrong.

What are the songs of your life? What inspires you, makes you cry, makes you feel hopeful? Listen to some music today, and let it fill your soul. Let it enhance your world, and take a moment to remember when….

AUGUST 31st

August is a beautiful time in Iowa. The rolling hills, where the rows of corn follow the lay of the land and are in perfect symmetry. Green and growing plants as far as the eye can see. Perfecting themselves in preparation for the harvest season which will be upon us. Sweet corn season has ended, but we will enjoy the memory of that delectable summer treat until next year's season.

Time to slow down driving the highways and backroads of this glimpse of paradise. Farm vehicles are starting to appear more frequently, preparing for the work that lies ahead.

The farmer is an interesting breed. They can plan, estimate, plant, watch and wait. Their success on a crop farm is dependent on the vagaries of the summer weather. Too much rain, too little rain, too much heat, will affect the livelihood of the farmer and his family.

It is a very complex chemistry problem to achieve the perfect growing season, and the farmer has very little control after planting is done. Offering prayers and entreaties to the one who paints the skies and sends the rain is all they can do.

Farming is not just a job. It is a way of life for the whole family. Living hand in hand with nature is a wonderful way to live. "To everything, there is a season, and a time to every purpose under the heaven: A time to be born, a time to die; a time to plant and a time to pluck up that which is planted." Ecclesiastes 3:1-2 Nobody understands the cycle of life better than the farmer.

On your day's journey, thank a farmer. Who else looks at dirt and sees potential? Who else lives in such harmony with the land? Who else feeds America? Drive the backroads and appreciate the beauty of crops in the field, the cattle in the pasture and the work of a farmer.

SEPTEMBER 1st

As a "guest" teacher for many years, I have walked in the shoes of many different teachers. I understand the daily frustration of students coming to class without paper, pencils, textbooks, and other necessary supplies-day after day after day. Repeat offenders may seem like they are doing this purposefully.

I recently read an article titled, "Give the Kid A Pencil," by Chad Donahue which struck a chord deep within me. He is also a middle school teacher and not a stranger to the no supplies phenomenon! He feels that it probably does more harm than good to nag, embarrass, or scold the student repeatedly. These students are, after all, kids and kids make mistakes. Don't we all?

The result could be that the student will dread coming to class. He may get less out of class and could have bad feelings about the subject and the teacher. He may feel humiliated or embarrassed. We don't know what happened at home last night or at school this morning. He states "I will always give the kid a pencil."

After reading this article and doing some thinking, I made a decision. I ordered a large number of personalized pencils that say, "Mrs. Lacina loaned me this pencil." So I, too, will always give the kid a pencil. If they keep it, that is more than okay with me. Maybe I made their day just a little easier, just a little better, and just a little more positive. At least, I hope so.

Sometimes, the world is a harsh place for all of us. Anything we can do to help each other carry the load even for a step or two helps. I truly enjoy middle school age students and want to help them succeed. A "pencil" can symbolize a whole lot more. I hope someone gives you a pencil today.

SEPTEMBER 2nd

DEAR READER: Today seems like a day to share quotes or thoughts to ponder, appreciate, agree or disagree with, analyze or memorize, so here goes!!

"How cool is it that the same God who created mountains and oceans and galaxies thought the world needed one of you too." Unknown

"The best time to plant a tree was 20 years ago. The second best time is now." Chinese Proverb

An evocative example of forgiveness that takes my breath away: "The fragrance of the flower bloom after it is crushed." Unknown

"Coincidence is God's way of remaining anonymous." Albert Einstein

"Yesterday is ashes, tomorrow wood. Only today does the fire burn brightly." Eskimo Proverb

"Those we hold most dear never truly leave us. They live on in the kindness they showed, the comfort they gave, the memories they created and the love they brought into our hearts." Lori Lacina

"Even the still wind has a voice." Navajo saying

"The Future is no place to place your better days." Dave Matthews Band

Hope some of these ring true to you, move your heart, feed your soul. Interesting isn't it that some of the oldest sayings hold ageless truths that stand the test of time, location, and in a different world?

SEPTEMBER 3rd

TODAY, I am thinking about my next book. Just kidding!! The amateur writes one book and thinks she can tackle another one. Thinking about my life and the many gravity storms I have survived. How does the title "Gravity Storms for Dummies" sound to you? I am sure that my vast experience could be useful to others who also have a gravity deficiency.

My mother used to say that I was an accident going somewhere to happen. Not very maternal, but unfortunately true. It all began at the tender age of 4 during a kindergarten nature walk around the neighborhood. Allegedly, I was walking with my hands in my pockets and tripped and broke my fall with my chin. It happens. 10 stitches.

The next incident I remember involved playing tag in the backyards and tripping over a garden hose. Fractured arm. I didn't go to the doctor till two days later when my mom asked me why I was holding my arm that way. Cast. Negligent neighbor.

At the age of 13, staying with relatives on the farm. Decided to sleepwalk down the steep, narrow steps. Not a good idea. 12 stitches inside my mouth, broken nose, black eyes, and a broken toe. Bad steps!

I only want to spend one page on this painful topic, so to list a few other events, broke my ankle on the way to a business lunch, fell off my front porch backward, and another broken toe after an incident.

I have to laugh at myself. Everyone else does. I need a support group for the gravitationally challenged. Mary Pickford said, "Failure is not the falling down, but the staying down." Can't keep me down!! I pick myself up, dust myself off, get a ride to the ER, and start all over again.

SEPTEMBER 4th

SOME YEARS AGO, I had an interesting adventure. I was asked to teach 2nd grade, Religious Education at Regina in Iowa City. I had a phone message from the Director at the time, Sister Mary Fran, telling me I had been recommended to her as someone who would be good at this. I am quite puzzled at this but return the call. She repeated her request, and I said to her, "Sister, do you know that I am not Catholic?" I was overwhelmed with the volume of the silence that ensued. After she gathered her wits about her, she said, "Well, if that didn't matter, would you do it?" to which I responded yes. She said she would think about it and get back to me. And she did and I taught. (I speculated she probably had to call the Pope!! Friends in high places...)

I really enjoyed these lively second graders. One night, Sister Fran stopped in our classroom to take pictures and visit. After I had called her "Sister" a few times, one of the children asked me why I called her that. I explained that Sister is part of her name, she is a nun. Which of course made the little guy ask "What is a nun?" I replied, "Sister, would you like to answer that?"

She told them she was married to Jesus, showed them her ring. She didn't have her own children, but they were all her children. Violet (names have been changed to protect the hysterically funny) says, "Well that's weird." So I chimed in, explaining she is one of God's helpers to do his work, like a priest. Jacob (the original questioner) states very seriously, " Well, that doesn't sound like much of a job to me." Sister Fran laughed uproariously, as did I. The thoughts and comments of second graders, uncensored, honest and forthright.

On your journey, look at life through the eyes of a child and remember a more innocent time.

SEPTEMBER 5th

AUTUMN....SIGH....HOW often can I sing your praises??? Today is about the fruit of fall, the apple. In this day and age, we can certainly purchase apples year round and they are normally pretty good. But they don't compare to the quality and abundance of the apples of fall that you can pick at the orchard. There are also more varieties to choose from. My favorite apple is one that comes and is gone before you know it, the Song of September. It is hard to describe the flavor, but it is very sweet, aromatic, and a little bit like cherry candy.

What can you do with all these fall apples?? There are many lovely recipes for apples, and best of all, most of them are desserts!!

To name a few.....

Apple Crisp	Apple Cake	Apple Pie (ala mode of course)
Apple Bread	Applesauce	Waldorf Salad
Baked Apples	Apple tart	Apple Pie Muffins
Apple Turnovers		

Warning: I am just here to share information. I am not responsible for what you do with this information. Any baking and dessert overload that you may experience is not my fault.

Enjoy some apples this time of year. Grocery store, farmer's market, apple orchards can all provide you with this tasty and healthy treat. However, there is nothing like a trip to the apple orchard on a sunny fall day for a great family outing. The beauty of the orchards and the smell of apples are a treat for the senses.

> Anyone can count the seeds in an apple, but only God can count the number of apples in a seed.
>
> — ROBERT H. SCHULLER

SEPTEMBER 6th

I SURE HOPE you are not tired of me celebrating holidays in general, or certain types of holidays. I am a celebrating kind of girl!! Welcome to National Read A Book Day!! As far as I am concerned, any and every day could be read a book day, but let's make this a special day. When my grandson Josh was a wee, small child, I would stop to see him when I left the bank, and spend 30 minutes or so reading with him, snuggling and getting some quality time. This also gave him mom a chance to figure out dinner. I didn't do it as much as I should have, but the times I did are very fond memories. As this book goes to print, Josh will be in graduate school having acquired a chemistry major/math double major as an undergrad. Our taste in books may have diverged...but maybe I could read him a chemistry treatise???

Take today to treat yourself to reading a book that you always meant to read. Classics are good for this, "Little Women," "A Tree Grows in Brooklyn," "Gone With the Wind." If those aren't your cup of chai tea, try a mystery writer that you haven't read; James Patterson, Agatha Christie, Lisa Scottoline, Lisa Gardner, Sue Grafton or P.D. James. Search a book you like and find similar ones.

Read to be entertained, to take a journey to a world unlike yours, to experience and to enjoy. Life is short and there are so many wonderful books to choose from.

On your journey today, have an adventure, support your local bookstore, grab your drink of choice and escape the daily obligations and chores we all have. They will still be there when you return!! Trust me on this, I am very good at escaping the demands of daily life, and darn if they aren't still there when I re-enter my world!!

SEPTEMBER 7th

I WAS HAVING A VERY productive day, you know the kind. I was checking things off my to do list right and left. Feeling so good about my progress on life's mundane chores and some extracurricular activities as well.Then I had one of my many life experiences that teach me things I didn't know, and if I were a more cautious person things I should never need to know.

Listen and learn….Hypothetically speaking, if you put a staple all the way into your thumb pad, you can actually remove it with your everyday office staple remover, looks like a tweezer on steroids.. I am not saying it wasn't painful, but it can be done. You may not want to try this at home, unless you have my vast experience with strange and unusual predicaments.

I am a hard worker, fairly intelligent, creative and a lot of energy. Somedays I am truly amazed by what I can do...and then there are the days when I staple my thumb….I could go on….So, if you are also someone who has "these" kind of days, welcome to my club!!

Thc good news about these kinds of days, you never know when they will happen, so if you enjoy the element of surprise, jump right in, I am never bored!! As Maya Angelou said, "This is a wonderful day. I've never seen this one before." I have a lot of days like that, and still, I appreciate each and every one. After all, if I were someone who wasn't an accident waiting to happen, where would I get my material??

SEPTEMBER 8th

Tyrannosaurus Rex, Velociraptor, Triceratops, Giganotosaurus, Roget's Thesaurus...oops, I guess Roget's Thesaurus is not a dinosaur but it sounds like one to me. It does have some characteristics in common with them, I think.

It is ginormous, my copy has 1,282 pages, printed in microscopic letters. I am not sure, but I can imagine the printed version could very well be on the way to join the dinosaurs in the land of the extinct.

It is very easy to find a synonym or antonym on the internet with a simple search. For those writers who want to go old school, carrying around a tome that weighs a good six pounds is fine. It could also help get the weights part of your exercise routine done as you go about your day. There is also the senses you use turning the pages of a book, the smell, the paper cuts, the painful broken foot after you dropped the thesaurus on it.

A thesaurus is a good tool for a writer's toolbox, or for a student writing a paper. There are only so many times you can use the word great, really good, or amazing in your text. Might need to learn some new words, hence the mighty thesaurus.

Voltaire said, "Writing is the painting of the voice." In that case, use all the paintbrushes in your toolbox, including the mighty Thesaurus Rex!!

On your journey, use all your words, write a letter, write a note, write a song. Read something you enjoy and relish the words the writer chose especially for you. Go to the bookstore and lift a thesaurus just to say you did!!

SEPTEMBER 9th

WESTWARD, Ho!! Road trip to the Rocky Mountains, where the scenery is on steroids, and you need to grab some attitude for the altitude!! A hiking trip, my companion, the experienced hiker, me, the novice hiker, going to take the trails by storm. People have often told me to take a hike, but I don't think that is the same thing.

We start the hiking in the Badlands on the way to Colorado. Some unforgiving territory here, but I am determined and confident. Starting out, the trail is not so bad, and enjoying the weather and scenery, until I spot the next leg of the trail. It is a rope ladder attached (somewhat) to a rock wall that is straight up. I am determined and confident. I climb the rope ladder with a crowd of strangers watching and cheering me on. Done!! The trail continues and is ours to conquer!

A wonderful hike, but day is done, time to return. The rope ladder descent looks more intimidating than the ascent was. I am determined, but not so confident. I watch others descend, but can't quite work up the courage to start. However, as my companion reminds me, there is no other way down. I slowly inch down the rope ladder, with another crowd of hikers/strangers watching me. I make it to the bottom with much relief and applause from the onlookers.

Off to conquer the Rocky Mountains. Lots of trails to hike, most of them straight up to a place where there is no air. They call it altitude there. The silence on the mountain is as breathtaking as the scenery and the altitude. Throw in the possibility of bears crossing your path, no bathrooms and no air. All kidding aside, I absolutely loved it, and loved the accomplishment I felt when we were bone tired every night. I was not too old to do this! Rocky Mountain High, Colorado...you were right John Denver!

SEPTEMBER 10th

"School Days, School Days, Dear old Golden Rule days. Reading and writing and 'rithmetic.." Those were the days!! Much to my dismay, they are no longer teaching cursive writing in many schools. Really?? This means that this generation will be standing in the Rotunda of the National Archives in Washington, D.C. and will be unable to read the original words as they were written in the Declaration of Independence. I am sorry for them, as seeing and reading the actual words that you have learned, on a historic document is pretty amazing.

Penmanship, in general, is a lost art. There are so many of my students who have such illegible handwriting I can't read it. How will they write a grocery list, a note to their boss, wife, daughter or anyone? Every aspect of your life can involve the physical act of writing something down. There is a different feel when you put pen to paper, a different reaction and perspective.

The other concern I see is note taking. Most of them don't take notes in class at middle school. This will not serve them well in the future. Writing (not typing) words helps you to remember them.

One last point to illustrate my concern is that printing and cursive writing activates different areas in your brain. I am led to believe using different areas of your brain is a darn good thing!! Or possibly, they just tell me that because I am "old", and they want to keep me busy.

Mahatma Ghandi said, "I saw that bad handwriting should be regarded as a sign of an imperfect education." Mahatma, I am singing the same song.

SEPTEMBER 11th

Most people reading this will remember where they were on that fateful day in 2001....I was at work at the bank. I heard on the radio that a plane had hit one of the towers. I thought to myself, some pilot just made a huge mistake. Then, I hear another plane has hit the towers. At that moment, I felt fear. I called home to my husband and said turn on the television, something is happening. The rest of the day at work is a blur to me. We were all in shock.

The rest, as they say, is history. Remembering a day that changed our nation and the world forever. The worst day in our nation's history since December 7, 1941. Technology in the form of videos showing this tragedy meant we had to see it over and over and over again.

If you haven't seen the movie *Extremely Loud and Incredibly Close,* starring Tom Hanks, it is definitely worth viewing.

The shining light in this tragedy is the American spirit. People from all walks of life, races, religions pull together and do what needs to be done when there is a disaster of any kind. It will take more than planes hitting the Twin Towers, the Pentagon, and crashing into a field in Pennsylvania. to break us down. Eternal thanks and gratitude to all those who responded to the call for help that day, some giving their lives in service of their fellow Americans.

Today, thank a police officer, a firefighter, all first responders and those serving in the military. They are the reason you are able to live your life free of fear and enjoy the freedoms their service affords you.

SEPTEMBER 12th

LIFE WHIZZES by us like a speeding train. We can let our appointment calendars drive us and be oblivious to the world around us. I am an egregious offender of this and can schedule myself into craziness with very little effort. So, I decided to slow down today and make a list of things worth noticing and giving attention.

- Stars on a clear night
- The sound of water, fountains, crashing waves, rippling lake
- The color of someone's eyes
- Smell of the rain
- Lights of a city at night
- Aroma of freshly brewed coffee
- Sound of laughter
- Wind
- Your inner voice
- Flowers that grow impossibly between rocks
- Sound of autumn leaves crunching underfoot
- Scent of a passerby's perfume or aftershave
- Savory aroma of dinner in the oven
- Tinkling of wind chimes
- Listen between the lines in a conversation
- Church bells
- Slowly enjoying one ooey gooey caramel
- Haunting sound of a train whistle in the distance

Today, take time for yourself. Take time to listen, look, smell, see, hear and appreciate. Make your own list. Just the making of my list slowed my heartbeat and made me smile at the thought of these treasures life offers up. Give yourself the gift of experiencing the smallest treasures.

> It is the sweet, simple things of life which are the real ones after all.
>
> — LAURA INGALLS WILDER

SEPTEMBER 13th

SIGH....GROCERY shopping....the bane of my existence....or at least one of them.. Grocery shopping irritates me like sand in your eye, a rock in your shoe, a paper cut on your finger, or a long, much repeated commercial about the latest pharmaceutical drug that will improve your life unless the side effects kill you.

I am very familiar with grocery stores, especially our Heartland mainstay, Hy-Vee. I got my first job at sixteen and worked there for five years. Loved that job, loved the customer service training and the "helpful smile in every aisle" that I was proud to be.

That's where the love ended. I make a list, which I often leave at home. Then there's the trudging through all the aisles of the super store, where they frequently move products around so you can't find them...which is made more difficult by the fact that you may not know what you are looking for because you have no list. Hide and seek is not a game I enjoy while shopping for food. Then there is the long line at the checkout, loading and unloading the car and last but still annoying putting the afore mentioned groceries away.

The one thing I do get a chuckle and a warm fuzzy from when I am shopping is the older shoppers, usually men who need help.. I must still have the Hy-Vee "aura" or special aisle smile. Almost every shopping trip I am approached by older men with a list and a puzzled look on their face. They ask me if I know what "that" is or where to find it.

I cheerfully decipher, locate and place the item gently in their basket, knowing their wives will be happy that they came home with sour cream instead of cream cheese or celery seed instead of caraway seed. Thinking of asking Hy-Vee if I could get my name tag and blue smock back.

SEPTEMBER 14th

IOWA CONNECTIONS ARE SPREAD FAR and wide, from sea to shining sea and beyond. A favorite Iowa born celebrity of mine is Meredith Willson.

Born in Mason City, he based the Tony Award-winning musical, "The Music Man," on memories of his hometown.

For those of you not fortunate to have seen the movie of this great hit, you are missing out!! A con man, a love story, and hope for a small town makes for a good movie. Every time I hear "Seventy-Six Trombones," I can picture Robert Preston leading the band down the main street in the final scene!!

Meredith Willson wrote two other Broadway musicals, "The Unsinkable Molly Brown," and "Here's Love." Many of the songs he wrote became standards and have been sung by many successful singers. Remember the song, "Till There Was You?" The Beatles (a small group you may have heard of from the UK) sang that song, written by Meredith Willson.

His talent and career took him all over the country, but his heart was always in Iowa. It has been said about him that he was a walking commercial for Iowa. You can take the boy out of Iowa....but you can't take Iowa out of the boy. That's a good thing. He passed away at his home in California, but his final resting place is in Mason City, Iowa.

There is one final song that I think you all will recognize, written by Mr. Willson. I did not know this was written by our famous son, until just recently, "It's Beginning to Look a Lot like Christmas." I believe he was writing from the heart, and remembering Christmas in Iowa.

Iowa, it's a land that steals your heart and keeps a piece of it no matter where you roam.

SEPTEMBER 15th

SOME TIME AGO, I saw a story on the news that made my heart glad and renewed my faith in the goodness of the human spirit. Two middle school girls acted on an idea to make their fellow students feel welcome and more comfortable at school. Each morning they arrived at school early and held the school doors open and greeted each student by name. They asked questions in greeting, that showed they knew the student and their interests. "How's band going, Lewis?" "Happy Birthday Abby!" "What did you do over the weekend, Sammy? Simple acts. Kindness. Goodwill to all.

It speaks to the essence of my mantra. If each person did something to make their little corner of the world better, the cumulative results would be mind-boggling. These girls started something that will change their lives forever, and have an impact on hundreds of others. They are role models. Leaving nothing to chance, they have recruited their replacements when they move on to high school!!

We can all take a page from their book. Be more inclusive. Step outside your clique or comfort zone and talk to those that seem to be lonely or on the outside at gatherings. Invite someone at work to join your lunch group. If traveling for work, invite people who seem to be alone to join your dinner table.

Be a strong voice in the world, not a faint echo. Set an example and make the world a better place, for others and for yourself. Kindness is a commodity that is plentiful and the more you give away, the more there is. Mark Twain, American author and humorist, never at a loss for words had something to say on this subject, "Kindness is the language which the deaf can hear and the blind can see."

SEPTEMBER 16th

"TRYING to be happy by accumulating possessions is like trying to satisfy hunger by taping sandwiches all over your body." George Carlin. This certainly paints a very vivid picture for me!

Things....objects....possessions....all things which complicate our lives. I have been trying to simplify my own life by downsizing the things I own. Clothes are a particular problem for me. Have I worn that in recent history? No, but I might, is my thinking. The true answer is that I won't wear it, so I need to set it free. Multiply this and the closet will look better and be more user-friendly.

If we try to think about the things are truly valuable, what would you take if you had an hour to evacuate your home, with the knowledge that it might be destroyed? Where to start??

So, not giving this much thought because if this really happened, there would not be much time to think, here is what I would grab:

1. Sentimental/special jewelry
2. Some of my quilts
3. My purse
4. Recipe box
5. Laptop, iPad, iPhone (I know these can be replaced, but I would like to keep my contact with the world intact.)

At this point, I am probably out of time. Looking at my list seems like many of the possessions are just that, things. Another reason to simplify and declutter and keep what is truly necessary and important.

On your journey today, be content, be present in the moment and pay it forward...

SEPTEMBER 17th

One of my favorite things, is the interesting, unique facts that you accidentally learn about people. I had participated in several Beth Moore bible studies at my church, and really enjoyed them. I then took training to become a bible study leader. I was excited to lead my first bible study and planned for the first session.

So as I prepared for the first night of the study, I included an icebreaker that I thought was clever and would get us off to a good start. I wrote on the board 3 colors. I then passed around a bag of skittles and told people to take as many as they wanted but they needed to take at least 5. After everyone had taken their Skittles, I explained the ice breaker. For example if they took 3 orange candies, they would have to answer 3 questions in a particular category.

The first person was to tell us something unusual about themself that no one would expect. Grace, (names have been changed to protect the innocent) proceeded to tell us that she had not one, but two dead animals in her freezer. Pets, that had died, but the ground was too frozen to bury them, so they froze them until they could be buried. ARE YOU KIDDING ME?? So, as you might expect, there was lots of laughter and teasing.

We move on to the next victim. Let me preface this with, I am not making this up….she has also had dead animals in her freezer for similar reasons. Okay, you have food in there you are going to eat, ARE YOU KIDDING ME?? I was almost afraid to continue the ice breaker, but the rest of the answers did not include dead animals in a kitchen freezer.

Disclaimer: I don't keep dead animals in my freezer, but I am trying not to judge.

SEPTEMBER 18th

I COULDN'T RESIST INCLUDING some fun one liners that I have heard (or used over the years!!) Sprinkle these in your conversation for some colorful additives!! Warning: The content on this page may be hazardous to your funny bone!! (Or to be medically correct, your humerus bone!)

"Butter my butt and call me a biscuit!"

"Bless her heart, who would have thought to wear that?" Or just "Bless her heart" with a certain intonation makes it clear there is no real blessing going on here!! (Talk to your Southern friends about this one!)

"If the good Lord's willin' and the creek don't rise…." (A personal favorite!)

'Always drink upstream from the herd."

"Life is simpler when you plow around the stump." (This one applies to many situations in life, sometimes there is no need to climb over something when it's easier to go around it!)

"If you're not the lead dog, the view never changes." (Think about it!)

"Never lick a steak knife." (Wise words, indeed)

I must include my favorite quote about our language., which of course is not really about language!!

> The nine most terrifying words in the English language are: 'I'm from the government and I'm here to help.'
>
> — PRESIDENT RONALD REAGAN

SEPTEMBER 19th

I WAS OUT RUNNING ERRANDS, one of my least favorite things to do, but sometimes you just have to get out there and get it done. I stopped at Walgreens to pick up a few items. There was quite a line at the checkout counter, so I had ample time to people watch. The gentleman in line ahead of me had a bottle of Glenlivet, a fine Scotch whiskey. I, on the other hand had Prilosec and Gaviscon (not fine Scotch whiskeys). I thought to myself, wonder who is going to have the better day? I will let you be the judge, but I am guessing you know what I was thinking. I chuckled all the way home!

So, the question is, what makes a day good or bad? Most days by nature are not over the top spectacular or horrible beyond words. Most of us have days with ups and downs, wins and losses, highs and lows. It has taken me a long time to realize that it is not always the events of the day that makes it good or bad but our reaction to those events.

Concentrate on the good and deal with the bad things, then put them to the side.

On your journey, get up every day with the attitude that you are going to do great things and make a difference in the world. You only need to touch one life in a positive way to start a ripple of waves that could affect hundreds. Drop that pebble in the water and watch what happens.

SEPTEMBER 20th

For those of you reading this that are from Iowa, here are a few more things to give you bragging rights!! Loving the history in the Heartland.

The Delicious apple was discovered in 1875 on a farm in Peru, Iowa by farmer Jesse Hiatt. It was a red and yellow apple which he called the "Hawkeye." In 1892 Stark Nursery ran a contest and the Hawkeye was the winner. They purchased the rights and changed the name to the Stark Delicious.

Here are a few other things that were invented in Iowa:

- Gasoline powered tractor(the inventor went on to form a little company you may have heard of called "John Deere"
- Trampoline
- Eskimo Pie
- Screen Door
- Buffered Aspirin (University of Iowa, Pharmacy Department)
- Helicopter
- Gallup Poll
- First automatic, electronic digital computer (Iowa State University)
- Bread Slicing Machine
- Vending Machinc
- Pinterest (the app that eats up hours of your time!)

This may be a rural state, but the diversity, ingenuity and work ethic of the people who call this home is extraordinary. Such an interesting and diverse array of Iowa's gifts to the world; products that impact lives every day all over the world. If you are not from Iowa, do a little digging and find out what your state has contributed to the world.

SEPTEMBER 21st

Good Morning, Friends!! What silliness should we stir up for today? I love the start of a new day, so many possibilities.....Let's do a little English lesson today, but never fear, you can also have fun with this at your next party! (Hey, I can hear those groans! Remember I love words and what can be done with them!)

A pangram (from the Greek. Pan gramma) or holoalphabetic sentence contains every letter of the alphabet at least once. Yep, all 26 glorious letters in one sentence. The real challenge is to try to use the fewest possible surplus letters in creating your sentence.

The most well known pangram, at least for people my age and older is the sentence we had to type in typing class: The quick brown fox jumped over the lazy dog. This is a pretty succinct pangram, with only nine surplus letters.The challenge is to use as few duplicate letters as you can, and still have a sentence that isn't gibberish!!

Here are a couple more examples…

Pack my box with five dozen liquor jugs. (How many times have I said that while packing for vacation?)

Here is one I created, with too many surplus letters to count:

For goodness sake, please, can you kids just be very quiet so the fox, zebra and wombat are okay. (Sad isn't it?)

Give this a try, it is a good puzzle to give your brain a workout. Have friends over for a game night and include this.

On your journey today, use your brain, make it work hard at something new and have some fun along the way. You are never too old and it is never too late to try something new.

SEPTEMBER 22nd

WELCOME TO THE AUTUMNAL EQUINOX…SORT of!! This event in September happens when the sun crosses the equator, which can happen on the 22nd, 23rd or 24th. Evidently, the celestial events have their own timeline which is not tied to a specific date on the manmade calendar!

Just a note, in case you are not as obsessed with these kinds of dates as I am….we have two solstices and two equinoxes each year. The solstice happens during our spin around the sun where the sun is the greatest distance from the equator, conversely, the equinox is where the sun is at its shortest distance from the equator, and making days and nights of equal length. Regardless of all that meteorological mumbo jumbo: Hello Autumn! It is official, I can start my public adoration of my favorite season in print and in person.

The first glorious day of fall, my favorite time of year. Bring on the brilliant colors of trees, the harvest, pumpkins, sweaters, boots, bonfires, Pumpkin Pie Blizzards, apple crisp with cinnamon ice cream, chili in the crockpot, Maple Pecan Frappuccino, pleasant days, and crisp cool nights. Whew, that was a long one, but a well-deserved tribute to this cozy season.

What does autumn mean to you? For me, it combines lots of emotions and changes. It means reflection, giving thanks, finding balance in my life, recharging creative energies that may have fallen dormant during summer's playtime. It is an ending and a beginning all at the same time, as are many things in our lives.

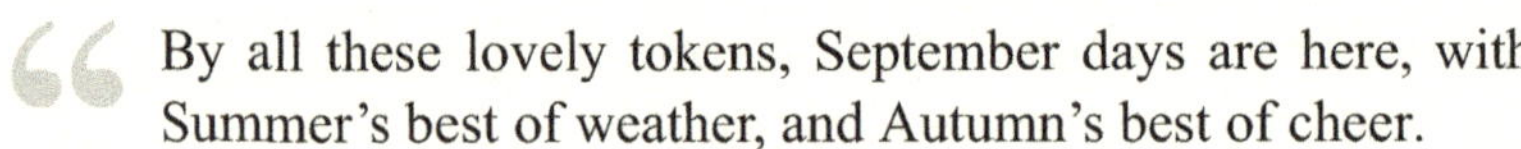

> By all these lovely tokens, September days are here, with Summer's best of weather, and Autumn's best of cheer.
>
> — HELEN HUNT JACKSON

Start today, embracing your life and plans in this season.

SEPTEMBER 23rd

I DECIDED to devote this page to helping my fellow man. I mean that literally….if you are a man reading this, take notes. If you are a woman reading this, leave this book open at this page for the man in your life with a well- placed note!! Men often don't truly understand women in general, and the woman in their life in particular. I am here to help.

I would like to share the following:

5 Actions guaranteed to get you into hot water with your wife/special woman in your life

1. Forgetting an anniversary: wedding, the day you met, the day you proposed, the day she cooked you dinner for the first time. Actually almost any day in your life as a couple, this is a hard one to "win" if you are the husband/man.
2. Calling her by your first wife's name. This should need no further explanation.
3. Saying, "Those pants really do make your butt look fat." Again, if I need to explain this, you are in more trouble than I can help you fix!
4. Buying her a lifetime membership to Weight Watchers.
5. Comparing her cooking (unfavorably) to your mother's. Please don't go there, I fear for your safety.

This has been a public service announcement brought to you by the Heartland Girl. Guys, I sympathize with your plight, do the best you can. May the force be with you.!

SEPTEMBER 24th

I HESITATE to tell you about today's holiday because most of you will want to go back to bed and bury your head in the covers. Welcome to National Punctuation Day! A few of you, (mostly some of my teacher friends) will truly appreciate it. Maybe they will bring treats for their students today!! Or maybe they will treat them to a surprise quiz on punctuation, it's just the way they roll!

This is a relatively new holiday, originating in 2004. The purpose is to celebrate the correct use of punctuation. Some of you may scoff at this, but this is posted in one of our Middle School classrooms and illustrates the importance of a well-placed comma. Punctuation can save lives.... "Let's eat Grandma" or "Let's eat, Grandma"

Or

"Julia Child found joy in cooking her family and her dog."

"Julia Child found joy in cooking, her family, and her dog."

If you find this subject as exciting as I do, you might want to check out the book by Keith Houston, "Sh@dy Characters: The Secret Life of Punctuation Symbols & Other Typographical Marks."

Speaking of other typographical marks, the much-overused pound sign, # number sign, or the cool kid's name for it"hashtag" has invaded every aspect of our life. The actual name for this symbol is the octothorpe. # In the early 1960s, scientists that worked for the telephone industry invented this name for the symbol. They added it to send signals to the telephone operating systems. Octo for the 8 points. No one seems to know exactly where the Thorpe came from.

So much more to say, so little space. Happy Punctuation Day from one who cares....

SEPTEMBER 25th

I AM ALWAYS MAKING DAILY/WEEKLY to do lists. Usually mundane things, household chores, return library books, miscellaneous errands are what you would see on my list. I started thinking (I know, dangerous when that happens), about what might be on the personal to-do list for the President. Wasn't thinking about a particular president, but just anyone who might be President of the United States.

Here is what I came up with:

- Ask the First Lady to hum "Hail to the Chief" when I come home
- Change the name of Camp David-Camp Constitution or Camp Seclusion?
- Get a better office chair.
- Remind the 1st Lady to buy more microwave popcorn for the residence.
- Call in sick.
- Declare the national vegetable to be french fries.
- Ask lead Secret Service agent to change his aftershave.
- Buy a new "power tie."
- Make a prank call to Montenegro or Croatia.
- Find out what the Secret Service did with my credit cards.
- Smell the flowers in the Rose Garden.
- Host high school reunion at the White House.
- Decide where my Presidential Library will be located.

I know they have important and world changing decisions to make every day, but I am sure they have a secret list of personal items to do....and if they don't, I bet the 1st Lady has a honey-do list!!

On your journey today, throw out the lists, throw caution to the wind and wing it!!!

SEPTEMBER 26th

SIGH....IT is that time of year again. The season of television shows filing away summer's reruns and showing off what twists and turns the new season of shows will hold for their viewers.

Sometimes I yearn for the days when television viewing was less complicated. I think we have too much of a "good" thing in today's world. When I became aware of watching TV, there were three networks. (Yes, I am older than Iowa or National Public Television, thank you very much for noticing.) That meant three choices of shows.

Whatever we watched, the whole family was watching. There was no channel surfing. When the channel needed to be changed, whichever kid was closest to the TV got up and turned the dial. Parents had remote controlled TVs long before the technology was invented!

Today, we have cable tv, satellite tv, Netflix, Hulu (is that like the hoop I used to have, oh wait that was hula), Roku, TIVO, Amazon Firestick, and probably many other things I am not aware of. The first time someone asked me if I had Roku, I had no idea if they were inquiring about my health, phone, or credit card! I feel rather hip now, being able to fling those terms around, yet having experienced none of them except TIVO. Too many choices, too much sitting and staring at a box in the living room or bedroom.

Wishing you a day or more a week, listening to music, walking, reading, baking, cooking, creating and conversing with real people! I enjoy select TV shows, but I also like living my life instead of watching others pretend to live a life. In the words of Groucho Marx, "I find television very educating. Every time somebody turns on the set, I go into the other room and read a book."

SEPTEMBER 27th

It seems fair to say that it has been established that I have an affection for words, the use of them, both properly and improperly. I also have lots of questions. Always looking for answers, good, bad, wrong, crazy, just give me an answer. I am flexible about information.

My question today is about the word "unruly." If a group of people can be unruly, does it logically follow that they can also be "ruly." I may have been called unruly at times, but I have never been called ruly, so is it a word? That might not be a fair demonstration of the word, using myself.

So, as inquiring minds need to be satisfied, I went to the source. I checked with Merriam-Webster, a company known for their dictionary publishing, since 1831. Guess what? Merriam and his friend Webster tell me that yes, indeed, "ruly" is a word. Their definition of the word does indicate the opposite of unruly. Ruly means obedient and orderly. No wonder I have never heard that word in common usage.

I can hardly wait til I am in a classroom where every student is working hard; and I can say, "Wow, girls and boys, you are so ruly today." That made me laugh out loud while typing. Their reaction could be interesting. I am thinking they will look at me, give each other sideways glances or eye rolls and continue working. Still might break it out someday and go for the gold.

On your journey today, use the words unruly and ruly, be the words unruly and ruly, share your unruly and ruly sides with the world. Be inventive, use your imagination and be yourself, whoever that is!!

SEPTEMBER 28th

I KNOW that all of my readers are facing the same challenge I am. Regardless of your age, the facts seem clear, we are getting older. Getting older is an everyday journey, some days are uneventful, and on other days there is evidence that our age is affecting our daily lives.

The brain is one of the many working parts of our frail, human bodies that can betray us. It becomes harder to remember dates, events, tasks and more. According to numerous reports by journalists across all media, there are some things that we can do for ourselves to slow this process.

Brain puzzles, as I like to think of them include suduko, crossword puzzles, and word searches. I am not a fan of word searches, but love suduko and crosswords. Card games that use strategy to win are also great for the brain. I like Euchre, Rummy, and Pinochle. I am sure there are many others to try if none of these things is your piece of cake.

I stumbled (figuratively this time) across a website called "Mental Floss." This is a very interesting place to visit. The site features facts, quizzes, and trivia. Mental Floss has about 20 million visitors a month to its website. I love the name, mental floss is such a strong image to me, I can see the floss cleaning out the crevices in a brain!!

Do something creative, think outside the box, in fact, stomp on the box and kick it to the side. Draw, write, paint, or sing. The world is yours to conquer. C.S. Lewis, author and essayist wrote, "You are never too old to set another goal or to dream a new dream." Yes, indeed!! Keep challenging yourself and please keep on dreaming!!

SEPTEMBER 29th

Laundry is my least favorite household chore. It is unending. It seems I just finish and there is already more dirty laundry. Having an empty laundry hamper is the best 19 minutes of my week. I am very good at doing laundry. I am a master of laundry. I might even deserve a Doctorate in Laundry. However, I am very bad at putting away the clean laundry. I have a very bad habit of doing the laundry, but not folding and putting away the things that don't have to be hung up. Hence, when I do more laundry, the towels, underwear, socks begins to take on the shape of a very high mountain. Bad girl. I know.

I was taking clothes out of the dryer the other day, and was once again amazed at the amount of lint in the filter. I clean out the filter every time I use the dryer. So I got to thinking……At this point of the story, my close friends are shaking their heads, saying, "Oh, no, here we go again, she's thinking."

With this amount of dryer lint, at some point shouldn't the clothes start disappearing? It might explain the age old mystery when you put a pair of socks in the washer, and only are able to retrieve one out of the dryer. Then the light bulb over my head lit up!! Another mystery has been solved, my clothes are shrinking in the dryer!! I always knew the darn scale was lying to me!!

I hope this has helped. Solving life's mysteries one at a time, that's my mission.

SEPTEMBER 30th

WEEKEND-JUST THE WORD itself can make a gloomy day sunny, can put a smile on the face of almost everyone and is a big piece of wedding cake and ice cream. For the Monday-Friday workers of the world, it is a much-anticipated break from the drudgery of the work week. It looms just over the horizon, a tantalizing chunk of unstructured time beckoning us to come hither. A weekend can be ANY couple of days that a person has that belong to them a little more completely

For informational purposes, for those of you still working, being retired does not dull the luster of the weekend. It seems as if it would not be such a big deal, after all, retired people have a seven-day weekend or so it would seem. But do they really? Inquiring minds might want to know.

Business appointments still need to take place during the normal work week, whether you are retired or not. Bankers, doctors, lawyers, dentists, accountants, you name the profession, they have regular office hours during the week. Another hitch in the giddy-up of the retired is the volunteer work one might decide to do. Family needs, grandchildren, you name it, someone needs you during the week.

So even for the retired, the weekend still promises fewer restrictions and obligations on their time. Sporting events, concerts, leisure time activities often are scheduled on the weekend. Something to look forward to after whatever the weekdays held in store.

There might be 48 hours in a weekend, like any other two days, but their elusiveness still confounds us. Weekends are like holding a pile of sand, no matter what you do, it will slip away, quietly into the past.

OCTOBER 1st

Happy International Coffee Day!! Join me in lifting a mug of the life-saving brew that assists many of us in making it through the day!!

I enjoy meeting friends for coffee and conversation, but ordering coffee these days has become very complicated if you visit a coffee shop. I am far from an expert on all the different options. I have discovered, however, it's good to know what you want before you reach the barista!! Seems like there is also always a line behind me as I stutter and stumble around in my pre-coffee fog trying to order something I will actually be able to drink!

Cappuccino	Latte	Mocha
Mocaccino	Flat White	Americanos
Espresso	Frappes	Coffee- cold or hot

Frappuccino-separating this one, as this name is a Trademarked Starbucks drink, so you might be able to get a similar drink elsewhere, but it won't be called by this name.

Remember the days when we all had a Mr. Coffee on our kitchen counter? We drank it black or with some cream. It wasn't very fancy but it served the purpose. Some might order coffee after dinner when eating out, or gasp, order an Irish coffee. That was the big time.

Now going out for coffee is an event, sometimes social, sometimes part of the daily routine on the way to work or class or everywhere.

Coffee quote of the day:

> Coffee is a beverage that puts one to sleep when not drank.
>
> — Alphonse Allais

OCTOBER 2nd

Do you have one of those old-fashioned, or maybe I should say retro hand mixer that is not powered by electricity but by human power?? The one that has a handle and the two mixing beaters at the bottom, and a handle to turn it?? I do, and it is rarely used, but is a part of some great memories, so keep it I must!!

When my granddaughter Allison was as young as 2 years old, she wanted to help me cook. I wanted to let her do as much as possible, but couldn't let her use the electric mixer. So I purchased the hand mixer and a few other items to make baking and cooking more Allison friendly! If you have little sprites that want to help in the kitchen, I would also recommend the "shot glasses" that are actually liquid measuring cups with teaspoons and tablespoons labeled.

One of our standard morning-after sleepover breakfasts included bacon, eggs, orange juice, and Mickey Mouse pancakes, with chocolate chips to decorate for facial features. She loved helping with those. I was never really sure if she actually liked pancakes, but she definitely loved playing with and eating the chocolate chips.

As she grew older, her baking skills improved, she is a natural!! She is not afraid to try things and can whip up a batch of pretty much anything with no problems. I enjoy letting her take over my kitchen, as I take her former role as the sous chef.

We have made many things over the years since those days; dinners, cookies, pies and more, but the best thing we ever made was memories to last us both a lifetime. Memories never grow stale, don't need refrigeration, and have no expiration date. I keep them filed away in my heart, and frequently pull one out and remember when…

OCTOBER 3rd

CRISPY, crunchy air...clear cool nights and warm sunny days... Bonfires and pots of homemade soups...Farm fields are in various stages of harvest and are gorgeous against the autumnal sky and riotous colors of the trees. The landscape looks like a patchwork quilt of many colors. If October was a color, I would wear it every day. If October was a perfume, it would be refreshing and energizing with a hint of nostalgia. If October was a song, it would be a love song played on an acoustic guitar. If October was a taste it would be apple cider and pumpkin treats. If October was a poem, Robert Frost would have written it. If October had a sound, it would be the golden aspen trees shaking in the wind. October is a celebration for the senses!!

I embrace October and wish it had more than 31 days...says a November birthday girl who if born eight hours earlier would have been a Halloween baby. I might be okay with just missing a Halloween birthday. It would give my friends and enemies alike way too much fodder for jokes about me, and they don't need anymore.

> October made the leaves on Main Street fit for a crown. They dripped from the trees in jewel-toned shades: yellow and orange and fiery red. The cool wind sent a confetti-cluster of leaves down around us.
>
> — NATALIE LLOYD

So many quotes about October, I am not alone in my fondness for this month!! In the 1908 novel, "Anne of Green Gables," Lucy Maud Montgomery wrote, "I'm so glad I live in a world where there are Octobers." Me too, Ms. Montgomery, me too!!

OCTOBER 4th

MERCY ME!! Before I let too many October days pass by, it must be noted that October is National Cookie Month! I am not a big consumer of sweets or desserts. I have many vices, most desserts don't tempt me. However, cookies are in a category all by themselves. The variety, the portability, the perfect size, what is not to like? They are also an easy treat to make.The word cookie evidently originated from the Dutch word koekje.

Many people favor the chocolate chip cookie, which was invented in 1937 by Chef, and owner of a restaurant called the Toll House Inn.

Ruth Wakefield subsequently sold the rights to Nestle's to allow them to print the recipe on their packages of chocolates. Hence, Nestle's Toll House Cookies were born. Mrs. Wakefield was hired as a consultant and received free chocolate for the rest of her life.

It's hard to beat a good chocolate chip cookie! I also enjoy peanut butter cookies and oatmeal cookies. However, one must be aware of raisin cookies masquerading as chocolate chip cookies. I have been fooled more than once. I find it to be a very unpleasant surprise. Raisins should not be baked in cookies, in my opinion. They should be eaten as a snack by themselves, if you must have them!

Have a cookie bake-off!! Share some cookies to celebrate this month. Bag up some cookies to give out to friends, family, the kids in your neighborhood and your local fire and police departments! It will be very much appreciated!

Wishing you a warm chocolate chip cookie kind of day!

OCTOBER 5th

IF YOU ARE LOOKING for a reason to party today, find a teacher!! Today is International Teacher's Day. In my retirement career, as a guest teacher for over a decade, I have so much more appreciation for the job that teachers do. Life is a great deal more complicated than when I was a public school student, and the job of a teacher has certainly followed suit.

Paperwork, reporting, school politics, children with behavior disorders, special individual educational plans, limited funding for necessary supplies, detention, recess duty, lunch duty, school shootings, pay scale, active shooter drills.....and more. The work life of a teacher is fraught with stress, and an unbelievable responsibility not only to educate children, but to protect their very lives.

Fortunately, there are still a great many dedicated educators who show up day after day after day to make a difference in the lives of children. There are still rewards in teaching, knowing that you have made a difference in the life of children. Interactions that a teacher has with students can impact them for the rest of their life.

Take a stroll down memory lane, remember teachers who made a difference in your life or the life of your children. Send a thank you note to any teachers you might be acquainted with.

To all the teachers in my family, my friends, those whose desk chair I have filled as best I could, thank you. What you do for the children of our communities is beyond compare. You prepare them to go out into the world and become mechanics, lawyers, doctors, plumbers, soldiers, electricians, cosmetologists, and teachers. I salute you and will enjoy an adult beverage in honor of you and what you do!!! Give everyone an A and take the day off!! If you need a permission slip, call me...

OCTOBER 6th

HAVE you ever had one of those days when all the puzzle pieces fit together, your underwear and socks match your outfit, when anything seems possible? Yeah, me neither, but every once in awhile, I get close!

I was driving all over the county a few days ago. Sirius Radio had a fist-pumping, barn burning stream of songs. I love singing along in the car. The acoustics are very good, and if I must say so myself, I was in fine voice. I was hitting the high notes, rolling with the low notes and having a grand time. I probably should insert a disclaimer here, for those that don't know me. My singing voice is one of a kind.....the kind that can barely carry a tune. Much to my regret, I am not a good singer. If I could have put in a request before I was born, I would have asked to be a good singer. I guess I was in the wrong line. No wonder I can never pick the right line at the grocery store.

The positive side of this is, I don't let it stop me from singing along to my favorite tunes, at home, in the car, or wherever else I have the opportunity. I am considerate of others, when I am not alone in the car or other places, to turn down the volume and sing softly to myself. It is not the same as belting out a song with Brooks & Dunn, Rascal Flatts, Elvis or Frank, but I don't want to torture those folks within hearing range.

The moral of this story is, as a song popular in the 1970's proclaimed, "If it feels good, do it, do it if it's what you feel." Sing, dance, write, create and live life out loud and in color. Be a Fruit Loop in a bowl of Cheerios. Embrace this gift of life and give the world the best version of yourself everyday...even if your socks don't match your underwear!

OCTOBER 7th

Movie theaters....who doesn't love going to see a story on the big screen?? Of course, the other draw is the movie theater popcorn that is horrible for you, but such a treat. We go to movies somewhat frequently, often matinees, because we can. The price is cheaper and the theater less crowded, sometimes even empty.

Nothing to mar your enjoyment and escape in a fabulous adventure tale or romance or chick flick......insert here the theme song from the movie "Jaws." Please explain to me why a person or persons would choose to sit directly behind me when there are only 15-20 people in the whole place. A regular buffet of seats to choose from...Color me annoyed.

I will admit I do like my personal space, maybe more than some. I don't think it is unreasonable to be irritated when this happens. Especially if said person or persons plans to talk throughout the movie, and occasionally kick my seat...Don't take it personally, but if you do this, I will probably give you a dirty look (or as my granddaughter labels it, my teacher look) and will move.

The best story about this occurred when I went to a movie with some friends, there were 5 of us. We were the ONLY people in the theater. Guess what??? Yes, you got it, someone came in and sat directly behind us. So, my conclusions are: 1) People are clueless, 2) Don't understand social contracts/constraints, 3) They just want to sit by me and are drawn by my magnetic personality!! This whole thing is rather funny to some, but not to me! My space is my space, and your space is your space, and never the twain shall meet! So, the next time you go to the movies (or really anywhere!), think before you sit!!! Don't be a space invader!!

OCTOBER 8th

I HAVE OFTEN WONDERED how my life would have turned out if I had made a different career choice. I was in banking for 27 years, purely by accident!! I loved it and was fortunate to have moved up the ladder nicely, and broke a few glass ceilings along the way. Here are a few unique jobs in today's working world!

Video game tester or Waterslide tester: Self-explanatory jobs and the pay isn't bad for basically "playing" at work!

Live mannequin: Have seen these in large department stores, and even tried it out!! Old Navy in Minneapolis allowed me to get in the display window with one of their live mannequins for about 10 minutes. It was very fun to hear the comments when passers-by realized a couple of the mannequins were real people!

Bounty Hunter-: Cowboy wannabes, this might be for you!

Hippotherapist: Also called therapeutic riding instructors This is the practice of riding horses for therapy, for disabled people of all ages. Perfect job for the lover of horses!

I saved the best for last….Oscar Mayer is always looking for hot doggers: folks to drive their fleet of Weinermobiles. I believe they describe the job as "navigators delivering joy." I would love to do this for a week or so!! Handing out hot dog whistles, enjoying the looks as you drive down the freeway in a vehicle that looks like a hotdog on a bun, singing the song that never gets old, "I wish I were an Oscar Mayer Weiner…"

> Alas for those that never sing, but die with all their music in them.
>
> — OLIVER WENDELL HOLMES, SR.

Find the song in your heart, and sing it out loud and proud for all to hear!!

OCTOBER 9th

TIMING IS EVERYTHING, isn't it? We had planned a weekend trip to travel north about six hours to see some fall foliage. The forecast was promising rain, rain, and more rain, but that did not deter us. We are glass-half-full people, so off we went! I know this will surprise you, but meteorologists are not always accurate...

It was cloudy and overcast, but no rain. We drove the hills and valleys of northern Wisconsin and saw hundreds of miles of the most spectacular fall foliage I have ever seen. There aren't enough superlatives to describe the vibrant array of colors displayed by the trees and other foliage. Around every bend in the road was another vista that deserved exclamations of wonder and delight.

After hiking in the forest at a small park, the park ranger taught us how to throw a tomahawk at a target outside. That was so much fun, and I can't tell you how often I have wished I had this particular skill. I am sure this will come in handy in the future.

After that, we took a drive on the Cranberry Highway. Wisconsin is the second biggest producer of cranberries in the world, behind Massachusetts. We had never seen a cranberry bog, and it was harvest time. A cranberry farmer stopped to talk to us when he saw me posing by the bog for a picture, and shared some information with us.

Ended the day with a stop at Bucks and Berries, the town diner, which offered three kinds of cranberry pie for dessert. We had the Cran-raspberry pie which did not disappoint.

I have learned, you don't have to travel far to have great adventures. Sometimes the greatest treasures are just down the road. Take a drive, take a walk and be open to the sights and sounds of life.

OCTOBER 10th

A FEW YEARS AGO, after moving I decided I wanted to put out a finch feeder and see if I could attract the goldfinches. The American or Eastern Goldfinch is the Iowa state bird, so it seems there should be a good population of them to feed.

So, got the finch feeder and hung it on my deck. It wasn't even 20 minutes and I had a finch having lunch!! I built it and they came….and came….and came…. Sometimes they would come in pairs, but usually the place was standing (or hovering) room only!! So much fun to see the activity and so many birds. I had to fill the feeder frequently, so I put out a second feeder...and they came...and came….and came… Then I added water, and well I think you have the picture.

The goldfinch is a small, somewhat delicate bird, larger than a hummingbird, but equally graceful. Guests marvel at the spectacle when they spot my herds of birds!! I like to think of them as Hawkeye Finches since they are such a nice gold and black.

Unfortunately, my patio is directly under my deck and my feathered friends were leaving me lots of deposits there….I can hose it off easily, but it is still rather annoying. I saw a quote that made me laugh out loud, and although I didn't try this, part of me really wanted to….

> Whenever a bird poops on my car, I eat a plate of scrambled eggs on my front porch, just to let them know what I am capable of.
>
> — UNKNOWN

On your journey today, live a life filled with laughter , love and the promise of what is to come...and don't forget to feed the birds.

OCTOBER 11th

LIFE USED TO BE SIMPLER, I think. We have many modern technological advances and gadgets to help us, but just plain life is harder. I came across this creed that was printed on the back of a grade school report card circa the late 1940s or early 1950s.

"A Creed for Country Girls and Boys"

"I am glad I live in the country, I love its beauty and its spirit. I rejoice in the things I can do for my home and neighborhood.

I believe there is much I can do in my country home. Through studying the best way to do my every-day work I can find joy in common tasks done well. Through loving comradeship, I can help bring into my home the happiness and peace that are always so near us in God's out-of-door world. Through such a home I can help make real to all who pass that way their highest ideal of country life."

I have to admit the first time I read this a song kept circling in my mind. Anyone who is a John Denver fan will probably recall the song, "Thank God I'm a Country Boy."

This was also a time when Deportment was a category you got a grade in!! I am pretty sure if that grade wasn't a B or higher for most students, their home life wouldn't be all that happy for a while!

Simple values, appreciation for work, our surroundings and our family, seems like a good thing to me.

On your journey today, give thanks for the work, family, and surroundings that make you the unique individual you have come to be.

OCTOBER 12th

I CONTINUE to be amazed by the multitude of inventive and wacky ways people choose to entertain themselves and lower their stress levels. As you may remember, we have had a discussion about goat yoga. I thought I had seen everything. I was wrong….so very wrong….Grab the liquid beverage of your choice, take a seat, and let me entertain you with the latest crazy thing I have come across.

Interacting with animals has been shown to comfort and lower stress for people. A farm in upstate New York is offering folks the opportunity to interact with horses and cows in new and different ways. Evidently, cow cuddling is the latest form of therapy. You, too can cuddle with a thousand plus pound farm animal. Cows have a slightly higher body temperature than humans, and a slower heartbeat, so "cuddling" them is very relaxing. I am not sure how you get the cow to lie down so you can rest against them, but I am pretty sure they are not going to do it if they don't want to. I am not sure how I feel about this, but it has to be better and safer than cow yoga. Don't worry goats, I think you've captured the market on animal yoga.

I am obviously making light of this subject, but I have some serious concerns about what is making people need to go to such extremes to be comforted, happy and less stressed. Viggo Mortenson, Author/Actor/Painter/Poet tells us this: "One of the best pieces of advice I ever got was from a horse master. He told me to go slow to go fast. We live as if there aren't enough hours in the day, but if we do each thing calmly and carefully we will get it done quicker and with much less stress."

So, friends, play more, laugh more, don't stress about the things over which you have no control. Respond to hate with forgiveness, respond to anger with peace, respond to the world with joy and love.

OCTOBER 13th

By now, you have grown used to my obsession/fascination with words in the English language. Something I have always thought interesting, is what groups of animals are called. Some cluster names are well known, others not so much. It may also depend on what source is listing the groups. Here are a few of my favorites:

- Convocation of Eagles -doesn't that sound majestic?
- Parliament of Owls - Perfect for the winged wise bird
- Prickle of Porcupines-Pretty clear!
- Thunder of hippopotamuses-Love, love, love this one!!
- Glare of Cats-Cat owners, could this be any truer?
- Shiver of Sharks-no explanation needed
- Scold of Jays-great description for them
- Intrusion of Cockroaches-Invasion might be better, but this works.
- Tower of Giraffes-Descriptive
- Stand of Flamingos- Shout out to the creator of this one!
- Scurry of Squirrels-Alliterative and expressive!
- Quiver of Cobras-Vivid and evocative picture
- Cauldron of Bats-Scary
- Crash of Rhinoceroses-Good visual

Drum roll please.......my favorite and sometimes so relatable to what happens in our nation's capital, year after year.....Congress of Baboons. I did not make this up, I am simply reporting the facts.

There are many more and if I have piqued your curiosity, look 'em up, or make some up yourself!!

Henry David Thoreau said, "The price of anything is the amount of your life you exchange for it." I hope the few minutes you spent reading this today was a fair trade!

OCTOBER 14th

Learning is a lifelong process, at least it should be. I am always on a quest for new things to learn and do. One of my more recent learning adventures was to seek an online ordination and certification to officiate at wedding ceremonies.

It wasn't as easy as it sounds, but it wasn't hard. There were forms to complete about your personal relationship with a church and with religion. An essay was also required, along with a fee for the documentation. I must have passed muster as I was issued a certificate of ordination. I did this, not knowing if I would every actually use it. Little did I know…..

It was only a few months later, that a friend texted me to ask if I would officiate at her son's wedding. My response was, "Are you serious?" Well, she was and I did! This young couple was a delight to work with. It was a small wedding, and the miniscule details didn't matter to them. They said more than once, "We just want to be married." The months flew by, and the big day had arrived. They were nervous, I was nervous, after all, it was the first time for all of us!

I can't begin to tell you how moving it was to stand there with these two young people as they started their life together. Watching them gazing into each other's eyes, observing the joyful tears of the bride and the steadfastness of the groom.

Weddings can take place anywhere, the venue matters not. The act of marriage takes place in the heart. It was an unbelievable honor to participate in the joining of these two hearts. If I never have this opportunity again, I will remember this forever with gratitude. Sometimes learning something new leads to more than you can ever imagine.

OCTOBER 15th

How often can I wax poetic about my favorite season? Frequently, I am sure. This is a warning, read on if you dare. I would call it a spoiler, but I am pretty sure most of you know about autumn.

There are college football games, pumpkins waiting to be carved, scare crows, homecoming parades, corn mazes, and witches. The paintbrush of the Master gives us a glimpse of paradise in the form of intoxicating fall foliage colors.

Picking apples at the orchard, then making a pie. It's time to wear your favorite jeans, jackets and boots. Tis the season to start baking, after your oven has been on sabbatical all summer. (Speaking for myself for sure) Sunny days and crisp, cool nights mean having a crackling fire.

If there is a cold autumn rain, good excuse to stay in and be cozy with a book or some projects. The smell of the roast in the crock pot all day, knowing your dinner prep is done.

TV series shows, old favorites and new surprises are back. Fresh air, rosy cheeks and a brisk walk are on the menu. Find a place to go for a hayrack ride. Watch the cornfields being harvested. Get out your favorite snuggly blankets for the sofa.

> Winter is an etching, spring is a watercolor, summer is an oil painting and autumn is a mosaic of them all.
>
> — Unknown

Discover what you like best about autumn, and partake. Scoop up a big helping of this season and enjoy every moment. Second helpings are encouraged.

OCTOBER 16th

Fondly remembering some of the joys of childhood. I have been a lover of books since my first memory. When I figured out those funny squiggles on the page were words, I was off to the races.

In my early grade school years, I was a huge fan of the the Happy Hollisters. The Happy Hollisters was a series of 33 books based on the author's family. Stories about young siblings going on wild adventures and solving mysteries. Highly unlikely happenings, but just the fuel for my young imagination.

I moved on to the series that still brings a smile to my face and has a special place in my heart, the Nancy Drew, girl detective with a splashy convertible, handsome boyfriend and her tribe of girls. She solved mysteries that baffled local law enforcement! I used to buy the hard copy books at yard sales. Such a triumph, when I found a new one.

While finishing my college education, I wrote a paper for a pop culture class about the Nancy Drew series. Gave me an excuse to re-read some of the books!! I also discovered that Mildred Benson the original author (Carolyn Keene) was the first male or female student to earn a Masters in Journalism at the University of Iowa….my alma mater.

I don't know if I am allowed to talk about comic books in the same breath as these classic children's books. They are called graphic novels in today's world, so I guess I can. Superman all the way!! Could not wait for the new Superman comic book to come out. I so wanted to be Lois Lane or Lana Lang. Loved alliteration even back then. So lovely when I married, my initials became LL….sigh…..dreams do come true!

Curl up with a childhood favorite and remember when….

OCTOBER 17th

RAISE your hand if you have ever shopped at the Dollar Store. Wow, quite a few of you! Actually, I am not surprised, even though I did not discover the Dollar Store for many years after one opened in our area. I didn't really know much about them, or what was available there.

Some years ago, I made my first trip to this amazing place. I don't remember why I went there, but may have accompanied a friend. As I may have mentioned elsewhere, I am not always the fastest car in the race. I was browsing around and saw some things I could use. There were no prices on anything, so I looked for an employee to ask how much something was. I am sure my surprise was evident when she had to tell me several times, "Everything is one dollar." What??? How is that possible? Sure saves them a lot of time putting prices on things!!

I was flabbergasted at what one could buy for a dollar. Everything from dishes to groceries, to toys, books, and a myriad of other items. It is a great resource to those people with fixed or limited income.

Everything you might need isn't available, but you can get many basic household items.

After my first visit, I stop in every once in a while. I may not always be the brightest, but you do not have to hit me over the head when I figure something out!! It is a great place to get party items, artificial flowers for the cemetery, inexpensive gifts for that Christmas saran wrap ball or gift exchange. This would also be a good stop to pick up small Christmas items to donate to the Salvation Army or some other organization that provides gifts for children and adults.

One single dollar for any item in the store.....amazing!!

OCTOBER 18th

On a recent, very long road trip, I had ample opportunity to see lots of interesting song titles on the Sirius Radio screen. Country songs definitely win the award for funniest titles. Willie Nelson says, "Three chords and the truth-that's what a country song is." Here we go, a list of "interesting" song titles and the icons who sang them!

"I've Been Flushed from the Bathroom of Your Heart" Johnny Cash

"Sick, Sober and Sorry" George Jones & Merle Haggard

"Wine Me Up" Faron Young

"If the Phone Doesn't Ring, It's Me" Jimmy Buffett

"All My Exes Live in Texas" George Strait

"Friends in Low Places" Garth Brooks

"Here's a Quarter-Call Someone Who Cares" Travis Tritt

"To All the Girls I've Loved Before" Willie Nelson

"She Thinks My Tractor's Sexy" Kenny Chesney

As Waylon Jennings said, "Country music isn't a guitar, it isn't a banjo, it isn't a lyric. It's a feeling." I agree, country music is about love, life, loss, family, patriotism and so much more.

On your journey today, turn up the music, belt out the songs and have a good time!!

OCTOBER 19th

Several things occurred to me while I was out among the populace running errands. Errands are my least favorite thing to do, particularly when there are multiple stops. I usually end up skipping one or more, as I did today. Today's undone errand was stopping at the grocery to pick up milk. Doesn't sound like a hard task for a college educated, semi-bright woman. However, after all the other errands, I did not want to traipse through a busy store to the farthest corner, almost in the stockroom refrigerator case where they hide the milk. So I skipped it.

This made me think, if someone came up with a drive-through window where you could get milk, bread, and eggs, I would be all over that. I can drive through the bank and get money. I can drive through the pharmacy and get medicine, and I can drive through McDonald's and get a coffee. This leads me to a confession. I may have, in desperation, in the past, driven through McDonald's and ordered two pints of milk that would get me through breakfast. I may or may not have been in my pajamas. Pathetic, I know!

The other random thought I had, which is not all connected to the milk crisis involves statues of deer in yards along the highway. First of all, we have more than plenty of real deer. Secondly, when the deer statue is placed just peeking out of a shrub or tree, my heart stops for a brief moment, thinking a deer is about to run across the road. I have had this happen too many times to consider the above event humorous. I totaled a car during one deer encounter. If you must have the deer statue(s), tie a bow around the neck, hang some lights on it, or put a Hawkeye sweatshirt on it...anything to show the innocent drivers passing by that it is not real. Drivers in the Heartland will thank you.

Wishing you a day of random thoughts and silly ideas!

OCTOBER 20th

TODAY'S TOPIC is one I have been pondering; things I will never understand. That is potentially one long list, so I will narrow it down and just share a few with you. Feel free to create your own list!!

Television-I personally choose to believe it is magic. My un-scientific mind does not understand how I can turn on this device, and instantly see pictures and sound that are happening live (or recorded) from thousands of miles away. The more I think about it, the more it confounds and astounds me.

Cat Videos-Evidently, there are people who watch hours of cat videos on Youtube or other sketchy sources. I do not understand the fascination. I am secretly a little afraid of cats, they are sneaky.

Car Bumper Stickers-I admit I have seen some hilarious ones. I don't understand the desire to stick something on your car that proclaims where your child goes to middle school, how many people/animals are in your family, somebody is an honor student, honk for Jesus and you supported Al Gore in an election decades ago.

Personalized License Plates-Some I have seen are very cute or clever. But I question who wants to drive around with a license plate that says, "Wifey," or "Palehoz," (took me years to figure out that was for the White Sox baseball team), or "GR8." In this part of the country, many proclaim their allegiance to the University of Iowa or Iowa State University. I admit I have been tempted to get some version of the University of Iowa Alumni on my plates, but that would be bragging…

I do believe that we are not meant to understand everything. I am trying to do my part to prove that statement true. I am a living, breathing example of puzzled!!

OCTOBER 21st

HOW OFTEN DO you check your junk email for spam? How often do you check your cupboard for Spam? Interesting that a junk email blast and a canned meat product have the same name...at least to me…

Some of the younger audience reading this might be confused, if so go to your local grocery store and find a can of Spam to purchase.

Spam, the meat, not to be confused with spam the mail, originated in 1937 and became a popular food product. Spam, the meat is made of pork and ham and other stuff. Spam, the mail would be more of a junk food. Spam, the meat has not had the best reputation in current times, but that is totally undeserved. It's a handy meal in a can, you don't have to cook it and the shelf life is good. Sources vary in their opinion about where the word Spam came from, but it appears to originate from the words "SPiced hAM."

Once you have introduced yourself or revisited your relationship with Spam, the meat, you will want to make a trip to Austin, Minnesota to the….wait for it…. the Spam Museum. Seriously….I can't make this stuff up. It is 14,000 square feet of Spam fun….and admission is free….yes, I said free!! Warning: If you sign the visitor log and give your email, you will probably get spam the email about Spam, the meat.

If that wasn't enough thought provoking information for you, did you know that ¾ of the people make up 75% of the population in the United States today. It is having access to information like this has made me who I am today.

On your journey today, stock up on Spam, the meat, delete spam, the mail and set your navigation system for Austin, Minnesota.

OCTOBER 22nd

LET me tell you about a love story today. It is about my love for the land I was born to and will never leave (except for traveling!). My roots are here, and they are deep. It would take many pages to tell about all the wonderful reasons to live here, raise a family here, retire here, and well….enough about that.

Iowa is the land between two rivers, the mighty and majestic Mississippi and the Missouri. It is a land of contradictions and contrasts, both geographically and culturally. We are a world leader in corn and hog production while welcoming writers, poets, Broadway plays, the Joffrey Ballet and Presidents, past and future.

The scenery in this beautiful state has something for everyone.

The bluffs in the northeastern part of the state, the river valleys, the gently rolling hills, the flatlands in the western region and of course the two rivers that border our state providing beauty and entertainment for many. If driving through our great state, get off of the interstate and take the state highways and county roads. That is where you will see the real Iowa.

Eat a Maid-rite or a loose meat sandwich at the local diner, or have a hand breaded pork tenderloin the size of a dinner plate. If you dare, top it off with homemade pie and ice cream. Strike up a conversation with one of us, we are very friendly! If you have car trouble here, no worries, we will call a tow truck, give you a lift, feed you lunch and pack a snack for the rest of your journey. If your timing is good, you might even get some homemade bread and a Scotcharoo!!

Feeling thankful, for this beautiful land I call home and the many fascinating characters who populate my life.

OCTOBER 23rd

ANOTHER THING I love about fall is baking foods related to the season. My family is particularly fond of pumpkin bread. My recipe makes 3 loaves and it will be gone in a day or less. One grandson in particular, not to mention any names, (Josh) can devour a loaf on his own. He is a tall young man without an ounce of fat on his body. That is so annoying.

The lovely, rotund pumpkin is actually a fruit, not a vegetable. Many fruits that are not sweet are called or considered vegetables. Most people use pumpkin as a vegetable. It may not be sweet on it's own, but enhanced with spices and sugar in the recipe it is a sweet treat. Warm from the oven, or slightly warmed in the microwave, with or without some butter on it, is a gastronomic treat for the taste buds.

The recipe I use came from my great-aunt Gladys forty some years ago.

Pumpkin Bread by Aunt Gladys

Ingredients: 3 ½ c flour, 2 tsp baking soda, 1 ½ tsp salt, 1 tsp cinnamon, 1 tsp nutmeg, 3 c sugar. 1 c Wesson oil, 4 eggs, ⅔ c water, 2 c canned pumpkin.

Mix ingredients in order, bake in 3 greased loaf pans at 350 degrees for 45 minutes to 1 hour, depending on your oven and how full the loaf pans are. It rises quite a bit, so I never fill the pans more than half full. This also freezes well, cool well and put in a gallon freezer bag.

Since pumpkin is the flavor mascot of autumn, it's a great treat to bake and share with family and friends. Bake some batches, share them around and you will be the Pumpkin Queen of October!

OCTOBER 24th

TODAY FEELS like another day dedicated to a letter of the alphabet. Let's talk about "Z" today. It is nice that the last letter of the alphabet has numerous words that are fun to say and use. Unlike his brother "X," who really struggles to have as many words, and certainly not ones that are useful in everyday conversation.

Zigzag	Zip code
Zany	Zoom
Zip	Zest (not the soap or the recipe kind)
Zumba	Zap
Zed	Zippy
Zebra	Zinger
Zombie	Xylophone-oops that's an X word
Zodiac	Zero

I could go on, but don't want to overwhelm you with "Z" words to use today. I wonder who decided "Z" should be the last letter in the alphabet. Why not the first or seventeenth? Another question for the universe. I imagine there might be some intellectual answer for the question, but that would be no fun., and as you may have noticed by now, this is not exactly an intellectual collection of essays.

On your journey today, zoom around your zipcode doing zigzags and shouting zingers to zebras and zombies. Or, alternatively, use a couple of these fun words today and do your best to put some zest in your day!

OCTOBER 25th

DREAMS ARE stories we tell ourselves, asleep or awake. I marvel at the miracle of the brain to do this, and millions of other things! There are lots of great songs about dreams, but none fit the dream I am about to reveal to you!

I have a recurring dream that I have had for thirty years or more. It is not a happy or relaxing dream, quite the opposite. I worked at our Heartland grocery store, Hy-Vee when I was in high school and college, for five years. Loved working there, still think of that job fondly, friends made, the fun we had, the customers.

The dream that I have usually starts with a vacation of some sort. I might be on a plane, at the pool, in a hotel, the venue varies. The one scenario I remember most vividly starts on an airplane. I am headed somewhere on vacation, when the cabin crew calls my name and asks me to come to the front of the plane. What awaits me there, is a cash register, and a long line of customers waiting to have their grocery order checked out. I am upset and frustrated, why did they call me up to check out? But what is one to do? My Hy-Vee customer service training is pretty ingrained, so I start checking out the grocery orders.

I wake up from this dream, exhausted...of course I do, I have been working all night!!

I have no idea what this dream means, if anything. It is part of my life because I have probably dreamed some version of this hundreds of times. It would appear if I was smarter, I wouldn't go to the front of the plane when my name is paged, but clearly I haven't learned!!

My wish for you, is that all the dreams and goals you have come true. Keep your heart and mind open to the possibilities.

> She (He) turned her can'ts into cans and her dreams into plans.
>
> — UNKNOWN

OCTOBER 26th

IT SEEMS like today is a good day to share some more stories about my second career, my guest teacher appearances at a middle school. The kids are so amazing, funny, sometimes challenging but worth every moment I get to spend with them. It is a privilege to have the opportunity to help them learn and maybe make a difference.

I decided to have some red added to my hair, but it didn't really work out. I had some streaks in my hair but not what was planned. The next day I am off to spend my day with 6th graders. This group is really my favorite age. One of the boys came up to me and said, "Did you dye your hair?" I replied, "I didn't do it myself, but someone else dyed my hair." He quickly realized he had the answer to the situation when he replied, "Was it a prank?" Color me deflated, but amused!!

Another day in the sixth grade (yes I keep going back for the punishment), the students were lined up to leave for the day. One gentleman was bouncing a basketball. I asked him to stop bouncing the ball in the classroom. He replied, "I'm not bouncing it, I am dropping it repeatedly." Seriously, these kids are quick on the rebound.

Last 6th-grade story for the day again involves a boy. Hmmm....is there a pattern here? I was explaining something in the lesson, and made a comment about "100 years ago when I was in middle school." We had a little more discussion, and a student raised his hand. When I called on him, he said, " Ohhhh, Mrs. Lacina, I don't think you are one hundred."

A compassionate little guy, although it appeared he didn't think I was that far off from that grand age.

I have to agree with Angela Bennett who said, "Teaching middle school is an adventure, not a job." I couldn't agree more!!

OCTOBER 27th

I AM sure that by now, you may have realized I am a very flexible person, and understanding of the foibles of the general public. If this is your opinion, you are so wrong!! Everybody has a goof up in public once in awhile, but my issue is with the group I will call "clueless."

Today's rant is about people who shop in herds. I will come across groups of anywhere from 5-11 people shopping together at the mall, or the grocery store, or the bank (well, maybe not the bank). Clueless at the mall. They are totally unaware of their surroundings, and how much physical space they occupy as they inch their way down the mall corridor. If I were a little better at algebra, I would calculate the area they take up. Most of these herds resemble an ellipse, in their shape and formation. I am not fast enough to figure that out while the ellipse is moving. I wonder if they would stop if I asked. Although, the average speed of a ellipse shaped herd is not quantifiable in any speed measurement I know.....color them slow.

Ignoring the fact that they take up the entire allotment of space for pedestrians, how do they accomplish anything? When one needs a restroom stop, do they all participate? Are they all interested in shopping for the same items? As you can tell, I find this concept very confusing and inefficient

Merriam Webster Dictionary: "Herd-A typically large group of animals of one kind kept together under human control. A congregation of gregarious wild animals.

On your journey today, break free from the herd and express your uniqueness.

> You laugh because I'm different. I laugh because you're all the same.
>
> — QUOTESLIFE101.NET

OCTOBER 28th

TODAY IT'S YOUR TURN. Fill this page with thoughts, sketches, doodles, ideas, it's all up to you.

There are 86,400 seconds in a day. It's up to you to decide what to do with them.

— COACH JIM VALVANO

OCTOBER 29th

THERE ARE SO many quotes that I hold close to my heart, and knowing I can't work them all into the remaining days of this epistle, here are some of the best.

"Make me aware that there is more to life than measuring its speed." The Quiet Mind Calendar, 1964

"The violets in the mountains have broken the rocks." Tennessee Williams, Playwright and University of Iowa graduate

"When you pass through the waters, I will be with you; and when you pass through the rivers they will not sweep over you. When you walk through the fire you will not be burned; the flames will not set you ablaze." Isaiah 43:2

"Walking with a friend in the dark is better than walking alone in the light." Helen Keller, Author and Activist

"Worry does not empty tomorrow of its sorrow, it empties today of its strength." Corrie ten Boom, Dutch watchmaker, writer and rescuer of Jews during WWII

"Birds sing after a storm; why shouldn't people feel as free to delight in whatever sunlight remains to them?" Rose Fitzgerald Kennedy, Philanthropist

"You may have to fight a battle more than once to win it." Margaret Thatcher, Former Prime Minister of the United Kingdom

"May you build a ladder to the stars and climb on every rung. May you stay forever young." Bob Dylan, Songwriter and Author

OCTOBER 30th

MANY YEARS AGO, before Rachel Ray had her own daily cooking show and became a well-known TV personality, she had a show called "Thirty Minute Meals." I really enjoyed the show, the recipes seemed simple enough and thirty minutes seemed like a pretty easy dinner.

I went to the store and purchased all the ingredients to make apricot chicken. Looked delicious on TV, and I thought we would really enjoy that. I chopped onion, dried apricots, and parsley. Had the required apricot preserves, chicken and other items standing by. I was ready to go.

Looking back, I am not really sure where I went wrong. I don't know what kind of stove she had, but my chicken was not browned in 10 minutes, or fully cooked in another 15. Frustrated, kept checking the chicken, calling to my husband in the other room, that dinner would be a little longer in the making. Finally, the chicken seemed cooked and added the other ingredients, simmered and served it.

The dish was delicious and we really enjoyed it. Total prep and cooking time for this Iowa chef, one hour and thirty minutes. I am wearing that like a badge of honor. It isn't everyone who can take 90 minutes to cook a 30-minute meal.

I enjoy cooking and am not half bad as a cook, but I do have adventures in the kitchen sometimes. As long as they are just adventures, not epic fails, I am good with that. I may need to heed some advice from the great chef, Julia Child: "I enjoy cooking with wine...Sometimes I even put it in the food." It's always wise to take advice from those who are at the top of their field!!

OCTOBER 31st

Happy Halloween!! I find celebrations of Halloween very strange. It is not a holiday I embrace, although I will admit as a child, the prospect of running around in the dark asking strangers for candy was quite exciting. The origins of this holiday, which I have limited knowledge about, was All Hallows Eve, the day before All Hallows Day, or also known as All Saints Day (my birthday, go figure.)

Superstitions abound concerning this day, many with origins in ancient times. Many have been "modernized" to fit today's times, and all are pretty silly. I am not a superstitious person, although I do believe spirits (not ghosts) are all around.

Now it is confession time...I have put in my time over the years, answering the doorbell every 28 seconds from 4:30 PM until 9:00 PM.

I have been chased down by crazy costumed children as I carried groceries into my house after work on Halloween. I have had my candy examined disdainfully, apparently not "treat worthy." Hey, kid, it's free candy, get a grip.

Here, is where it gets real. I make a point of not being home on Halloween these days, or I hide in my house with the lights off and watch television. I shudder as I hear the screams of all the ghouls and goblins running amok in the neighborhood. My name is Lori, and I am a fun hater....at least on Halloween!!

> Shadows of a thousand years rise again unseen, voices whisper in the trees, 'Tonight is Halloween.'
>
> — Dexter Kozen

On your journey, don't leave your broom in a no parking space, watch out for flying monkeys, and feel free to stop in for a spell.....

NOVEMBER 1st

Happy Birthday to me!! This is the oldest I have ever been....and unfortunately the youngest I will ever be again!! Or as I have been known to tell people, this is the anniversary of the day the world was graced with my presence. Feel free to use this version, it always elicits some kind of response!! I don't mind getting older, age is just a number, albeit a BIG number in my case. My stated age is 50 plus shipping and handling. (And we know how much that can add up to...)

And before you ask, no, you may not see my drivers license.

I am also celebrating National Author's Day. Yes, there is a holiday for pretty much everything, but this one is special to me, and falls on my birthday.

Age is a state of mind. It is your passion for life and love. It is letting your inner child come out to play now and then. It is skipping in the parking lot on the way to the grocery store. It is laughing, loving, sharing and caring. It is letting joy fill your heart and soul every day. So live each moment as if it is your last. We never know on what page of the Book of Life our story will end.

Celebrate your birthday the entire month!! Why not? Drink in every ounce of moments and memories, family and friends. Enjoy the cake and ice cream, cards and gifts! Get ready for another amazing trip around the sun.

Let me leave you with this quote today in celebration of all of our birthdays:

> Youth is a gift of nature, but age is a work of art.
>
> — Stanislaw Jerzy Lec

NOVEMBER 2nd

I HAVE MENTIONED that I am a quilter. Creating something beautiful gives me pleasure. It is productive, and the results are tangible. Spending time in my quilting studio is a little like meditation for me. I get in the zone of creation, it calms me and I have no sense of time. I am usually making a quilt for loved ones, someone who needs a boost or for charity. This is amazing to me that I can let go like that. I am pretty much a Type A personality, very time and schedule conscious.

There are so many ways we can express our creativity and feelings. Knitting, crocheting, drawing, embroidery to name a few. I have done all of those activities at one time or another in my life....except drawing. No one wants to see my lack of artistry in that category. Stick figures drawn badly are not a welcome gift.

My latest outpouring of creative work is, of course, this book. It is one of the most satisfying projects I have ever undertaken. The hours, weeks, months spent on this were wonderful. I don't consider writing work. It has become one of my greatest joys. The aspect that is not a joy are the logistics that happen after the writing to bring this book to life. Necessary but definitely not a walk in the park. I might compare it to cooking or baking. I love making things in the kitchen, but detest the dreaded clean up that follows.

Find an outlet for your creativity, dust off some old skills, take a class and learn some new skills. It will reward you in ways that you can't begin to imagine. Don't give up, the world needs you and your unique perspective and talents. Beverly Sills, internationally renowned opera singer said it well, "There are no shortcuts to any place worth going."

NOVEMBER 3rd

It's not a secret that I like lists, so let's make today a list day!!

I am thinking about the top 4 or 5 in different categories. So grab a pen and notebook, and make your lists along with me!!

Books: This is a tough one, as there are many books I love, and re-read.

1. "Little Women" by Louisa May Alcott
2. "Gone With the Wind" by Margaret Mitchell
3. The Women's Murder Club series by James Patterson
4. Agatha Christie books, Miss Marple editions
5. Marie Bostwick, The Cobbled Court Quilt Series

Movies: This is almost impossible, I have a large collection of movies and re-watch many of them. So this is pretty random.

1. "Bride Wars"
2. "The Book Club"
3. "Mama Mia" Original and the sequel
4. "The Perfect Murder"

Foods: This is easier.

1. Pizza (hold the pepperoni, please)
2. Italian
3. Mexican
4. Comfort food, ie mashed potatoes, meatloaf, potato soup, chili

Songs:

1. Elvis…. Anything he sings, particularly the ballads.
2. "Jealous of the Angels" Donna Taggart
3. "Heavenly Day" Patty Griffin
4. "Bless the Broken Road" Rascal Flatts

So, whatever it is you enjoy; drench yourself in it, share it, revel in it live life out loud!!

NOVEMBER 4th

I LOVE WATCHING MOVIES!! I love going to the theater, despite what you may remember from last month about one of my personal space issues!! I have a nice DVD collection and will re-watch a movie countless times if I like it. The nice thing about getting a little older is that I am sure at some point I won't remember them and they will all be new again.

Here are some of my favorite movie quotes:

"Houston, we have a problem." *Apollo 13,* 1995

"Frankly, my dear, I don't give a damn." *Gone With the Wind*, 1939

"I'm one stomach flu away from my goal weight."

The Devil Wears Prada, 2006

"You're going to need a bigger boat." *Jaws*, 1995

"If you build it, they will come." *Field of Dreams*, 1989

"Toto, I've got a feeling we're not in Kansas anymore."

"*The Wizard of Oz" 1939*

"May the force be with you." *Star Wars*, 1977

Some movie quotes strike a note with audiences, and those quotes become part of our daily language, often for decades. A few weeks ago, in anticipation of seeing *Gone with the Wind* in the movie theater for an 80th anniversary showing, a group of my friends were texting our favorite quotes from the movie in a very long group text!! Some movies and quotes you never forget.

Take a stroll down memory lane and try to recollect the iconic quotes from your favorite movies. Rustle up some popcorn, watch some of your favorites again and enjoy!

NOVEMBER 5th

As a native English speaking person, I feel I have the right to poke fun, ridicule, question, and guffaw about the idiosyncrasies of the English language. The only problem I face is where to start, there is so much material!!

840 million people speak English as their first or second language. That alone is a testament to the intellect of people worldwide who can learn and understand this crazy language!

The first thing I thought of when writing this, was the prefix "de." It generally means to undo something, ie: deemphasize, decompose, destruct. Following that train of thought, the word "delight" should mean to "unlight" something, when it really means something quite the opposite. My definition of delight is to fill someone with something wonderful in some way, in fact something that might make them "light up!"

When trying to achieve something, having a "fat chance" or a "slim chance" means the same thing. Doesn't seem right!! I would love to have a fat chance to win the lottery or have a best selling book!!

Another favorite of mine is that the long bone in your upper arm that connects with your elbow is called the humerus. That screams funny bone to me. Although when you whack your elbow, it's really nerves, not a bone that makes you wince, grimace or involuntarily exclaim in pain!

Thinking I should end this little frolic through the English language with a quote that I have enjoyed for years: "If the English language made any sense, lackadaisical would have something to do with a shortage of flowers." Doug Larson, Columnist and Editor

NOVEMBER 6th

I RECENTLY WATCHED a video that a friend had posted on Facebook.

It was done by a man named Bill Hart, and he shared a story, that he called "shoulder taps." The idea behind the story is that sometimes God taps us on the shoulder to get our attention, and "encourage" us to do something. As Mr. Hart was leaving a restaurant, he felt compelled to speak to an older lady he observed, who was all dressed up for a family dinner, and told her how lovely she looked. She was very touched and told Mr. Hart that her late husband would have said the very same thing to her.

This story hit home with me. I am from Iowa. We talk to people we don't know, perfect strangers in fact, and before you say it, no, most of them do not call the police. I started doing this about 10 years ago. Whenever I see a member of the military, or a police officer, fireman, I walk over and thank them for their service.

I branched out, and will tell someone their dress is pretty, or that they have a lovely family. Who among us couldn't use a boost on almost any day, but some more than others? This story made me think that I need to pay closer attention when I have the instinct to speak to someone. I think God has been tapping me on the shoulder.

I think God is tapping you on the shoulder as well. Follow your heart and instincts when you feel the need to say some kind words, help a harried mother in the grocery store, or pay for someone's meal.

On your journey, today, take note when the Keeper of the stars gives you a nudge or taps you on the shoulder. It's the way that the world becomes a better place, one act of love and kindness at a time.

NOVEMBER 7th

My retirement career as a substitute teacher, or as the schools label us now, a guest teacher has been rewarding in so many ways. This is not to say that there aren't any days when the behavior of middle school age students makes me want to run screaming from the building in search of a vodka tonic. Fortunately, these days are smaller in number than the good days.

Sixth grade might secretly be my favorite. Time spent with this group is delightful and usually educational. When they learn and I learn it's a good day. I thought I would share with you titles of some of their free reading books I spy on their desks as I walk around the classroom.

"The Christmas Dog," The Odd Squad," and last but not least, my personal favorite, "The Teacher's Funeral: A 3 Part Comedy." Good thing they like me….I think…

Seventh grade is fun and educational in a different way. They challenge me every day. I secretly enjoy the ornery boys and they do make me laugh in spite of their distracting behavior that sometimes earns them detention. A seventh-grade boy asked me for a band-aid one day. I asked him why he needed one. His answer: "I scraped my knee falling for you." How can you not laugh at that??

There is also a sweetness in the seventh graders as I see glimpses of the adult they will become. I observed a young lady sitting in a chair before class, in front of the flag with her hand over her heart, humming the "Star Spangled Banner." They do melt my heart frequently!

I am thankful for the opportunity to touch these young lives and hope that once in a while I can make a difference.

NOVEMBER 8th

I MAY HAVE MENTIONED I was a voracious reader as a child. I have two very distinct memories of "special" books read when I was eleven or twelve.

The first book was "Gone With The Wind," famous classic by Margaret Mitchell. I was staying at my Grandmother Detweiler's house during the summer. She had a copy of the book, large, beautiful hardback that was illustrated with beautiful color pictures from the movie, featuring Clark Gable and Vivian Leigh. I discovered it one day in an upstairs bedroom and began reading it. I couldn't read it fast enough!

Upon taking the book downstairs, Grandma saw what I was reading, and commented on her uncertainty if I was old enough/mature enough to read such a risque (in those days) novel. I think she was worried if my mom would approve. She asked me if I understood it and I answered yes. That was enough for her and she let me read it, and even gave me the book to keep. I still have it and it is a beloved treasure.

The second memory is staying with my cousin Sandy, on the farm her parents lived on. Her mother, Barb, had lots of books she gave us to read. We would take a pile of books, some blankets, and snacks and go to a wooded area on their farm and while the summer afternoons away.

I can't remember any specific books, but I remember how much I loved all the books and her encouragement to spend time reading. My Aunt Barb died at a very young age, and I have so many memories of her. She was very special to all who knew her.

Do you have memories connected to books or reading? If not, no time like the present to make some with children or grandchildren. They will remember those times with fondness forever. Oscar Wilde is quoted as saying, "It is what you read when you don't have to that determines what you will be when you can't help it."

NOVEMBER 9th

"FILL your paper with the breathings of your heart." William Wordsworth. I have tried to do this, between the silly stories and my misadventures, I have spoken to you from my heart. I have shared happy and sad moments and my feelings about lots of things. There is such a thing as over-sharing, and please accept my apologies for that!!

If you have any inkling in your heart that you would like to write something, I hereby give you permission to write like nobody's reading!! This is the easy part!! As I neared completion of this book, I began to realize that people, yes, even people I don't know are going to read my ramblings. That's enough to put you off your feed!!

Write a daily paragraph in a journal. Sometimes I write a word that I like (I have a whole page of those, and as you might have noticed I have been sharing them with you!!) If you come across a quote that strikes a note in your heart, write it down. Road trips can be great for writing inspiration.

Writing is not for everyone, and life is too short to do something you dislike!! But if you like to write, even a little bit, do it!! It is cathartic, it is creative, it is satisfying. There are lots of resources out there, books with writing prompts and ideas to get you started. It's never too late to try something new!!! Good for your brain and good for you!!

On your journey today, take some advice from Benjamin Franklin: "Either write something worth reading, or do something worth writing."

Well said, Mr. Franklin, well said!

NOVEMBER 10th

Do you enjoy an occasional meal of Chinese food? I certainly have for many years, but alas, something has gone amiss in the world of Chinese take out or eat in!! What is going on with fortune cookies?? There is no longer a fortune for you to ponder or aspire to, but merely a statement. Here are some typical "fortunes"...

A person is never too old to learn.

Don't confuse recklessness with confidence.

You have a friendly heart and are admired.

A friend asks only for your time not your money.

Seriously?? Those are not fortunes!!I want to break open that cookie and be amazed and excited by what may be in store for me! Maybe I could get a job as a fortune cookie writer...Here are a few of mine:

Take a walk tonight, love is waiting for you around the corner if you take the right turn…

You will live a very long life. Buy new towels.

Great wealth is in store for you. Buy a lottery ticket today!

A tall, dark, handsome/beautiful man/woman wants to meet you. Wait by the front door, I get off at 9:00.

On your journey today, eat some Chinese, stand up for your rights and demand a more meaningful fortune in your cookie.

NOVEMBER 11th

SALUTE to all veterans on their official holiday today. Happy Veteran's Day!! This holiday originated in 1919, to celebrate the end of WWI and was called Armistice Day. An interesting fact is that WWI ended on the 11th hour of the 11th day of the 11th month, in 1918. I find numbers that come together like that so fascinating. By chance or by choice, still meaningful.

On June 1, 1954, this date became a national holiday called Veteran's Day, a day that honors all military veterans of the United States. In Britain, Canada and South America, there are two minutes of silence at the 11th hour (United Kingdom time) to commemorate the time the armistice became effective. I like traditions that celebrate or commemorate our history. A quote that holds so much truth and has been paraphrased in many ways. It seems the original quote was from George Santayana, philosopher, writer and Harvard professor. "Those who do not learn history are doomed to repeat it." Unfortunately, sometimes even when we learn history, we seem unable to avoid making the same poor decisions again.

American history, as well as the history of the world, needs to be learned, celebrated, revered, reviled but not changed or forgotten. I don't think it's appropriate to remove statues of those important in our history. Times change, society changes, people change, but the events that made us who we are as a nation do not change and should be remembered and taken in the context of the era.

Thank a veteran for their service today, and every day. They have been the sentinels of our liberties and freedom since our revolutionary ancestors took on the British. The price of liberty is high, and these veterans have paid the bill for us.

NOVEMBER 12th

CAUTION: The following material may be offensive and hazardous to the mental health of any men who are reading this.

I decided it would be fun to take a random inventory of my purse (or as my dad calls it, my suitcase) and share it with you. So here goes, don't judge me, I am being totally honest here, and am frankly a little scared about what I might find.

In no particular order:

Verizon receipt
Trident cinnamon gum
Wadded up napkin
Lipstick
Travel hand lotion
Neon colored note cards
UIHC letter
Bottle of Zantac
Ibuprofen
St. Christopher Medallion
Underwear in a ziplock baggie
Travel toothbrush
Eye drops
Immodium
Benadryl
Pepcid AC
Wallet

Kleenex
73 cents
Phone
Pink highlighter
2 pens
Shout Wipe & Go
Crystal nail file
Business cards
Appt. calendar
iPad
Book
Travel manicure set
Granola bar
Mini box cutter
Tylenol Sinus
Raspberry Soft Lips
Keys

Crazy conglomeration isn't it? I do like to be prepared, you never know when you might have a simultaneous sinus/gastrointestinal attack with achy muscles in conjunction with a snownado that prevents you from getting home. For those of you laughing, wait til it happens to you!

NOVEMBER 13th

SINCE IT IS NOVEMBER, and the whole month of November should be a celebration of my birthday...notice the word should...never happens...but a girl can dream…..It seems only right that this month should be brought to you by one of my favorite letters "L." The family of words that begin with L is a loveable and likeable family. Here are some of my favorite "L" words.

Lilt	Levitate	Lark-2 meanings, both good
Libation	Liquidate	Legible
Lampoon	Linguistics	Lackadaisical
Language	Lanyard	Litigious

When was the last time you got together with friends and went for a lark and indulged in some libations? Just make sure you don't get involved in anything that could result in libel or litigation. Not likely, I'm sure.

On your journey today, embrace your inner child, be kind to all you meet, and take the high road, the view is spectacular!

NOVEMBER 14th

I THINK FONDLY of the days when my grandkids were much younger, and any activity or game I came up with made them think I was magical.

Sigh.....how quickly they grow up. Remembering those times, I thought I would share some ideas with you for your younger family members.

An easy activity is to create personalized word searches. The word search makers allow you to choose the words for the puzzle, how many words, and sometimes even a seasonal shape for the puzzle. I would include family names, pets, favorite foods, holidays. There are many websites that will help you create puzzles.

Christmas was one of the great times to use this. It would give my grandkids something to do between dinnertime, and the highlight of the evening for them, opening gifts. They love finding their names and other familiar items.

Treasure hunts that begin with a piece of different colored yarn for each participant that criss-cross and travel all around the house to find a treasure at the end, or clues to keep the game going. I am not sure who had more fun with this, but it was probably me. Seeing their excitement at having an adventure lit up my world. Spending time focused on them, is something they will never forget. Sometimes that means watching "The Lion King" 217 times, and loving it each and every time!

Grandchildren are the fountain of youth, the chocolate chips in the cookie, and a glimpse of heaven. They are picnics and tea parties. They are the reason to get up every morning and the reason the world goes round. They are the spring in my step and the flowers in my garden. Grandchildren are the love that fills in all the empty spots in your heart. Grandchildren, my favorite hello, and my hardest good-bye.

NOVEMBER 15th

EXCITING NEWS FOR YOU TODAY!! I bet you didn't know that today is a holiday for you to celebrate!! Welcome to Clean Out Your Refrigerator Day. I promise, I do not make these up!! Just goes to show you, that there are so many reasons to celebrate, big and small, let's celebrate them all!!

The origins of this holiday are unknown. Some claim that the Whirlpool Corporation started this special day. It seems very strange to me that anyone would think of this!! There are just so many ways to go with this, and none of them are good!!

Finding unknown, long forgotten objects in the refrigerator is the stuff of nightmares for me. I have a pretty high pain tolerance. I am a strong person. If you are bleeding profusely or being sick, I am not bothered and can take care of you. But if I find a container with moldy or otherwise spoiled food in the fridge, it is all over. I will not wash that container, it will go in the trash. I have no emotional attachment to any of these dishes. Done, over, moving on.

A clean, sparkling refrigerator is a thing of beauty. There are several ways this can happen: 1) Do it yourself. 2) Hire a cleaning service to do it. 3) Don't cook, or never have leftovers. 4) Buy a new refrigerator. I personally like the option of #2, especially if you have let this chore slide….for months….or years….#4 seems extreme, but do what you have to do. We will not judge.

On your journey today, be strong, clean the fridge, buy new storage containers. Maybe next year, we won't celebrate this day!

NOVEMBER 16th

AHHH……..NOVEMBER, a month I will never forget. I am not trying to make you jealous, but how many of you have a massage table in your living room? Not bragging, but let me tell you, that is the life...or is it?

One dark and stormy day in November, well, I don't remember what the weather was, but it became a dark and stormy day in my life. I was minding my own business, living my life, being as normal as I know how.

I noticed a little something with my eye, something wasn't right.

I called my friends at the University of Iowa Hospitals and Clinics where the eye clinic is internationally renowned. My doctor looked at my eye, took some pictures and proceeded to ruin my day. I had a detached retina. This is not a good thing. I needed surgery sooner rather than later.

Outpatient surgery sent home with instructions to lie face down until the next day when I would come in for a post-op check. I could be "up" for 15 minutes an hour which would allow me to eat, use the bathroom etc. Hence, the massage table to the rescue. The next morning I was grumpy, not feeling well, but not expecting the doctors to say that I needed to continue this procedure for another 5 days. Color me sad.

I had 7or 8 different eye drops to take every day. Thank goodness the tops were color coded. I was not well enough to figure it out myself, thankfully my loving caregiver was a highly organized individual. The drops were all a different number of times a day, 3, 6, 5, 2, 1, as needed. He created a spreadsheet….. I have recovered nicely. Do not have a detached retina. It is not as much fun as it sounds.

I learned from this experience. Patience. This too will pass. The love and kindness of friends and family. The blessing of good health. May you have all of these in your life when you have the need.

NOVEMBER 17th

I LOVE TECHNOLOGY, and I like to think I have some skills in that area. If there is a new gadget, sign me up. I do, however, have some nostalgic yearning for things from the past. At home, we had a kitchen wall phone with an extra long cord. I could stretch that to the basement steps and shut the door to the kitchen while I talked. Privacy was very important to this teenage girl!! When my parents were not home, or asleep, I could stretch the cord to the living room, where I could lie on the orange shag carpet (which we had to rake!!) and "watch" a movie with my boyfriend.

Sentimentally, I would love to have my Princess phone back. It was modern, sleek, and a favorite of young women. It seemed so special to receive calls on that phone. Part of the attachment might be related to the calls during that part of my life. Maybe I could still find a Princess phone. I am one of the holdouts who still have a landline. I need it to call my cell phone when I can't find it. Color me clueless.

What do you miss from a time gone by? Life was pretty darned good and much simpler before all the technology. I miss being surprised by who is calling me on the phone. There are too few surprises now. I miss receiving actual letters in the mail from friends and family. I miss common sense manners in personal interactions. I am very content with the woman I have become, but a part of me misses that young girl with all her hopes and dreams ahead of her.

On your journey today, embrace the past, improve the present and plan for the future.

NOVEMBER 18th

I HOPE your November is going well. Don't get too excited or annoyed, but I am about to use the word Christmas and it's only November. I wanted to share some ideas about gift giving, and if any of them tickle your fancy, I wanted you to have time to implement them.

I read a Facebook post from somewhere that suggested an idea I wish I had thought of years ago. The premise is 4 gifts for Christmas: Something they want, Something they need, Something to wear and Something to read. After talking with my niece, Jess about it, we decided it would be perfect if one more category was added: something homemade.

We are both quilters and love to make quilts and other items to give away. The beauty of a homemade gift is that it is from the heart and one of a kind. Before you say you don't sew, you don't have to sew or be "artsy" to give a homemade gift. I once typed 52 sayings or quotes about someone I loved, secured one on each card of a new deck of cards. Punched a hole in the middle of the top, and put a ring binder through it. Another version that is less labor intensive, write notes on different colored slips of paper and fill a jar with them for somebody. Decorate the jar, and voila a gift. This can work for kids, grandkids, spouses or anybody.

A little Googling or Pinterest will give you lots of other ideas. For me, this puts the heart back into Christmas and takes away some of the commercialism. Don't be afraid to try!! Life begins just outside your comfort zone!

So here's hoping this early encouragement for Christmas didn't make you get your tinsel in a tangle, cause your lights to twinkle or set your bells to ringing!!

NOVEMBER 19th

THANKSGIVING IS JUST around the corner. Thinking I need to share this Public Service Announcement again: "For every Christmas tree lit before Thanksgiving, an elf drowns a baby reindeer." I know, it's very bad, but the first time I heard it, it made me laugh out loud. I'd say rolling on the floor laughing, but then you might think I had a gravity storm. I don't know who said this, but seemed important to share, because I know it's tempting to light that tree!!

My tradition has been to start the Christmas decorating the weekend after Thanksgiving. I mean, after all, it is a lot of work to get all that fol-de-rol out, tree up, outside lights. So if I am going to do all that, I want to enjoy it for the whole month of December at least!!

My normal tradition for outdoor Christmas lights is to procrastinate until the whole neighborhood has decorated, while the days were warmer. I prefer to do it when it is very cold and when there is a wind chill. So much more challenging, and of course you get to use a lot more duct tape. And who doesn't enjoy that? Red is my Christmas duct tape color of choice… I think it makes a strong statement!!

So, here's hoping you navigate Thanksgiving smoothly, and transition to your Christmas decorating with no harm to elves or baby reindeer or yourself. I'm rooting for you!!

NOVEMBER 20th

I HAVE ON SEVERAL OCCASIONS, waxed poetic about Hy-Vee, our Heartland grocery chain. I worked there, I shopped there, I still provide customer service with a smile in the aisle, albeit sans paycheck. One of the interesting things about grocery shopping is "the list." A very important component to the shopping extravaganza. Sometimes I write a very detailed list, and leave it on the kitchen counter. A more interesting tale, is when I take the list. On a recent grocery shopping trip, here is my list, and what I actually bought….

List: milk, creamer, apples, cheese, rice crackers, breakfast cereal, hamburger, taco seasoning, sour cream, napkins, Benadryl, large black trash bags. I managed to purchase everything on the list except the trash bags. The rice crackers were actually almond nut thin crackers, and I found those.

Here are the additional items I purchased: english muffins, eggs, yogurt, Blue Bunny neapolitan ice cream, Cheetos, strawberries, lettuce, smoked turkey lunch meat, a can of pumpkin, cherry jelly, 2 boxes of weird rice and a lunch tote. In my defense, I bought the rice to donate to the University food pantry. Some students were asking for donations as you entered, and they suggested rice. I can take direction….occasionally….don't like to make it a habit…..

I am certain that many of you could tell a similar tale. I never compared my list to my acquisitions before, and thought it was kind of interesting. As Erma Bombeck says, "The odds of going to the grocery store for a loaf of bread and coming out only with a loaf of bread are three billion to one."

Wishing you successful grocery shopping, hope you can find the health market aisle as well as the potato chip aisle. I am still looking.

NOVEMBER 21st

It is that time of year. Thanksgiving is approaching, which makes me think of fall turning into winter. Not always true weatherwise, but definitely a checkmark that we are heading for the Christmas Blitz!!

I was thinking about a childhood song the other day. "Over the River and Through The Wood," written by Lydia Child in 1844. It was originally written as a poem. Somewhere along the way, it was set to music, and became a Thanksgiving song. Another somewhere along the way, it also became a Christmas song. I am not picky, it works for both holidays, but in all fairness, Christmas has lots of songs, let's leave this one for Thanksgiving!

> "Over the river and through the wood,
> To Grandmother's house we go;
> The horse knows the way to carry the sleigh
> Through the white and drifted snow."

The Thanksgiving version had twelve verses. The words have been changed over the years to make it more of a Christmas song. Either way, it evokes many emotions for me. It brings back many memories of those trips to my grandparent's homes for holiday gatherings. The road was never too long, or the weather too wrong to make that important trip. Arriving to a "grand" welcome, the aromas of pies baking, dinner cooking, cousins, chaos and pandemonium. Those were the days my friends!!

Even though I would never want to be younger again, a part of my heart aches for the days of grandparents, family and the simple things. Now, I am the grandparent, best job in the world, by the way. So, make the effort, make the trip, make the memories, it will be over in the blink of an eye.

NOVEMBER 22nd

CONFESSION TIME....WHEN I moved into my new townhouse, I was enthralled with the hardwood floor I had chosen for the main living area and kitchen. I am still enamored with it, but have had to agree to a love-hate relationship. Dust is our mutual enemy. Every miniature, microscopic, infinitesimally small particle shows, and they bring their friends. I can dust/vacuum until the cows come home, and the next day, the dust is back. If I were getting paid for this, the job security would be great....since I am not, wouldn't mind not playing the dusting game every day.

Today was one of those days where I had, ahem, let the dust pile up for a few days. I had a pretty aggressive to-do list, or should I say to-dust list for myself, along with some other cleaning and re-organizing chores. I applied my dusting tools with great vigor and enthusiasm and mad short shrift of the pesky dust. Unfortunately, when I completed the dust battle, my enthusiasm had dwindled. So, I thought to myself, a break would be a good thing. I deserve a break. I have earned a break.

Here is where the problem rears its ugly head. I may have turned on the television which just happened to be set on the Hallmark Channel, where this time of year, Christmas movies are being shown constantly. I am an easy mark for anything Christmas, especially Christmas movies. I am not apologizing, I recognize my weaknesses and take full responsibility for them. So, the afternoon has turned into a Hallmark Christmas Movie Marathon. However, in my defense, I am doing small chores during the commercials.

> Almost everything will work again if you unplug it for a few minutes, including you.
>
> — ANNE LAMOTT

So go ahead, unplug, refresh, and take a break! You deserve it!!

NOVEMBER 23rd

SIGH....WHERE does the time go? More importantly, where does YOUR time go? If you are like most people, there never seems to be enough time to experience the activities, travel, and other leisure activities we yearn for. Yet, on the flip side, there is also never enough time to accomplish the most simple daily tasks of living; chores, shopping, cleaning, going to our job and so on. So.........if we can't get our work done, we don't have enough time for fun, what ARE we doing with the 24 hours we are gifted each and every day?

Whether you have a Ph.D. in Procrastination or one in Organization, it is easy to let time slip away, and then wonder what happened. I happen to be a Type A personality, goal oriented, and very organized, but if there is time to be wasted, I get on the early bus and stay late. There really is nothing wrong with that, I think we all need some time to waste. However, I keep asking myself, "Where does my time go?" So it seems like it is time to wrestle this problem to the ground and get an answer!!

Join me in keeping track of time for the next two weeks or so. Grab a notebook, laptop, iPad, whatever and start logging your time. Track every single minute like you are getting paid for it! If you spend 7 minutes mindlessly staring at Facebook, write it down. Time spent eating, showering, cleaning, reading, working, sleeping, and absolutely everything that you do in a day. Hint: when you get done for the day, it should add up to 24 hours, or 1,440 minutes or 86,400 seconds!

I, for one, can't wait to see where my time goes!! Why didn't I think of this before? One of life's mysteries solved at last!!

The bad news is time flies. The good news is, you're the pilot.

— ANONYMOUS

NOVEMBER 24th

As I sit with my dying father, I have lots of time to think. Sometimes he is somewhat coherent, other times dozing and sleeping. When he is on the alert side of the fence, he wants to hold the hand of whoever is sitting in the chair next to him. It could be me, my nephew, his twin brother, granddaughters, sons or the caregivers who take such gentle and kind care of him. This is not something he normally ever did, but now nearing the end of his journey he seeks out this simple comfort.

This made me think about the act of holding hands: holding the hand of a grandchild to cross the street, the fifth-grade girls at recess who promenade, holding hands and proclaiming friendship. Then there is a new romance and the thrill of holding hands and starting a relationship. The new couple proudly showing the world and each other their connection.

We might be holding the hands of an elderly person to steady them as they walk and to guide them. (Beloved grandchildren of mine: I am not there yet, but keep this in mind for the future, as I aimlessly wander the Target parking lot looking for my car. In the interest of full disclosure, this might have happened...)

What is it about holding hands? I think it's the physical connection that demonstrates the heart connection. It is comforting and peaceful. I love this quote I found, from an unknown source, "Holding hands is a promise to one another that just for a moment, the two of you don't have to face the world alone." Such a beautiful sentiment.

On your journey, today, hold someone's hand and enjoy the comfort you give and the comfort you receive. A gift beyond measurable value....

NOVEMBER 25th

I WOULDN'T SAY I have an obsession with socks. I will confess that I have many pairs of colorful, fun, quirky, interesting socks. I like socks. There is nothing that jazzes up a conservative outfit more than a wild or slightly inappropriate pair of socks.

I like to think myself as curator of a colorful textile collection…..of socks. The blame (or credit) for my vast sock collection can't be laid solely on my doorstep. When others know your propensity for socks, you often receive unusual, fun socks as gifts. I do not have a one in one out policy for socks, and so the collection grows…..

I know the men reading this are shaking their heads and rolling their eyes. Many men believe black socks and white athletic socks are enough. They are wrong. Once they are shown the way, they can be converted to having a high fashion sock wardrobe.

A few years ago, I realized I was in a very serious relationship when I showed him my sock drawer. I don't show that to just anybody. If you see my sock drawer, you are part of the inner circle in my life. I must say, he was appropriately overwhelmed...at least that is how I interpreted the long silence as he gazed at the rainbow of socks, arranged by color. I am sure the seriousness of this event did not escape his notice. At any rate, he didn't run screaming out the door. He's a keeper!!

On your journey today, join me in rocking some socks. They don't even have to match, makes it all the more fun. A side benefit of wearing mismatched socks, doing the laundry is less stressful: no socks to "match!" There is no guarantee that you will have an even number of socks coming out of the dryer, some mysteries remain unsolved.

NOVEMBER 26th

THE QUESTION OF THE DAY, is this: What is the difference between I like you and I love you? There are some obvious differences and many different kinds of love. Buddha answered this question in the most beautiful way. "When you like a flower, you pluck it. But when you love a flower, you water it daily." Simple, thoughtful and very meaningful answer.

I have been thinking about this quite frequently, in fact, ever since I stumbled upon it. Do we "water" the people that we love daily? Or even weekly? Monthly? Probably not. I plead guilty, Your Honor.

How do we "water" our loved ones? Expand that term water to include: tend to, show visible efforts to care for, comfort, praise, appreciation, and affection. It really can be the little things. Actions that do not take a great deal of time, talent or money.

I have some ideas about actions. Some I am quite good at, others not so much. Here is a list I've compiled about things I do and things I need to do!!

1. Text wishing someone a good day, thinking of you, proud of you, miss you, wish you luck, or success, love you. Think of how many people one could touch taking a few minutes.
2. Random snail mail card. Could include a gift card, a bookmark or some other small items. I send my grandkids $2 bills sometimes.
3. Set aside 10 minutes for a quick catch up phone call.
4. An unexpected small gift when you meet up with a friend.
5. Treat the next time you have a coffee date.
6. Leave a message if you don't reach someone by phone. Just calling to say I am thinking of you.

I have no doubt that you can think of many more ideas, more creative than mine. Get your watering can, and be liberal with your sprinkling!

NOVEMBER 27th

I CAME across some words the other day that have fallen out of use for the most part. Children and young adults would have no idea what was meant if they heard them in conversation.

For example, when I was growing up, we sat on the davenport in the living room. I never hear the word davenport any more. Sofa seems to be used some, but most commonly this piece of furniture is called a couch. The definition of sofa and couch is identical. The definition of davenport uses the word sofa to describe it.

Here are some other terms for furniture that seem to be out of favor: wardrobe, chest of drawers, armoire, settee, chiffarobe. Another example of more specific words being ousted by more general language.

As a word lover, this annoys me. I love specific words for items, and the unusual word is always better than the usual.

At this point, most readers are thinking, this author needs a new hobby!! Who cares?? I compare the loss of language to the loss of our history if no one remembers it or knows the story. Language is part of our history and culture and should be treasured. I know, maybe I should spend more time playing tennis or doing hot yoga (whatever that is!)

On your journey today, sit out on the front stoop or take a seat in the parlor, and try to remember words that were used when you were a child, or heard your parents use. It's a trip down memory lane.

NOVEMBER 28th

> Winter is the time for *comfort,* for *good food* and *warmth,* for the touch of a friendly hand, and for a talk beside the fire; it is the time for *home.*
>
> — Edith Sitwell, British poet

This is very true in the deep, bone chilling coldness of a winter in the Heartland. We seek the warmth of home, we crave particular kinds of food that we generally only make in the winter. Comfort food, we call it. There is something so amazing about the aroma of the pot of chili simmering all day, extending the promise to us that a tasty, warm and comforting meal will be there at the end of the day. Lasagna, beef stew, casseroles, mashed potatoes are a few other comfort foods that come to mind. They seem to warm us from the inside out. There is also the nostalgia of the food, if it is something you ate as a child. How many times have I said or heard, just like mama used to make!

Winter is filled with hearty meals, the wish for home and hearth, and stirrings of the heart. There is more time for reflection and quiet conversations. I find I am much more content to miss or skip an activity that means leaving my cozy house and braving the winter winds and cold, than I would be another time of year. Time slows down. There is no need and sometimes no way to be in a hurry to go somewhere, especially if snow and ice have made our road a little tricky.

The roads of life are tricky enough, with their twisting, turning downhill curves and uphill mountains. I enjoy the happenings of winter that require and encourage me to slow down, stay home and just be. Family, friends, a fire in the hearth and a comforting meal garnished with conversation and laughter, these are the treasures of life.

NOVEMBER 29th

Every year I have a notion to plan a small holiday party for friends. I have thought about an open house format, drop in for snacks and drinks. Another idea is to have a Christmas Caroling party. I think this tradition is slipping away from us and needs to be revived. My CPR certification is not up to date, but there must be something I can do!

It has been a while since carolers have appeared at my front door, and it was a delightful surprise, and it would be nice to pay that forward.

I thought I would brainstorm a bit here, and come up with ideas to plan a simple caroling party. A repertoire of five to six songs should be enough. Choose songs that are easy to sing, in case someone like me is in your group, or it could be a very tortured performance. If you know someone who can strum the guitar, it would be a nice addition.

Song Ideas that are tried and true! I'm sure you can come up with others.

- "Silent Night"
- "Jingle Bells"
- "Here We Come A-Caroling"
- "Joy to the World"
- "O Come All Ye Faithful"

After delighting the neighborhood with the performance, serve your favorite homemade soup, bread, warm drinks, and Christmas cookies. Simple but cozy. A nice way to spark the holiday spirit in the hearts of those you touch.

After procrastinating about this for a number of years, the time has come! Party I must! Warming up my singing (?) voice, finding my mittens and makin' some soup!!

Wishing you a hearty meal on a cold night and someone to share it with.

NOVEMBER 30th

"STOPPING BY WOODS ON A SNOWY EVENING" by Robert Frost

Whose woods these are I think I know.
His house is in the village though;
He will not see me stopping here
To watch his woods fill up with snow.

The woods are lovely dark and deep
But I have promises to keep,
And miles to go before I sleep,
And miles to go before I sleep.

I thought I would share an excerpt from this lovely poem. There are four verses, I have teased you with the first and last verses, hope you will look for the entire poem. I love the simplicity of the words and thoughts. I find it calming to read. A dark, snowy woods would be a beautiful sight. I wanted to share this with you because classics are worth revisiting. I have always wondered, what promises does the mysterious man on the horse have to keep? Where is he headed? Is the village miles away? Is he running away from something or someone?

The never to be answered questions will haunt me!!

Only make promises you intend to keep. A promise is a pledge made in friendship and love, to help others on this bumpy ride we call life. Make some promises to yourself to better your life and keep those promises as well. Promise to smile, to laugh, to love, to cry, to walk in the rain and to play in the snow….promise to live life in the front row. You will never regret it.

DECEMBER 1st

AHHHH.....DECEMBER.....THE first day of December signals the first day of winter to me. Gone (hopefully) are the cold, raw, rainy days that November can give us. I think of December as a softer month, that brings us a winter wonderland. Snowscapes, Christmas lights, holiday celebrations with family and friends abound.

The colorful lights in all the neighborhoods make the dark evenings so cheerful. It is a lot of work to put up Christmas lights, and I always appreciate the efforts of people who put up a huge display, and also those with one string of lights. Together, we light up the nights!!

There is always a great comedy act in my neighborhood this time of year....oh wait, that was me putting up MY Christmas lights. I am the person who can't open child-proof anything, can't re-fold a map, well, you get the idea. The process for me is never easy, but I am usually determined to get them up. My weapons of choice lots of duct tape, many power cords and generally a tangle of electrical things that would make most men weep. But the end result is what counts!!

Here is another way to light up the world! Today is the day to start your reverse Advent Calendar. This can be done at work or home. Use a box, and every day place a food item in it. Continue to do this until Christmas Eve, and then make a trip to your local food pantry. Think of the results for the food pantry if we all did this!! Also a great way for children, teenagers and young adults to participate in the giving spirit of the season.

On your journey this season, make sure your lights are on, (both literally and figuratively!), embrace the spirit of the season and be kind to all you meet.

DECEMBER 2nd

TWENTY SIX (OR more) best things about the Christmas season….

- A-Angels We Have Heard on High
- B-Baby Jesus
- C-Church, Carols and Candy Canes
- D-Decking the halls
- E-Elves and Evergreens
- F-Fudge, Fir trees and Frosty
- G-Gingerbread people
- H-Holly berries
- I-Icicles, Ivy and Icing
- J- Joy and Jingle Bells
- K-Kris Kringle and Kringla
- L-Lights, Laughter and Love
- M-Miracles
- N-Nativity
- O-One horse open sleigh
- P-Presents and Peace
- Q-Quilts
- R-Reindeer
- S-Silver Bells and Sugar Cookies
- T-Tinsel & Trees
- U-Unwrapping gifts
- V-Vixen and reindeer crew
- W-Wonder of the season
- X-Xtra time with family
- Y-Yule log
- Z-Zipping (or dashing) through the snow

Making this list could be a fun Christmas game for all ages See how many words your family can think of for each letter, and be creative!!

DECEMBER 3rd

On this date, in 1968, Elvis Presley's Legendary Comeback Special aired on television. It marked his return to live performances, and it was an unprecedented success. The King was back, make no mistake about it!!

Elvis concluded the show with a very special song that was written specifically for him to perform, by his musical director, W. Earl Brown.

Elvis recorded it two months after Martin Luther King was assassinated. It was released just before the Comeback Special aired.

Elvis was very passionate about this song, and of course, knocked it out of the park. It was titled "If I Can Dream." Very appropriate title considering Martin Luther King's "I Have A Dream" speech.

If you haven't heard Elvis sing this, you must. It will give you the chills! Elvis felt the inequalities and injustices he saw in life very deeply.

Unfortunately, we still haven't figured out the answer to the question Elvis asks in the song. If we can dream of a better life where we all work together, why can't it come true? Progress has been slow as molasses on a chilly winter day.

We are the answer. We are the bridge to understanding. If we all try a little harder, open our hearts and help one another, the world can be a better place, one small act at a time.

DECEMBER 4th

Be strong, my friends. All good things must come to an end, or so I am told. I hate to have to tell you this, but it is December which means this is your last "letter" of the year. This month, the appropriate letter seems to be "J." So many of my favorite words seem to have a connection to this special and festive month.

Drum roll please..........J words of the month are:

Jingle	Jest	Jig	Jaunty
Jam-packed	Joyful	Jubilant	Juicy
Jocular	Jiffle	Jam	Judicious
Java	Jeep	Jag	Jinx

The only word in the above list that I think you might not be familiar with is Jiffle. Jiffle is a good word to describe me sometimes. I am definitely a Jiffler. It means to move around restlessly, fidget. I definitely have some students at school like that, I need to teach them that word!!

On your journey, may you have a joyful, jaunty, jam-packed day filled with java, jingles, and juicy jam.

DECEMBER 5th

IF YOU DO NOT ENJOY, or maybe I should say revel in the 24 hour/7 days a week Christmas movie marathon provided by Hallmark Channel on cable TV, you may want to stop reading now. Consider yourself warned and armed with the knowledge of what may follow!!

I personally enjoy Christmas movies. I will admit that the Hallmark Christmas movies are a genre unto themselves. One might say, they are predictable plots and always have a happy ending. I am very okay with this at Christmas. Life does not always provide a happy ending to your story, and I find these movies a relaxing respite from "real" life. I can relax, enjoy the cozy story without angst and dramatic turns of events that can leave a viewer breathless.

I have friends that poke fun at them and me for watching them. They crack jokes about the endings by saying things like, "Wow, who saw that coming?" in their most facetious surprised voice. I say to them, do not bring your negative feelings to make fun of my enjoyment of the Hallmark movies. My observation is that most men really struggle to watch them, while most women enjoy at least some time spent with Hallmark.

Hallmark is great at marketing. They offer shirts, socks, and mugs to name a few items that say, "This is my Hallmark movie watching shirt, etc." Genius, I say!! The other characteristic I have noticed is the stable of actors they have that they use repeatedly in many movies. These actors are generally very clean-cut, no scandal, family oriented people. They have a standard or brand to protect and more power to them. There definitely will not be any quotes like, "Merry Christmas, you filthy animal," ala the movie *Home Alone 2!*

Season your holiday with a little or a lot of these happy movies!!

DECEMBER 6th

One of the delights for me during the Christmas season, is reading books about Christmas. I start reading them after Thanksgiving to catch some holiday spirit. Not really necessary, as I am a blinking lights necklace with jingle bells kind of girl. However, I enjoy re-reading some old favorites and finding some new tales of the season.

I would like to share with you some good reads for Christmas. Here is a short list of cozy stories.

- The Christmas Train by David Baldacci
- Hope at Christmas by Nancy Naigle
- The 13th Gift by Joanne Huist Smith
- Twelve Days of Christmas by Debbie Macomber
- A Gift from Tiffanys by Melissa Hill
- A Vineyard Christmas by Jean Stone
- A Plain and Fancy Christmas by Cynthia Keller

To add a couple of classics to the list, I always enjoy re-reading "The Gift of the Magi" by O. Henry. An editorial published in the "New York Sun" in 1897 always deserves another read. The editorial was titled, "Is There a Santa Claus?" I never remember that title, I always call it 'Yes, Virginia, there is a Santa Claus," which is the famous line in the editorial. It is said to be the most reprinted newspaper editorial.

On your journey through the Christmas season, I hope you can find words of humor, joy, peace, faith, and comfort. Embrace your traditions, maybe start a few new ones, and more importantly treasure the time you have with family and friends. Wishing you all the blessings of the season.

DECEMBER 7th

REMEMBERING TODAY, the tragedy that occurred at Pearl Harbor in 1941. On a quiet Sunday morning in Honolulu, the Japanese Imperial Navy attacked the Pearl Harbor Naval Station without provocation, warning or a declaration of war. The attack sank four U.S. Navy battleships, killed approximately 2,400 and injured another 1,200. This is a day that changed our nation and the world forever.

President Franklin Roosevelt made a speech in front of Congress to talk about this outrageous attack. One of the lines from his speech has been oft repeated and has become very famous, "Yesterday, December 7, 1941--a date that will live in infamy, the United States of America was suddenly and deliberately attacked by naval and air forces of the Empire of Japan." He then asked Congress to vote declaring war with Japan, the vote was 82-0.

Today, the population that was actually alive on this day is dwindling. The descendants of those at Pearl Harbor on that horrific day, as well as the rest of the nation will never forget this day. I mourn the loss of life of the military personnel who made the ultimate sacrifice in service of this country, as well as the civilians who were killed.

Pearl Harbor Remembrance Day is just that, a day to remember and honor. Flags should be flown at half-staff until sunset, in case you need to know the flag protocol. Take a moment on this day to be thankful for those brave men and women who stand vigilantly, ever ready to protect the freedoms you enjoy.

President Harry S. Truman said, "America was not built on fear. America was built on courage, on imagination and an unbeatable determination to do the job at hand."

DECEMBER 8th

Christmas is the season for kindling the fire of hospitality.

— Washington Irving

I think sometimes we all feel like we need to do something to ignite our Christmas spirit's dwindling flame. What is Christmas spirit to you? What makes this holiday season meaningful to you? There have been years when I have felt that I am just going through the motions, and not participating in anything that celebrates the season. I have come up with some ideas that I have been experimenting with, and maybe they can inspire you to add some cheer to your Christmas!!

- Check your church calendar for special services, children's play, caroling and any other events that you can attend or help with.
- Find out what your community or surrounding communities offer for Christmas activities. There might be music, tree lighting ceremonies, things for families to participate in together and probably much more.
- Call the Salvation Army, Toys for Tots, or other agencies in your area that will need donations and help to create Christmas for families who otherwise would have no real celebration.
- Be a Secret Santa to a child or adult who might need a boost this year. Leave some surprises on the doorstep or mailbox.
- Host a holiday movie marathon open house. Get some snacks together and watch some holiday flicks.
- When planning family Christmas gatherings, focus on interaction rather than a pile of presents. Pinterest has some fun ideas for interactive Christmas activities for all ages.
- Host a potluck dinner with a white elephant gift exchange
- Get a group together and do a flash mob Christmas caroling event at a local grocery store or mall.
- Volunteer to serve a meal at a food kitchen.

Just a few ideas to inject some spirit into the Christmas holiday season. I am sure you can come up with many more. As they say where I come from, Make this Christmas one to remember.

DECEMBER 9th

THOUGHT I WOULD MIX things up today, and try to write a poem. I used to write some poetry, but then, I used to do a lot of things that I can't do anymore!! However, I never shy away from a challenge…..

The Joy of Winter

Winter snow crunches under my feet,
Like the caramel apples that I eat.
Stinging cold, frozen nose.
Still I love it, don't you knows?
Some may scoff and some may whine,
But they can't ruin this winter of mine.
Yes, summer is warm and summer is fun,
But the joys of winter can't be outdone.
So, this I ask you, if I may,
Please embrace my winter day.

Winter is a big part of life in the Heartland. It can be difficult, but if it were easy, California would do it. We secretly take pride in our 40 degree below wind chills and mountains of snow. (For a while anyway!!)

We think we are hearty, and tougher than the winter weather storms Mother Nature gives us. Winter is a fact of life here, and you pretty much have to love it or leave it. Embrace the sledding, skating, snowmobiling and building of snow people!! Of course, enjoying the fireplace on a snowy winter night is indescribable bliss!!

> In the midst of winter, I found there was, within me, an invincible summer.
>
> — ALBERT CAMUS

Let winter challenge you and inspire you. Find the beauty of the single snowflake, the joy of a child, a sled, and the first winter snow.

DECEMBER 10th

AHHHH....DECEMBER and all things Christmas!! I saw this quote somewhere, and liked it enough to write it down in one of my lists/journals of things I must remember. I wanted to share it with you so here it is!

"Lessons From a Christmas Tree"

- Be a light in the darkness.
- We all fall over sometimes.
- You can never wear too much glitter.
- Bring joy.
- Sparkle and twinkle as often as possible.
- It's okay to be a little tilted.

By Jane Lee Logan

I can identify with all of these things, especially the one about falling over....but my gravity storms are a story for another day!! Sparkle, twinkle, light up the world around you and bring joy to all those you meet.

My wish for you at Christmas is that you will never be too old or grown up to search the skies on Christmas Eve for the North Star and a bearded man with a sleigh full of gifts.

DECEMBER 11th

RANDOM ADVICE to shoppers this Christmas season...if you see me walking in the parking lot of the mall, grocery store, or pretty much anywhere else (other than my driveway), do not follow me hoping to get my parking spot. What you don't know, is that I usually do not know where I parked. It becomes a little creepy when you follow me up and down multiple rows of vehicles for fifteen minutes or more! It is like a game of hide and seek for me to find my vehicle. Trust me, it's all fun and games until you have to wait for all the stores to close and there are fewer cars. My name is Lori and I am parking challenged.

I have sharpened my skills in this regard after an incident at the airport. I flew home from North Carolina by myself, arriving around 10:00 p.m. Retrieved my luggage, and walked outside. It was dark, and with the added bonus of raining...hard….I walked to the area where I believed I might have parked. I was hitting my panic button periodically. It all looks different at night. I was close to tears and didn't know what I would do. No more flights coming in, airport closing down.

Walking back to the terminal I saw a man in a reflective jacket that had some sort of airport job. I told him my pathetic tale of woe. He said something to the equivalent of, "Don't you worry little Missy. This is why we have airport police." He called the policeman, who threw my bag in his SUV and drove me up and down every row till we found my car. My hero!!

When I park my car at the airport now, I take a picture of the nearest sign that is labeled for parking areas. Again, I must blame my directional dyslexia, it can't be me?? Can it?? Don't answer that.

DECEMBER 12th

THE YEAR WOULDN'T BE complete without mentioning how important comfort food is during the winter to those of us that are the frozen chosen in the Heartland. Frozen due to extreme below zero wind chills, and chosen because we made the choice to live here!

I love a winter day when I can put the makings for chili in the crockpot. The aroma is so tantalizing all day if I am home. If I am out, the thought that dinner will be ready when I return is so wonderful.

Make a pan of cornbread and we are good to go!!

Other comfort foods for a winter day; roast & potatoes in the crockpot, meatloaf and mashed potatoes, Ham & potato soup, biscuits warm from the oven, gravy on anything and warm Swedish rice (rice pudding) straight from the oven. Just to name a few. Basically, carbs, carbs, carbs and more carbs will do the trick.

The aroma of comfort food cooking can evoke very strong memories, times growing up, holiday events, special dinners and special people.

Cold weather is the perfect backdrop for comfort food. The hot and humid Iowa summers don't lend themselves well to chili or potato soup!!

Winter will always leave, but often not without a struggle!! Spring arrives and the memory of comfort food on a cold, snowy winter night that warmed our stomach and our heart will be with us.

On your journey, plan a comfort food meal with family or friends. Have everyone bring their favorite comfort food to share. Wear some stretchy pants, dig in and enjoy!!

DECEMBER 13th

My life continues to provide amusing moments for others. I was preparing for a busy and productive evening crossing things off my list. First up: make an apple salad for a Christmas party the next day. Had the ingredients all lined up, and was ready to start cutting up grapes, celery, and apples. Here is where the fun began….

I was reaching for something on one of the higher shelves in my pantry. I knocked something off the shelf below. I didn't see what it was for a few minutes as I turned around. All of a sudden, when what to my wondering eyes should appear, a large tsunami of golden liquid drenched my floor, wall, and pantry door.

A brand new, large bottle of vegetable oil had fallen off the shelf. The impact dislodged the lid. I have never been responsible for an oil spill before, but I can attest to the fact that no wildlife was hurt because of my actions. Thank goodness they won't let me pilot an oil tanker. I had no idea what to do, but I leaped into action. Moving things, grabbing towels, generally adding to the havoc of the moment.

Next, I made numerous trips to the linen closet after I emptied the kitchen drawer of towels. I managed to soak up the oil. No more puddles, but now the hardwood is well oiled up and slippery. Two rounds of scrubbing the floor (which of course had been mopped and cleaned two days prior) with hot water and it seemed the catastrophe was over….except for in my mind. Every towel in the house was now dirty, so off to the laundry room, to add an extra load of laundry to my chores for tonight.

Now, where was I? Oh, right, making apple salad. So back to the chopping, slicing, and mixing. Much later than I planned on, the festive salad is prepared, sampled and proclaimed good enough for company.

DECEMBER 14th

As I deck the halls this season, listening to my favorite Christmas songs, (which is all of them), I can't help thinking about the empty chairs in my house. The family and friends I once shared this time with who are no longer with me, are taking up space in my mind. They are always there in the background, reminding me of times past.

To ease the sorrow, I think of the loved ones we have added to our gatherings. The family grows with the addition of marriages, births, engagements and new friends. It is an ever changing story, with the comings and goings of people who help tell the story of our lives.

Life is like a quilt made up of many different colors, textures and fabrics. Each one adds to the beauty of the quilt in its own special way. The quilt comes together with hours of work, stitches to hold it together, and the love that goes into the making of it. I am holding on tightly to the quilt of my past, and eagerly working on the quilt of the present and future.

I am thankful beyond measure for those that have shared the journey with me for a time, and those who will join my journey someday. Those who are gone have taken a piece of my heart with them, but those who are new travelers on my journey bring with them a sewing kit to add new pieces and mend the frayed edges.

During this holiday season, remember those who have gone before us with love and joy knowing they are having a heavenly Christmas. Embrace those sharing your life today, and the love they bring with them. May the peace and blessings of the Christmas season be yours today and always.

DECEMBER 15th

ONLY TEN DAYS until the birthday celebration of the One who was born in Bethlehem. I love the month of December leading up to Christmas. It means hope and peace to me along with the elation of spending time with family and friends. It means the beautiful colored lights that chase away the darkness on a cold winter night. Also love Christmas music, lots of it...24-7 is not too much for me. I mean who doesn't want to hear Elvis singing "I'll Be Home for Christmas??" Or anything else he wants to sing for that matter...

One of my favorite Christmas songs has lyrics that speak to me, and the tune is so uplifting, if you haven't heard it, give it a listen.

The song was written by Alan Jackson, "Let it be Christmas."

Here are a few of the lyrics: "Let it be Christmas everywhere, let heavenly music fill the air. Let every heart sing and every bell ring the story of hope, joy, and peace."

I admit it, I am that friend who reminds people how many days until Christmas, starting in about March. I love to post it on Facebook to figuratively hear the groans of my friends!! I think you can never start thinking about something good too soon. A wise older gentleman, by the name of Lou who had a gift shop on Melrose Avenue in University Heights gave me some good advice about this when I was a child. I would have to save my money for things I wanted in his store. When I had enough, my mom would take me there to make the purchase. It was hard to wait sometimes, and that is when he said this to me, "Anticipation is often greater than realization."

I think of those words often and they always strike a chord with me. Anticipating a holiday, a vacation, a visit from a friend is often more than half the fun!! Anticipate away, my friends!!

DECEMBER 16th

Recipe for a Blustery Winter Day

Ingredients:

- Hot coffee, tea, or hot chocolate in your favorite mug
- Cookie in a Cup (recipe below)
- Warm, snuggly blanket or quilt
- Brand new book or an old favorite
- Cozy reading nook
- Fireplace (optional)

Directions:

Assemble all ingredients and enjoy being warm and snug.

Repeat as often as necessary!

Recipe for Cookie in a Cup

1 T melted butter
1 T sugar
1 T brown sugar
1 egg yolk
¼ cup flour
2 T chocolate chips

Mix together and microwave for 60 seconds!! Repeat as necessary!!

Reading gives us someplace to go when we have to stay where we are.

— Mason Cooley, Professor and American Aphorist

DECEMBER 17th

FOR MANY, life is about a journey "home," or finding "home." What is this mystical place called home? Home is a commonly used word to describe where we physically live, and where we store our possessions. I think home is something entirely different.

Home is an idea, a comforting thought, a warm spot in your heart, and people you love. It is an emotional place where you belong. There have been a number of books, songs, and movies about finding the way home, sometimes literally, but often figuratively. I have a couple of favorite songs that are heartbreaking dreams of going home.

"Green Green Grass of Home," tells a story of all the wonderful things that he will see, touch, and experience when he is at home. The ending changes the tone of the story, as it turns out the man is dreaming in his jail cell and will never see home again.

The iconic song, "I'll Be Home for Christmas," was written and recorded in 1943, from the viewpoint of a soldier away at war. The soldier recounts all the things he is looking forward to at home, but ends with the words, " I'll be home for Christmas,if only in my dreams."

My hope for you is that you have found home. We all need to have a place that is our emotional sanctuary, that nurtures our minds and heart. There are often obstacles to going home, family estrangement and distance being two of them. Never give up the search for home, and help others in your life find their way home. Read the words of Emily Dickinson, American poet: "Hope is the thing with feathers that perches in the soul, And sings the tune without the words, And never stops at all." Keep hope alive in your heart and mind always. Find your way home.

DECEMBER 18th

DECEMBER, the time for many friends to get together to have a cookie exchange!! It is a fun night, and everyone goes home with a nice assortment of Christmas goodies for their family.

Eight years ago, one of my best friends hosted a cookie exchange for about ten of us. The treats everybody brought were amazing, we had adult beverages and it was a riot!! It was unanimous, we would do it again next year. The next year rolled around, the hilarity commenced and it was again pronounced a success.

Here's where things went south...we were chatting and having so much fun, and somehow the conversation turned the corner about how much fun it would be to do if we didn't have to make the cookies….the seed had been planted, and trust me folks, that seed grew and was prolific.

Third year, spouses were invited, potluck dinner and adult beverages were the entertainment and no cookies were baked! Another wonderful party and even the spouses were looking forward to the next year.

So…....I just got my invitation for this year's "8th Annual Non-Cookie Exchange & Yankee Swap." I mean if you are not going to do something, do it right!! The Yankee Swap is a trading, stealing, coveting kind of gift exchange that creates much plotting, planning, and laughter.

Last year some Christmas clothing and decorative headgear showed up on a few people, so we are upping our game again. I have purchased a wonderful "fascinator" covered with colorful Christmas ornaments to adorn my head, along with a red, green, and white fedora for my better half to wear. Thankfully, he is a good sport and will wear the fedora with style and panache. Just the attitude needed for a non-cookie exchange party!

DECEMBER 19th

For the pathway that lies before me, my Heavenly Father knows — I'll trust him to unfold the moments as he unfolds the rose.

— Ellie Claire

Getting a little closer to Christmas, and I have been thinking about Christmas Miracles and how God unfolds them every year in His proper time. He unfolds the blessings of our lives and causes us to look at things from a different perspective.

Christmas Miracles I am thankful for:

Tidings of great joy.....hearing from family and friends
Faith...a chance to listen to the Christmas story and believe
Angels on High....the only way I can explain some happenings
Truth...discovering the truth about what is truly important
Sounds, scenes and scents of the season...music, lights, trees
Love...to hear the word of God and know his love
Magic...the wonder of little children as they behold the beauty of Christmas and wait for Santa
Hope.....for Peace on Earth, Goodwill to Men
Eternity...God's promise of our forever home

As you make your way on this journey to Christmas Day, slow down so you don't miss the Christmas Miracles that surround you. Visit the festive light displays and see them through the eyes of a child. Give an unexpected gift to someone you know, and to someone who is alone. Revel in the sights, sounds and scents of the season, and remember there is no such thing as too many Christmas cookies!

DECEMBER 20th

As I now have one book under my belt, so to speak, I have had some ideas sneak in for a second book. I am not sure I have the stamina for another book, but I can confidently tell you about some books I will never write.

1. Marathon Running for Dummies-I do not run, I hate running, if you ever see me running, get your track shoes on, it's the apocolypse!
2. Graceful Dance Moves-We took a social dancing class (twice) to master the art of dancing at social events. We actually did pretty well, but to retain that information, one must use it all the time, and we don't.
3. Folding Pizza Boxes-I had a short stint as a waitress at Iowa City's famous family owned pizza place, Pagliai's Pizza. When we weren't busy, we were supposed to fold pizza boxes for takeout orders. I couldn't master it or even do a passable job.
4. The Ancient Art of Map Folding- Folding a map in the car, I find a near impossible task. Not enough room if the map is entirely exposed, and I again, can't do it very well. I blame all these folding issues on my directional dyslexia and spatial perception issues. (Self-diagnosed)
5. Advanced Origami (see a pattern here?)-This involves very complicated folding, at which I am again, an utter failure.
6. DIY Anything-Particle board bookcases, lamp poles, Christmas trees, you name it, I can't construct it. The directions/pictures might as well be written in Chinese pictographs.
7. French Cooking for the Masses-I am a passable cook, but would not venture to try "fancy " cooking!

This is the short and quick list of the many subjects I could not and should not be allowed to write about!! The total list could be a book in and of itself….hmmm...there's an idea. Brilliant, if I do proclaim that myself!!

DECEMBER 21st

WINTER SOLSTICE IS HERE!! It is also known as mid-winter and is the shortest day of the year...well actually, the day still has 24 hours, but it is the least amount of daylight in the year. Here in the Heartland, it also usually means cold weather. But as John Steinbeck so brilliantly noted, "What good is the warmth of summer, without the cold of winter to give it sweetness?" Indeed.

Since Winter Solstice is such a popular holiday, I am certain that you have your normal celebrations scheduled for today. I would like to think there would be parades and spontaneous outbreaks of dancing in the streets, but alas, for most it is just another day. To me, the "shortest" day of the year means that the days will get "longer" (translate to more daylight) and every longer day gets us closer to spring.

On your journey today, put your sassy pants on, kick up your heels, rock the boat and make it a day to remember.

Somehow this next quote seems to fit today, and it always makes me giggle.

A day without sunshine is like, you know, night.

— STEVE MARTIN

DECEMBER 22nd

"SCOTCH TAPE" is actually a brand name that has come to be used as a generic tape for all transparent, cellophane tape. I used to like scotch tape. I have known scotch tape my whole life. Prompted by an advertisement, my mom used to tape my bangs to my forehead and trim them above the tape. Works great, if you get the tape on straight....It's okay, Mom, lots of the kids had goofy hair cuts. It can be a very useful product in the home, school and office settings.

So, back to my original statement, I used to like scotch tape. I will blame myself for my issues with this product. Although, in the back of my mind, I am thinking maybe the quality has declined, as in many products today. Wrapping Christmas presents has become a battle of me versus the tape. I tear the tape off the roll, ready to jump into action, as I move it towards the package, it rolls up and sticks to itself. Sometimes it wraps around my finger and refuses to come off. Not to mention, if the placement of the tape on the wrapping paper is not quite perfect, one doesn't dare try to lift the tape to adjust. The paper (which is not the quality it used to be) will tear and have a huge hole.

I am willing to accept the blame for my inability to use this product correctly. It probably goes into the category of my uselessness at folding maps. It also takes patience, which is not something I am famous for.

Middle school students find lots of inappropriate uses for scotch tape, mostly taping it to their face, taping their fingers together, and making a huge loop to wear as a necklace, to name a few. Their creativity and passion for this product are unmatchable. Once in a while, they even use it for actual school work! What can you do with your scotch tape today???

DECEMBER 23rd

HERE WE ARE, only 2 days until Christmas!! More importantly, we are only one day until most men start their Christmas shopping. Helpful hint to those fellows still procrastinating: jewelry stores are your friend!!

To be fair, it is not just men, but I do think they will be awarded the trophy every year. It always amazes me, Christmas is the same date every year, yes, every year. It would seem difficult to not know the holiday is approaching when Christmas fol-de-rol starts showing up in the stores about Halloween. Maybe, it is because of the early advertising etc., it seems like there is a long time to get that Christmas shopping done.

Reasons to shop early:

1. More selection
2. Finding sales
3. Less stress
4. Stores less busy
5. "You may delay, but time will not." Benjamin Franklin

Reasons to procrastinate:

1. Never do today what you can put off till tomorrow

Sorry, that's all I got.

It is so hard for me to understand the methodology. I am a list maker and nothing is better than crossing things off my Christmas to do list, or any other list!!

Here's to our differences which make us unique and interesting!! Have a holly jolly Christmas and get your shopping done!!

DECEMBER 24th

HAPPY CHRISTMAS EVE!! May you have a joyous and special night, as we approach tomorrow's celebration of the birth of Jesus!

Many people will attend church services tonight, have family gatherings, or maybe just a special night at home. I have recently learned of a Christmas Eve tradition in Iceland that has tickled my fancy. It is called Jólabókaflód, pronounced Yo-La-Bok-A-Flot. The meaning of this phrase is Yule Book Flood!!

The holiday began during WWII when foreign imports were restricted, and paper was cheap. During the final weeks of the year, Iceland publishers flooded the market with new books. Hence, the tradition began. Not surprisingly, Iceland ranks as the third most literate country in the world.

Mid-November, Icelandic Publishers send a catalog of books to every home, which kicks off the Christmas season!! Icelanders use the catalog to order books as gifts for family and friends. The tradition is to give books and chocolates as gifts that are opened on Christmas Eve, and then spend the evening reading the new books. I can't even express how much I love this idea!! Christmas, chocolates, and books all wrapped up together!!

Wishing you a Happy Jólabókaflód! May your home be flooded with love, joy, peace, and of course books and chocolates!!

DECEMBER 25th

AS THE DAWN breaks on this Christmas Day, embrace your faith, family and traditions as you celebrate the birth of Jesus Christ.

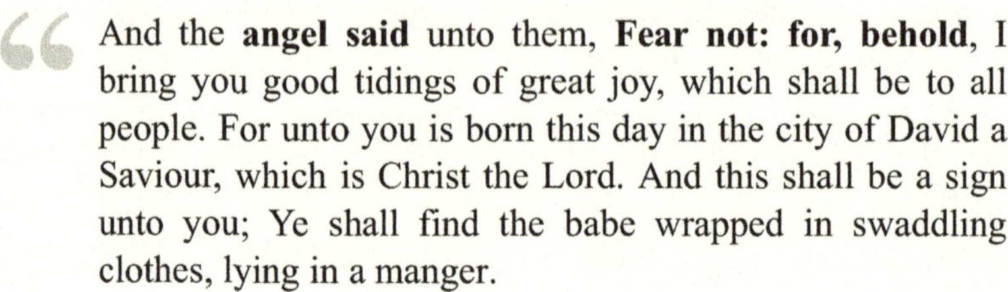

> And the **angel said** unto them, **Fear not: for, behold**, I bring you good tidings of great joy, which shall be to all people. For unto you is born this day in the city of David a Saviour, which is Christ the Lord. And this shall be a sign unto you; Ye shall find the babe wrapped in swaddling clothes, lying in a manger.
>
> — THE GOSPEL OF LUKE, CHAPTER 2, VERSES 10-12 KJV

May this day bring you peace for today, hope for tomorrow, and God's love for eternity. Fill your heart with the joy and light of the miracle of Christmas Day. Have a blessed Christmas!! Joy to the World, indeed!!

DECEMBER 26th

CHRISTMAS HAS COME and gone again, just like that. How does the season pass so quickly? Probably because you have been working your fingers to the bone! Baking, decorating, eating, shopping, work, cleaning, wrapping gifts, Advent Services and Christmas services, family traditions, family obligations…..Whew….Have I forgotten anything?

The day after Christmas, to me, is like exhaling a big sigh after holding your breath for a really long time. The hard work is over, your calendar is not so full, the relatives have gone home. For some, the day after Christmas is a big shopping day. Somehow, fighting the crowds to buy wrapping paper on sale for next year, bargains on leftover gadgets and whatnots just doesn't ring my bell.

To me, it's a good day to put your feet up, watch another Christmas movie, admire your gifts, and eat some Christmas treats that managed to escape the ravages of the crowds at your house. Also, a good day to go out to a movie, have some popcorn, escape, do something not related to Christmas.

The bad news that I feel compelled to relay to you, however, is coming.

Time to return the gifts that don't fit, can't be used, don't want, or seriously hate. Many happy returns!! Only 364 days until Christmas, so better start your planning and shopping now, time's a 'wasting!!

DECEMBER 27th

FIVE YEARS AGO, the new (but already special) man in my life, asked me for some ideas for Christmas. One of the ideas I gave him was "something romantic." Now many men would run for the hills at this point, but this guy is a trooper.

Christmas arrived and we were opening our presents to each other. In my stocking was a blurb from the nearby community college describing a "Social/Ballroom Dancing Class" that started in January. This prince among men had met the challenge head-on and hit the ball out of the park. I was delighted with this very romantic gift!!

Classes began and we danced our way through Monday nights for about eight weeks. The instructors were a husband and wife team who had been teaching dance for years. They were very experienced in dealing with all kinds of wannabe dancers and were very helpful in demonstrating the error of our ways. Not to brag, but once I stopped trying to lead, we were cutting a pretty wide swath on the dance floor.

We were sent out into the world to use our new skills. As time passed, we discovered if you aren't practicing the twirls, steps and moves, it is easy to forget how to do them. So, being the whiz kids that we are, we signed up for another class. Well, technically it was the same class, we were taking it for the second time. We thought it would be a good review, and the new students would gaze at us admiringly at how quickly we caught on. We received glances, that is true. Admiring, probably not!! We had such a good time, Laughter abounded! I wanted to sign up again, but even the most romantic of partners have their limits!!

Let the music play and get up and dance!! I do some of my best moves spontaneously when home alone! Anyway, I think so, and that is all that really matters!!

DECEMBER 28th

Many people have probably read or re-read "The Christmas Carol," by Charles Dickens this past week or so. In some homes it is a tradition to read it aloud, others may just read it alone for their own enjoyment. I feel Mr. Dickens tricked us with the title because what one might expect from a Christmas story titled thus, is not what the reader receives. As I struggle with a title for this collection of essays, I wonder how he came up with that.

The theme of the story is many-faceted. forgiveness, transformation, memories, regrets, and guilt. The story is brought to us by Ebenezer Scrooge's scary encounters with three ghosts, who represent his Christmases Past, Present, and Future. He sees the error of his curmudgeonly ways through these encounters and transforms himself and his life for the better.

I think it is a good story to read every year. If it makes us stop and think, even just a little about our actions and how they affect others, that is a positive thing. The story reminds us that it is never too late to change our ways for the better, which I know I certainly can never have too many reminders.

When I think of Christmas Past, it is not with regrets for actions taken or omitted, but about those people who no longer are here to be with us at Christmas. I can look around the room and see the "empty" chairs, with wonderful memories of those gone, but with sadness in my heart that I can feel. Broken hearts are real. These people have taken a piece of my heart with them when they left, but in exchange, left me a piece of theirs to hold in my heart and soul forever.

Next Christmas, take a moment to reflect, to remember and to acknowledge those that live in your heart now, and hold them close.

DECEMBER 29th

I AM WRITING from a new environment today. I am sitting in a place called the Bird House, The Bird House is a hospice house in my area, and I am sitting bedside by my dad, listening to him breathe. After some weeks of struggle with medication and pain, he is comfortable and peaceful. He sleeps a lot but wakes to call us by name and talk a little.

This morning it is very quiet at Bird House. It's morning, and there is only one other "bird" here besides my dad. By lunchtime, there will be noise and laughter, conversation and maybe a few tears. My brother from Ames and family will be here, and some family members of the other bird. Staff is cooking a big lunch and the smells of something Italian are wafting through the home.

This place is a sanctuary for my dad to spend the last days of his earthly journey. It is a cozy home in the woods, with beautiful views out the window, including birds at the dozens of bird feeders, deer and other critters that traverse through the woods. It snowed yesterday so we can see their tracks. It is also a sanctuary for family members. The staff cooks for us, the kitchen and pantry are to be treated like they are ours and there are peaceful nooks and crannies to read or talk while Dad is sleeping. I feel comforted knowing how well he is cared for when I am not here. It gives me respite to not be here hours and hours every day, knowing he is okay. I can call day or night, and the staff will tell me how is he doing at that moment in time and how he has been doing.

If you have a Hospice House in your area, be grateful for its existence. I hope you will never need it, but if you do, it will be a Godsend. If you feel inclined, volunteer or donate. Anything you do will give solace to a family, as they walk with their loved one the final steps of their journey.

DECEMBER 30th

How did we get here? On the brink of a brand spanking new year, almost time for me to say: cheerio, adios, au revoir, ciao, arrivederci, shalom, sayonara, aloha, until we meet again….But don't go away yet and don't stop reading…. all is not lost, we still have tomorrow!

Tomorrows are not promised to anyone, but the natural faith and optimism we have encourages us to count on and plan for our tomorrows. I am sure you all know someone who had their tomorrows cut short. So, in their honor, let us squeeze the life out of each day that we are given until we have wrung it dry!

It has been an honor, and a privilege to share this year's journey with you. Writing my first book was liberating, heart wrenching, silly, fun, hard work and a labor of love. It is one thing to do the writing, but when you start imagining that people are (you hope) actually going to read your thoughts, it is frightening, panic attack inducing, humbling and every other emotion one can think of. But as I am nearing the completion of it, I would do it all again in a New York minute!

My hope is that I have made you smile, made you cry, made you think and made it worth your time to read my ramblings. As one of my favorite humorists and comedians said, "I think I did pretty well, considering I started out with nothing but a bunch of blank paper." Steve Martin

See you tomorrow and thank you from the bottom of my heart for the time you have spent reading these essays.

DECEMBER 31st

I THINK many people find New Year's Eve anticlimactic, disappointing and often a letdown. It seems all the hoopla surrounding this day leads us to believe that if we don't have exciting plans or parties complete with hats and whistles, or romantic evenings, we are in the minority. So not true, and I have come to treasure a quiet dinner at home with that special someone, family or friends. In the Heartland, weatherwise it is usually a good night for fuzzy socks, cozy blankets and a warm fire..not to mention a hot or cold toddy and some reflection on this trip around the sun.

A year ago, disregarding the weather possibilities in Iowa on New Year's Eve; a few couples had big plans for dinner and a band that we all liked. Bought tickets a month ahead of time to make sure we could get in, and planned for a night of frivolity. When the night arrived, it was 21 degrees below zero without windchill, and the party venue was very chilly. We all made it and of course, we had a good time, but the cozy night at home sure sounded good as we were preparing to brave the frigid temperatures to meet our friends.

So, here we are again...a new year is waiting just around the corner...so many possibilities ahead of us. So goodbye, my friend, Old Year. You've been a good and trusted partner in this journey, but it is time to start saying our goodbyes. Even though we will never meet again, I will treasure the time shared and the memories made. I will plan to write passionately in the Book of my Life next year, and take advice from this quote:

> Maybe this year we ought to walk through the rooms of our lives not looking for flaws, but looking for potential.
>
> — ELLEN GOODMAN

ACKNOWLEDGEMENTS

After decades of harboring this secret desire, and months of working to make it happen, I am hovering between delighted and disbelief! Thrilled to know this dream has come to fruition, yet amazed that I finally accomplished it! So it is time to thank those who believed in me, encouraged me, and were my labor coaches for the birth of this book.

Verne Nelson-You fanned the flames of the hidden fire within and gave me that gentle, loving push off the cliff into the abyss. You laughed at my stories, encouraged my idiosyncrasies and ignored the thousand or so notecards scattered everywhere. Your love and faith in me were steadfast when the seas were stormy. There are not enough words to express my thanks. (I know, you are laughing now about my "lack" of words. You should be so lucky!) You are my world.

Beth Howard-Thanks for sharing your time and talents with me, the excellent coaching, referring marvelous resources, and for cheering me on to the finish line. Beth is the author of three fabulous books; "Making Piece," "Hausfrau Honeymoon," and her cookbook, "Ms. American Pie."

Ellie Firestone (Fiverr)-Thanks for being so patient with me, and helping me jump the technical hurdles to finalize the manuscript.

Morgan Krehbiel- Thank you for excellent cover designs and being the final check and step to making my dream of publishing a book come true!

To all my friends and family-Thanks for providing me with abundant material from which to choose! Your stories are my lifeblood and my heartbeat. Thanks for being there for the good times and the not so good times.

To my readers: I hope this collection of essays, serious and silly will make a connection with your heart. I hope on the days when you need a laugh I can provide that. I hope we can also connect through the laughter and tears provided by life's journey.

ABOUT THE AUTHOR

A lifelong writer and avid reader, the author grew up in Iowa City, Iowa, home of the University of Iowa, her alma mater. As a child she dreamed of becoming (in no particular order) a writer, librarian, FBI agent, cowgirl, and talk show host. Her actual career turned out to be twenty-seven years in banking, retiring as a Vice President.

Share the memories, misadventures, and musings of the author in her first book. She shares her experiences and life, growing up in Iowa, the Heartland of America. The 365 daily essays include reflections, humor, recipes, lists, and ponderings. This book will inspire you, make you laugh, make you shed a tear, and make you think.